D0604828

ART GLASS

HOW TO COMPARE & VALUE

LOUISE LUTHER

ART GLASS

HOW TO COMPARE & VALUE

LOUISE LUTHER

Miller's
ART GLASS
How to Compare & Value

A Miller's-Mitchell Beazley book
Published by Octopus Publishing
    Group Ltd.
2–4 Heron Quays
London E14 4JP
UK

Miller's Commissioning Editor:
    Anna Sanderson
Miller's Executive Art Editor:
    Rhonda Fisher
Miller's U.S. Project Manager:
    Joseph Gonzalez

Produced by Deborah DeFord
    & Barbara Marks
Stony Creek, CT 06405
USA

Volume Editor: Deborah DeFord
Copy Editor & Indexer: Joan Verniero
Proofreader: Fredric Sinclair
Graphic Design: Barbara Marks
    Graphic Design

Library of Congress Cataloging-in-Publication Data Applied for
ISBN: 1 84000 542 4

Set in Bembo
Produced by Toppan Printing Co., (HK) Ltd.
Printed and bound in China
Miller's is a registered trademark of Octopus Publishing Group Ltd.

*On the cover: Green on Gold King Tut Vase, Durand Art Glass, c.1929; back cover: Cameo
Etched and Enameled Vase, Burgun, Schverer & Cie, c.1895.*

Contents

▶ *A.D. Nash Ribbed*
Polka-Dot Vase, c.1930.
$1,500–2,000.
9in/22.9cm tall.

An Introduction
to Art Glass

How to Use This Book

The unique compare-and-contrast format that is the hallmark of the *Miller's How to Compare and Value* series has been specially designed to help you to identify authentic antique art glass on the American collectibles market and assess its value. At the heart of this book is a series of two-page comparison spreads—64 in all. On each spread, two examples of a studio or artist's work are pictured side by side and carefully analyzed to determine not only the market value of each art glass piece, but *why* one is more valuable than the other.

In the comparison section, you'll be able to consider the context in which the pieces were created, their intended uses and relative condition, and their importance in today's art glass market. By comparing and analyzing a wide variety of art glass, you'll gain the knowledge and

skills you'll need to find and evaluate art glass pieces and assess their worth with confidence. The illustrations and call-outs, below and opposite, show how the various elements on a typical two-page comparison spread work.

The book's introductory chapters offer an overview of the art glass market and practical pointers on the care and display of your acquisitions. A fascinating history of art glass in Europe and the United States is illustrated with a superb array of examples, and a guide to looking at art glass offers a brief tutorial on how to begin.

And, finally, at the back of the book, you will find further information on where to see and buy art glass in the United States, other sources of information that may advance your knowledge and understanding of the field, a glossary of art glass terms, and a detailed index.

The *introduction* presents an overview of the studio or artist in the context of time and region, and the place of the line in the art glass market today.

The *featured art glass pieces* include one good example and one relatively better example from the same studio or artist.

The *call-outs* highlight each example's "value features"— key factors such as design, technique, condition, and provenance that account for an art glass piece's relative market value.

The small *value boxes* (blue for the good piece, pink for the better piece) contain the size and potential value range of the featured examples.

Mount Washington Glassworks—Variations

The Mount Washington Glassworks was among the most prolific of the American glass companies, despite innumerable business problems that eventually resulted in its takeover by Pairpoint. The firm created many different product lines, each one comprising a wide variety of forms: pitchers, bowls, sugar bowls and creamers, lamps and lanterns, trays, biscuit and tobacco jars, dresser sets, and others. In fact, Mount Washington was able, more than most, to make form follow function. The items sold well, partly because American buyers could perceive utility in their "art" purchases—an important incentive for the pragmatic and conservative New England market.

The most important Mount Washington art glass product line was the Royal Flemish (pages 62-63),

sometimes bearing the Mount Washington winged dragon, or griffin, with which the company was so closely associated. The main characteristic of the Royal Flemish line is a body of colorless, clear glass. Other Mount Washington lines, such as Napoli and Verona, also used clear glass.

One may question whether the punch bowl seen opposite is part of the Royal Flemish line, or if it is a one-of-a-kind item, simply using Palmer Cox's Brownies (see feature on page 65) to decorate a colorless glass blank item. The consensus among collectors seems to be that the punch bowl is unique, but decorated in the typical Mount Washington manner. Unquestionably of Mount Washington origin, this rare piece probably will not be found again in the collectibles marketplace.

Royal Flemish Flying Griffin Vase, c.1900

The raised rim has a classical scrolling, gilt-enameled, repeating motif—an elegant British Victorian-style touch.

The graphic impact of this restrained and perfect oval form increases the value of the piece.

Note the background that simulates "stained glass" in amber, russet, and ochre.

This piece skillfully presents the full menace of the griffin: the horns and ruff, the scowl, beak and tongue, sharp claws, scaly body, and long tail.

When found intact, early labels showing the flying griffin motif increase the value of a piece.

Although there is no mark or label on this example, collectors would not be deterred.

Height: 7in/17.8cm
Value: $5,000–7,000

The *headline* is a brief descriptive title for each featured piece, followed by an approximate date.

The *feature box* provides further information on the featured art glass items and their studio, artist, or history.

The *bulleted points* offer further specific information about an art glass piece's design and background.

Punch Bowl with Palmer Cox Brownies, *c.*1894

Note the rim, crimped in 12 evenly spaced notches; a dozen such punch cups would be a treasure.

The wear on the gold rim and base decoration does not detract from its accent value or the piece's overall desirability.

An elaborate pink framework separates three vignettes of Brownies in humorous postures.

Each scene includes several broad-bellied Brownies with long, spindly legs, wearing odd hats and carrying strange tools.

Characters in the droll scenes are in recognizable roles, such as the policeman and the Irishman.

The punch bowl is inserted into the matching base, with typical Mount Washington scrolling devices, outlined in gold accents.

Neither bowl nor stand is signed or marked, but collectors would still be happy to find this rarity.

Size: 13 x 16in/33 x 40.6cm
Value: $25,000–35,000

• *Design, condition, and rarity affect appraisal. These pieces score high on all.*
• *Color is another major value factor; the multicolor Brownie decoration above adds impact, value, and collectibility.*
• *The rarity of both pieces here increases their value. As the punch bowl is extremely rare, value is extremely high.*
• *The "trademark" Mount Washington vase is rare, but not one of a kind, and not as important in terms of size. Dragon/griffin collectors of the 21st century could drive the price higher.*

Palmer Cox and His Brownies

Palmer Cox was born in 1840 in Granby, Quebec, a small town settled originally by immigrants from the Grampian Mountains of Scotland. Cox grew up with stories from the old country, including the much-embroidered folk tales about "little people," or "Brownies."

Palmer Cox set out from his Canadian home in 1857 to seek fame and fortune in New York. Minimally successful, he sailed for California in 1863. There he sought work as a writer, adding to it his talent for illustration and drawing. In 1874, he appeared in print for the first time in *Squibs of*

California, but response was weak. Two years later, he returned to New York.

When he began working with children's books and magazines, he found the acceptance for which he had hoped. In 1880, the highly regarded *St. Nicholas Magazine* published his stories. Searching for inspiration to create a book series, Cox recalled the Scottish tales from his childhood. He first introduced the popular Brownies, named for their coloring, in 1883 in a story published in *St. Nicholas*; they were an immediate hit. Cox's first book, *The Brownies, Their Book*, was published in 1887.

Brown and Stretched Gold Vase, *c.*1912

This oval form was ornamented with an elevated and flared collar.

The top has been tooled and widened while hot, giving the "stretch" effect and a rough-textured, irregular edge.

The gold iridescent top shows dimpled marks of tooling where it was applied to the brown base, a rare and tricky maneuver.

The dark honey-colored brown body is cased to an opal-white interior, giving it weight and enhancing its color.

The flat-disk, pedestal foot was formed and applied to the base at the furnace, a fine finishing touch.

The "L.C. Tiffany Favrile 8719 G" inscribed on the underside of the base adds value.

Height: 5in/12.7cm
Value: $4,500–6,000

• *Two-toned vases are scarce in freeblown art glass, because two "batches" means two rates of expansion at the fire, decreasing the success rate.*
• *Tiffany vases that are 5in/12.7cm tall decorate well, please the eye, display easily, and are relatively affordable.*
• *The mahogany-brown color, seen on the vase above, was popular in Arts and Crafts style and early 20th-century designs.*
• *Freeblown stretch glass achieved great success at Tiffany in the 1910s. It was copied inexpensively as Depression glass, which is also collectible today.*
• *Fluctuations in market value for collectible art glass are inevitable; ups and downs follow the economy. Tiffany pieces of good design, and in excellent condition, are A-1 investments.*

Charles Hosmer Morse Museum

One of the most important collections of the works of Louis Comfort Tiffany is that of the Charles Hosmer Morse Museum in Winter Park, FL. The museum was established in 1942 by Jeanette Genius McKean and her husband Hugh F. McKean, the latter a friend of Tiffany's and director of the museum until 1995.

A visit to the extensive Morse collection offers insight into Tiffany Studios' scope. The museum brochure states: "At its peak the Tiffany furnaces

produced 30,000 items annually—most of them lampshades, which reached a production rate of four per hour from each of five 'shops,' or 1,000 per week. There were 200–300 tons of glass stored at the plant and it was classified into 5,000 different colors and varieties. Distributed by the Shreve Co. in San Francisco, Neiman Marcus in Dallas, and, of course, Tiffany & Co. in New York [and] . . . Tiffany Studios, his blown glass was as commercially successful as it was artistically superb."

Sometimes, the *feature box* offers additional information that relates to the art glass market, production techniques, or art glass venues open to the public.

Understanding
the Art Glass Market

Like most commodities in a free market, the value of art glass is ultimately determined by the buyer. When the price tag exceeds the amount a buyer is willing to pay, the object does not sell. Mr./Ms. Seller can ask whatever he/she wishes, but the true value is determined by the amount the collector decides is fair. That purchase price then becomes the standard by which others, including the seller, evaluate the item. When an item comes to market in an auction situation, the auction house places an estimated value range on that item and publishes it in a catalog. When the item sells, the post-auction price list tells all who wish to know exactly what the item is actually *worth*. Like it or not, the value of the item depends on the price it commanded.

In a gallery, shop, or studio, the price ticket may read $2,000 for an art glass vase. A collector may want to buy, but not at that price. The collector may offer $1,500 for the item, only to have the seller refuse and counter-offer $1,750. If the collector agrees to the new price, the true value of the item is neither the tag price of $2,000, nor the offered price of $1,500, but rather the final sale price of $1,750. The compromise satisfies both seller and buyer, and the value of the item is established. You may not see this value in any price guide, but it works its way into the marketplace by natural processes.

Art glass as a collectible has come a long way from the time when its ownership was limited to royalty and the wealthy. The production of glass was difficult and required

▼ *Carder Steuben, c.1927. This amethyst quartz bowl is a Frederick Carder classic. It shows pink and blue Cintra flecks, and applied frosted, colorless glass leafy twigs and feet. $1,500–1,800. 7 × 8in/ 17.7 × 20.3cm.*

▶ *Quezal, c.1920. This piece is a typical Martin Bach floriform with a delicate Nouveau ruffled top, iridescent interior, and a precise pulled feather motif. $2,500–3,000. 6¾in/17.1cm tall.*

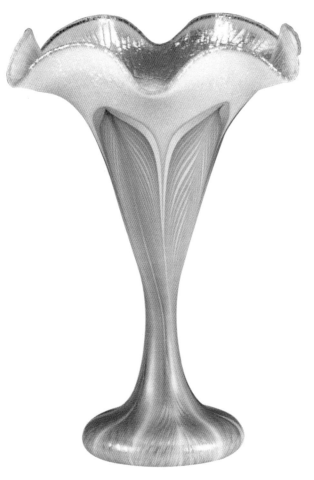

great quantities of materials, equipment that included furnaces and fuel, and, of course, skilled workers. In time, glass vessels became available to the general population, but the collecting of non-functional glass items as purely decorative works of art remained a privilege of the fortunate few. Not until the 19th century did middle-class Europeans and Americans gain access to glass artifacts for purposes of pleasure rather than pure function. Collecting became a sign of affluence and prosperity associated with the erudite elite, an association that some might say drives certain collectors to this day.

At times, collections of art glass have been used to barter in exchange for goods and services. They have been put up as collateral for loans or payment of debts. The value of collections has often followed the ups and downs in the stock market, fluctuating with the Dow Jones and NASDAQ as surely as Pepsico and pork bellies. The value of a collection of art glass changes not only with international economic indicators, but also with what I like to call the "style du jour." Collectibles in general go in and out of fashion, just as do Barbie dolls, Beanie Babies, and Cabbage Patch Kids. There have been occasions when I have suggested to potential consignors that they wait until their collectible art glass comes back into fashion before offering it for sale. Cut glass, Carnival glass, Victorian, Venetian, and even Tiffany, Gallé, and Webb have all had their highs and lows, with periods when frenzied collectors vied for every available piece and times when collectors consistently passed them by. The public has never been known for its loyalty; in fact, the public is notoriously fickle. So if you find yourself with a cabinet full of out-of-fashion, collectible art glass, just wait it out.

◀ Durand, c.1925. This ribbed blue iridescent "stick" vase is also called a Genie vase. Its dark cobalt blue glass enhances the effect of the coloration. $2,800–3,500. 15 1/2 in / 39.3cm tall.

▼ Mount Washington, c.1887. This Lava vase is an early American example of inserted decoration with bits of red, blue, pink, and green glass picked up at the fire. $2,000–2,500. 6in / 15.2cm.

Good stuff always returns to favor and once again becomes the "style du jour."

There's the key: Good Stuff. If you intend to acquire a collection of art glass with even one squinted eye toward its potential for increasing in value over time, always buy the best you can possibly afford, and then some. It will certainly repay you in the joy you have with it, the pride you feel in displaying it, and the knowledge that it will sustain you in your golden years, or your children in theirs.

This puts the onus squarely on you, the collector. You need to do your homework. No other party—no dealer, advisor, auction house, glass artist, or museum director—can make the decisions you need to make to gather a collection that truly pleases you and yours. All the material you need to make intelligent decisions is available, however, from those aforementioned people, and from libraries, museums, and websites. Search for knowledge in the area of collecting you have chosen and you will take home the Good Stuff.

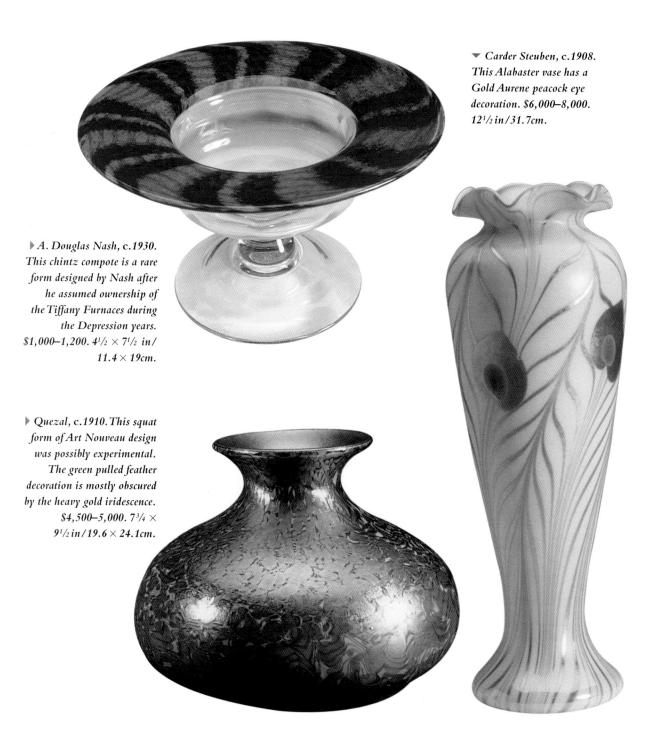

▼ *Carder Steuben, c.1908. This Alabaster vase has a Gold Aurene peacock eye decoration. $6,000–8,000. 12¹/₂ in/31.7cm.*

▶*A. Douglas Nash, c.1930. This chintz compote is a rare form designed by Nash after he assumed ownership of the Tiffany Furnaces during the Depression years. $1,000–1,200. 4¹/₂ × 7¹/₂ in/ 11.4 × 19cm.*

▶ *Quezal, c.1910. This squat form of Art Nouveau design was possibly experimental. The green pulled feather decoration is mostly obscured by the heavy gold iridescence. $4,500–5,000. 7³/₄ × 9¹/₂ in/19.6 × 24.1cm.*

There are a number of particulars that collectors need to watch out for. For example, condition always counts. An increasingly high level of technology has provided restorers and conservators with amazing new tools for repairing damaged art glass. Acrylics can plug holes and fill chips like never before. Super adhesives and glues can put back together what the saddest art glass accidents have taken apart. But these and other high-tech techniques are available to unscrupulous people as well as legitimate professionals. It has become all the more important for collectors to examine potential buys before they pay the price for supposedly perfect art glass items. Use your strongest light source, a magnifying glass, and black light to check any piece for which you harbor the slightest suspicion of repairs. Buy from reputable sellers, and always get a fully detailed receipt with a complete address from the seller. Only by standing firm on this can you buy confidently and return the item, if necessary.

Collectors must also be aware that fakes and forgeries abound in the collectibles marketplace. Some are blatant and obvious, but some are much more subtle and insidious. Again, knowledge is your best weapon against criminals who take advantage of the unwary collector. When you have taken the time to learn what the real art glass looks like and have made a point of knowing what the real mark looks like, the chances of being deceived are few and far between.

The biggest problems occur when collectors assume authenticity because of pricey surroundings or quasi-normal situations. I personally have seen fake art glass being sold in shops in America's most prestigious hotels, giving an air of legitimacy to the rogue dealers and owners who pay the rent. Attending "traveling auctions" in similarly accredited locations also tends to reassure collectors that the material being offered has equally reputable credentials. Not necessarily so! The art glass illustrated on page 25 came from similar situations over a period of time and were purchased at prices the collector should have known were "too good to be true." Watch out for the old green-eyed monster when you make your appraisal of these kinds of offerings. Greed affects both sellers and buyers in the world of valuable collectibles.

▼ *Durand, c.1928. This crackle glass vase of transparent amber glass has red vertical ribs and is iridized overall. $2,000–2,500. 6in/15.2cm tall.*

▶ *Quezal, c.1920. This morning glory vase recalls Tiffany design. Green pulled feather decor contrasts with the opal exterior. $1,500–1,800. 7³⁄₄in/19.6cm tall.*

▼ *Corning Glass Works, c.1887. This Brilliant Period cut glass light bulb envelope accentuated and radiated the light from the bulb within. $600–800. 5³⁄₄in/14.6cm.*

Displaying and Caring for Art Glass

There are surely as many ways to display art glass collections as there are collectors. Consider collections by style, technique, color, size, age, form, artist, company, country, function, decoration, texture, history, value, and potential. Add all variations and combinations of attributes, and you discover an infinite number of possibilities for collecting. It is a personal, fulfilling, and expressive activity that many people begin in childhood and continue through their adult years. And if anything appeals as much or more, it is displaying a collection for others to enjoy.

Art glass cries out to be displayed by virtue of its beauty of color and ability to refract and reflect light. For the collector, the most significant consideration in planning how to display is simply this: "What do I want to express by this display?" You may focus on the brilliance and clarity of the glass. Alternatively, you may want to emphasize the decoration, whether internal to the glass itself or external. Decoration such as iridescence, crackle, or surface texture, invites attention, as does artful "cold work" such as etching, engraving, or sand blasting. You may

be more intrigued with the proportions of your pieces, their massive size or diminutive stature. If you appreciate sculpture, the shape or form of your art glass will have special meaning. Some collectors find the functionality of art glass pieces compelling and collect rose bowls, toothpicks, salt cellars, perfume bottles, or inkwells. Others find the color the most significant factor, as in "the redder the better."

For many art glass collectors, design rules. For others, the skill involved in the execution of the design is paramount. In each case, the display focus can be remarkably different. Subtle backlighting might silhouette the design most effectively. A more direct and illuminating light, on the other hand, may be desirable to show the details of workmanship involved.

Which brings us to the most important element of displaying art glass: light. Light is always the answer to bringing out the best attributes of an art glass collection. Once you have determined what it is you want to accent, you need to direct your light source accordingly. This tends to be a personal, subjective consideration—something that

cannot be learned from a reference book on interior decoration, illumination, or even photography, however insightful they may be. In the end, it is up to you to set up your display as carefully as any stage manager sets a scene. What you choose to accent will not only illuminate your collection, but also how you respond to it yourself.

Caring for Art Glass

Art glass is unequaled in its amazing ability to affect its immediate environment. It is also fragile, as any art glass collector knows. It chips, cracks, or shatters under stress. It has a low tolerance for abuse and requires careful attention to its idiosyncrasies. In return, however, glass can warm and beautify a home with its form, color, and brilliance.

Consider, for example, American Brilliant Period cut glass. Thousands of Americans have inherited a piece or two of grandmother's cut glass and may even store it carefully in the same china cabinet she used to display it. Whether tucked inside a case or displayed on a sideboard, cut glass needs a light source so it can sparkle and glow, showing the facets its designer and engraver planned for the purpose. Given light from a window, a spot, or even a bare bulb, cut glass will offer a display that uses all the colors of the spectrum.

But do not let the glass touch the piece next to it. Cut glass is its own worst enemy. Bring two pieces together,

This tight display of British Cameo glass by Thomas Webb and Stevens & Williams is placed against an unobtrusive background to emphasize the color and form of the art glass. Note how the transparent glass at center catches the light to simulate the lakeside scene.

The subtle artistry of René Lalique's work is beautifully presented in this arrangement of his frosted and opalescent art glass. The deep red background is used as accent, and the indirect lighting highlights the pieces, both effective display techniques.

and both will come away chipped. The very factor that makes Brilliant cut glass beautiful—that is, its high lead content—is also the characteristic that makes it vulnerable. Never stack it or it may crack from the weight. Never wash it in hot water or it may crack from the sudden change in temperature. For the same reason, never take it from a cold area to a warm one, or from warm to cold. Wash it gently, dry it carefully. Never leave liquid in it, even overnight, or it may stain. In short, treat it like an heirloom, and it may well become one.

Brilliant Period cut glass makes an excellent example for discussing art glass care because it is the most vulnerable of all collectible glass. When you understand how to care for "cut," you know what is needed for virtually all collectible glass. More than anything, collectible glass is fragile, and it demands the special attention and precautions that fragility implies; but it is also complex, textural, chromatic, and alive with light, which is exactly why collectors continue to choose art glass, its fragility notwithstanding.

▼ *This extensive collection of Steuben and a few Sinclaire American art glass candlesticks allows for a single theme that can be rearranged in many configurations: by pairs, color, height, design, pedestal or bobeche form, and more.*

▶ *Displaying an extraordinarily large art glass vase by Quezal (18in/45.7cm) with a small, faceted agate vase by Tiffany (8½in/ 21.6cm) emphasizes both. Placing them against the cool blue cloth provides contrast that heightens their color.*

Glass Care Basics

Wash your art glass gently. Remember that light refraction will be increased when you remove dirt, dust, and fingerprints. Add a touch of softening agent to lukewarm water with a little mild dishwashing soap. Always avoid harsh chemicals.

To remove really stuck-on dirt or grease, use a little gel toothpaste on an extra-soft brush. Easy does it. Rinse the piece well with the same temperature water—no abrupt changes. Buff dry with a soft lint-free cloth.

Don't expect to remove the cloudy stain from an art glass vessel in which flowers, wine, or vinegar have been allowed to sit. The acid that forms in such a case etches the glass; the glass needs the attention of a professional conservator, who may or may not be able to help. "Sick" glass can seldom be cured.

Keep art glass away from strong, unfiltered sunlight. The glass can get hot enough to crack. It can also be affected by ultraviolet rays over time. It may even act as a magnifying glass and ignite nearby papers or cloth. No kidding.

Anchor your art glass to the display shelf with the pliant wax material recommended by museums. This medium may not hold the glass object in place through an earthquake, but will steady it when the children turn up the volume.

Keep your insurance policies up to date. Take photos or video tapes of your collection. Store both policy and records out of the home.

If your art glass has applied decoration, take special care with cleaning or polishing. Silver or gold accents, hand-painting, enamel decor, beads, or butterflies must be preserved; loss detracts from both appeal and value.

Never pick up or carry your art glass by its handles or applied protuberances. These represent the most vulnerable areas of your collectibles. During the annealing process, when your piece was cooled, tiny fractures or weaknesses may have occurred that could result in significant damage if exposed to undue stress. Treat your art glass with care.

◀ *This display of late 19th century art glass from Mount Washington and New England Glass Co. uses graduated light intensity to accent the Burmese and Peachblow color and Royal Flemish medallions.*

▲ *Similar design and decoration hold this arrangement of Carder Steuben vases together. The green Aurene, Tyrian, and blue Aurene Intarsia pieces complement one another, projecting a powerful image of the genre.*

An Art Glass Primer

The art of glass-making dates well back into the ancient past. The first evidence of glass comes from Mesopotamia around 2500 BC. Early glass-making centers of antiquity were Egypt and the Middle East, whose wares were highly prized. The glassmaker's art reached new heights in Islamic Middle East, Renaissance Europe, and Czarist Russia. But for the purposes of this book, art glass of the 19th century, commissioned by royal families and owned by the wealthy few, is the starting point of a story divided into three distinct sections—American, European, and Contemporary. Art glass became available to a broader population only as the world moved into an era of technological and economic advances. Population growth, greater productivity, and the industrial revolution

of the mid 19th century, brought new methods of glass production that introduced more of the product to the general population. At first, the trend was reflected in purely functional glass—tableware, lighting devices, and occasional decorative pieces. Then, in the late 1870s, art glass began finding its way to the homes of the working classes. Glass was revered, tended, and lovingly displayed.

The American glass industry borrowed heavily from earlier European craftsmen and glass masters. American immigrants, business owners, and working class families brought skills and training with them from their home lands. Glass factories sprang up where ready access provided raw materials, workers, and potential buyers. Virginia, Ohio, New Jersey, New York, and New England

Mount Washington Crown Milano, c.1893. $15,000–18,000. 38in/96.5cm tall.

▼ *Pairpoint/Mount Washington Burmese lamp with ducks, c.1898. $14,000–16,000. 19½in/49.5cm.*

▼ *Tiffany Studios Laburnum, c.1899. $140,000–160,000. Adjustable height to 30in/76.2cm.*

became centers of the burgeoning industry. Windows, bottles, and early glass—necessities of the colonial period—became mainstays. In Massachusetts, the Boston & Sandwich Glass Co., the Mount Washington Glass Works and the New England Glass Co. competed, not only for potential profits, but also for available workers and their skills. During the late 19th century, new processes revolutionized the industry, making possible both mass production and major expansion. Increased capacity led to new designs, and throughout the United States, marketing lagged behind production. The "fancy glass" companies were not always adept at selling their new wares.

While art glass of the late 1880s was widely admired then as now, consumers offered resistance to buying it. To the conservative New Englander or Midwestern resident, art glass for art's sake seemed shockingly frivolous. Sensing this attitude, local glass manufacturers produced art glass in more practical, usable forms. All manner of tableware, vases, and especially lamps were made in the complete range of Americanized Victorian-style art glass, including Amberina, Burmese, Lava, Peachblow, Agata, Green Opaque, and Pomona, sometimes patterned with hobnails, drapes, ribbing, and coin spots. Transparent, translucent, and even opaque glass lamps appeared in great quantity and in all colors. Many Tiffany leaded glass lamps sold in the late 1890s and after were bought as "practical" purchases. They are now the foundation of collections.

Americans were certainly primed for collecting art glass by the time the 20th century arrived. Three remarkable men were poised to produce the lustrous golden iridescent art glass that set the style of the 1900s. Louis Comfort Tiffany, Frederick Carder, and Martin A.

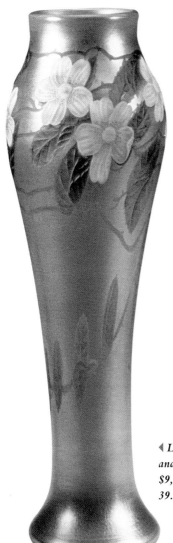

◀ *Louis C. Tiffany Inc. padded and intaglio cut vase, c.1910. $9,000–12,000. 15^1/$_2$in/ 39.3cm tall.*

▲ *Carder Steuben Tyrian disc, c.1916. $25,000–28,000. 16in/40.6cm diam.*

Bach directed the most successful American companies: Tiffany Glass and Decorating Co., the Steuben Glass Works, and the Quezal Art Glass and Decorating Co. For the next 20-some years, these three produced the most significant art glass of the United States, often copied and frequently maligned by critics. While similar, each had his own style and branched into other artistic expressions. All three were profoundly affected by World War I, and later, by the economic swings of the 1920s. Tiffany retired in 1928 and died in 1933. Carder was replaced in 1933, and Steuben reorganized. Bach died in 1921, and Quezal ceased production by 1925. An era had ended, but its art glass lives on in American art glass found throughout the world, and in replications by many artists of today.

The stories of other American art glass producers—equally interesting to the history of art glass—also tell of the whims of the public and the influences of history. Whatever its form, art will always be affected by the world in which it develops. The artists and designers who create art reflect the forces that formed them.

European Art Glass

Meanwhile, a different scenario created a different kind of art glass in Europe. The traditions of the past built an industry with an elite establishment of glass masters, designers, and artists who advanced through an apprentice system. In England, during the surge of art glass development, from 1880 to 1914, the glass-making industry centered around the region of Stourbridge, home to the glassworks of Northwood, Thomas Webb & Sons, and Stevens & Williams. Their collectible glassware evolved at a time when the industrial revolution was having a tremendous impact on the glass-making industry.

England's major contribution to the collectible art glass market is the extraordinary cameo glass, created mostly in the late 19th century and epitomized by the work of the great masters John Northwood, and the brothers George and Thomas Woodall working for Webb. No other country came close to the British mastery of this particular glass technique, although others such as Gallé and Burgun &

▶ *British cameo glass, featuring miniatures, scent bottles, and vases, ranging from $200 for the smallest to $20,000 for the tall tricolor bird vase (18 1/2 in / 47cm). The George Woodall portrait vase (7 1/4 in / 19.6cm) at center is valued at $25,000–30,000.*

Schverer had their own approach. It was a function of the times that the British glass industry could profitably allow the creation of cameo glass masterworks that required months, even years to complete. In addition, glass artists resisted the pull of new machines, clinging to the old model of the artist as hand-crafter. Many of the resulting pieces were made primarily for exhibition and the prestigious awards and commissions they could earn—standard procedure in 1890.

This is not to say that the controversy of art versus industry did not find resolution. The introduction and acceptance of acid-etched cameo glass allowed the execution of thousands of designs and production of cameo glass for lucrative foreign and domestic trade. The United States became the largest importer of British cameo glass from 1890 to 1914; in fact, much of the Webb and Stevens & Williams production was made specifically for the American market. British art glass remained popular in the United States, excepting the war years, until the late 1920s, when the economy slipped into depression.

Collectors of British cameo glass find mostly the typical white on colored glass vases and decorative art forms in the American marketplace because that was mostly what had been exported. On the other hand, at least one major collection of made-for-home British cameo glass, gathered in England, came into the United States in the 1980s and was dispersed into private collections and public museums shortly thereafter. Historically, when great examples of a glass venue become suddenly available, collectors respond positively, and values for the ware increase significantly. These increases soon trickle down into the general collectibles marketplace. The network of collectors is a major force in changing prices.

In France, the history of art glass resembles that of Britain, affected by economic factors and wars that damaged their homeland but not their spirit. As a result of the Franco-Prussian war of 1870, many formerly French glassworks and workers were now in German territory, and repatriation was a long time coming. It was not until after World War I that the affected region of Alsace-Lorraine

▶ *Daum cameo glass vase, c.1920s. The acid-etched design shows three dancers wearing fashions in the Art Deco style. $18,000–20,000. 12in/30.4cm tall.*

▲ *Quezal vase, c.1910. This piece was blown into a ribbed mold, giving it a striped appearance as the opal white inside shows through the green exterior. $6,000–7,500. 8in/20.3cm tall.*

◀ *Thomas Webb cameo glass sculptural vase, c.1900. Minor damage to this piece lowers its value by about half. $2,500–3,500. 7½in/ 19cm tall.*

became French again. During the interim, many glass workers fled to the Nancy area where Gallé, Daum, and others created the art glass so highly regarded throughout the world. In each of the French art glass companies of the period, positive economic factors of the late 19th century allowed the development of art glass as a viable commodity, both as an artistic medium and as a decoration for the home.

France's glass artist-craftsmen expressed their talents without relying too much on industrial techniques. For example, Jean Cros rediscovered the ancient art of *pâte de verre* (paste of glass), but did not share or exploit the knowledge in his lifetime. It was left for Decorchmont, Argy-Rousseau, and Walter to redevelop the same techniques independently, and to benefit artistically and financially from their skill and knowledge of this ancient art glass technique. In any case, while glass artists resisted industrial mass production techniques, the technology marched forward.

Virtually all the French glasshouses were closed for the duration of World War I, 1914 to 1918, except for work required for the war effort—French at first, then German during the occupation. The post-war period moved France steadily back to normalcy, but times had changed. The styles of the early 1910s, the scenic cameos and Franco-Art Nouveau florals, had lost favor, and an exuberant vivacious

new style was gaining ground. Between the wars, from 1919 to 1939, art glass thrived. The Art Deco style and spirit renewed faith in the arts and with it the art glass industry. Preeminent designer René Lalique's work inspired a number of Art Deco designers to greater heights of creativity in glass, lighting, and architecture.

Highly sophisticated studios and clientele established an environment in which designer-artists could produce their work without "selling out" to the industrial establishment. French art glass artist Maurice Marinot is a case in point, perhaps surpassing the genius of all French art glass artists. On the other hand, his work seldom appears in the collectibles marketplace, in part because of his fierce independence. The industrial establishment did perfectly well without Marinot and those like him. There was room for both the elusive artist and the entrepreneur.

Unfortunately for both, the coming of World War II crushed the expansion of the arts and, economically or literally, destroyed many of the glass factories and related businesses. The period of post-war reconstruction of French glass factories incorporated still more industrial methods and techniques. As in Britain and the United States, production of significant art glass was slow to make a comeback. Meanwhile, modern art glass innovations from Italy and the Scandinavian nations sent a breath of fresh air into the art glass milieu.

◀ *Venini Murano patchwork vase, c.1950. In the Vetri Pezzati series. $5,000–7,000. 8¼ in/20.9cm*

▼ *Venini Murano patchwork vase, c.1950. $5,000–7,000. 5¾ × 7¼ in/14.6 × 18.4cm.*

◀ *Argy-Rousseau veilleuse/ night light, c.1925. This is a popular collectible form with conforming wrought metal mounts. $7,000–8,000. 8½ in/21.6cm tall.*

Venice is a city of 118 islands, separated by 160 canals and connected with 400 bridges. Virtually all the Venetian glass factories are located, for fire protection, on the island of Murano. The businesses are historically interrelated and highly competitive, with a symbiotic relationship that mysteriously improves the artistic performance of each. After World War II, the Murano glasshouses—led by, but not limited to Venini—created a king-sized commotion with their colorful, often whimsical, design-centered glass art. Not quite Art Deco in style, their works were more closely related to the Secessionist school of art combined with Italy's own Novecento style. The Italian glass of the 1950s and '60s led the world in a resurgence of art glass and provided a bridge for the international Contemporary Studio Glass Movement. It is no wonder that collectors around the globe seek the mid-20th-century art glass from Murano to satisfy their obsession for original art glass designs with which to decorate their homes, offices, and retreats. Nor is it surprising that Dale Chihuly suspended chandelier/lanterns from so many bridges in the Venetian lagoon in tribute to the leadership of their glassmasters.

Austrian-Bohemian art glass is also a product of 20th-century political and economic upheavals. The Loetz and Moser glass companies have been the most significant and prolific of the many glass factories in the area. Today's extraordinary interest in Austrian-Bohemian glassware is due in no small measure to the art glass's availability in the marketplace. You can't collect what you can't find! The Bohemian companies, and later the Czechoslovakians, discovered early on the importance of a strong continuing business relationship with the countries of the Americas. They established import-export commerce with the United States, Canada, Mexico, and certain South American countries. Coming from a great tradition of virtuosity in glass-making, the companies could produce whatever the client preferred in design, style, size, color, or function. They were masters of technique and their decorating skills were unsurpassed. They had, after all, centuries of preparation behind them.

Contemporary Art Glass

The Contemporary Studio Glass Movement began roughly 40 years ago. That seems a long time to be tagged "contemporary," but the name remains. The Studio Glass Movement really took off after 1962, when the Littleton–Labino workshop built the first small furnace for blowing glass *(see pages 158–159)*, and, suddenly, studio glass courses appeared at universities and art schools virtually everywhere. Young and old alike joined enthusiastically in the development and support of this modern art form.

The Littleton-Labino workshop achievement was a significant breakthrough. Never before had artists been able to create their designs themselves, working in their own studios with small furnaces and tools of the art. With the new innovations, they could take the glass-making process from beginning to end, as thoroughly and professionally as any painter, potter, or poet. The glass artists were able to elevate their craft to an art with the same potential for technical virtuosity and aesthetic expression available to artists in any medium. This was the true beginning of the Studio Glass Movement and it has spread throughout the world like wildfire.

▶ *Five "Charder" vases by Schneider, c.1930. Collected for their form, color, and technique, these pieces are decorated in the Art Deco style. $1,800–3,500. 5–19in / 12.7–48.2cm tall.*

Looking at Art Glass: An Identification Guide

Imagine that wonderful moment when you come across a table full of art glass available for sale. Perhaps you are the first one into the consignment shop when a dealer is changing the display. Or you drive into a country auction where nobody bothered to advertise the art glass available. Maybe you make it to a little antique show in the middle of a blizzard and find yourself the only customer there. These are the novice collector's dream situations. So, what do you look for? Which item is valuable and which can be passed by? Here are some essentials to take into consideration.

Form is basic. Also called shape, and even design, the form is of paramount importance. This raises the first and most important tenet: the collector decides. Your favorite form may be asymmetrical and angular, or a perfectly balanced classical shape. You may prefer a straight-sided cylinder or a curvaceous baluster body with handles. Good form will catch the appraiser/collector's eye; it's decisive, comfortable to live with, and aesthetically pleasing to you.

Style is another part of the same equation. Style can refer to a very specific school of artistic expression, such as Art Nouveau, Art Deco, Arts and Crafts, Secessionist, Modern or Moderne, or Revivalist—Greco-Roman,

Egyptian, Islamic, Japonesque, Venetian, and so on. If you care to pursue it, some study will teach you to identify a variety of decorative art styles in a heartbeat. Style also refers to what matters to the collector/appraiser. Good art glass has a lot of style—pizzazz, aplomb, or savoir faire. This, again, is a matter of personal judgment. The collector of satin glass rose bowls has a different reference point for style from the collector of Victor Durand crackle glass.

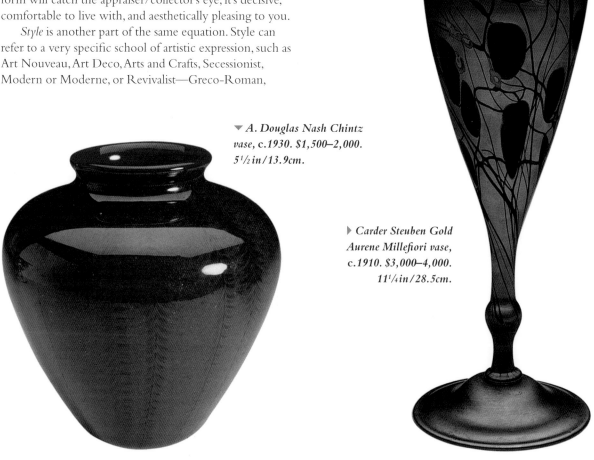

▼ *A. Douglas Nash Chintz vase, c.1930. $1,500–2,000. 5 1/2 in/13.9cm.*

▶ *Carder Steuben Gold Aurene Millefiori vase, c.1910. $3,000–4,000. 11 1/4 in/28.5cm.*

Condition matters as well. Check the top of a piece of art glass. Run your finger around the rim. It should feel smooth, without nicks or chipping. It will be either polished or rounded, depending on how it was made and finished. If it is polished, you must determine if the piece was sheared at the time of making, or was cut down to eliminate a chip and then polished to hide the repair. Next hold the item to the light to see if there are any flaws or cracks within the glass. Note that flaws such as a grain of undissolved sand or a flake of carbon are considered "in the making" and, if minor, generally are acceptable to collectors without detracting a great deal from the value. Flaws or damage that occur later, however, are less acceptable and definitely detract from the appraisal value. Check the base also to make sure no chips or evidence of repair exist. On cameo glass, run your finger around the decoration as well. Chips on the outer layer of glass may not be obvious in a quick inspection. Don't wait until you get the item home to check.

Marks can help you. They can also break your heart. Much of the art glass from the golden period of 1880–1930 was not marked. When it was, the marks were often sloppy, executed in an offhand manner that make forgery easy. As you study the marks on legitimate art glass pieces, you will probably be surprised to see how crude and amateurish many of them look. You may find a beautiful, intricately designed masterwork made by the Tiffany Studios, then find the original mark "L.C.T." on the base looking as though a 9-year-old child had made it. Or you may find an extraordinary Orrefors Ariel vase with engraved markings on the base rim that defy translation into the Swedish "artist, number, and date" that you know should be there. Take heart. Marks are easily copied. Use them, but do not depend on them.

Note the illustration of fakes and forgeries below. These pieces of art glass were not made to deceive. They are perfectly legitimate pieces of modern studio glass that once may have been signed by the original studio: perhaps Orient & Flume, Lundberg, Correia, or Lotton, for example, all of which are reputable artist studios that do fine work. Some rogue dealer looking for profit changed the mark to L.C. Tiffany, not the original maker. Again, use the marks, but do not depend on them.

Finally, *rarity* affects value greatly. Short of traveling with personal computer and reference books (and some collectors do this), you may be confronted with an item you do not recognize, a signature you do not know, or a design that defies your knowledge. In such a case, go back to the basics. Check form, design, style, and condition. See if a mark can help you. Most importantly, decide whether you like the piece well enough to live with it. If your answer is "Yes," know that later you can study it, learn about it, and make it your own. Understanding the rarity factor requires expertise and the time to acquire it.

▲ *Durand King Tut vase, c.1928. $800–1,000. 6¼ in/ 15.8cm tall.*

▶ *American art glass pieces with fake signatures. Made by modern studio artists, the original marks were later replaced with forged Tiffany signatures.*

Comparing Art Glass

Now, think of the numbered illustration below as your table full of art glass. Notice the two blue iridescent double-bulbed vases: **#2,** the smaller vase, is Steuben blue Aurene, a nice diminutive example; **#15,** is a Tiffany vase. The color and lustre on the two pieces is quite similar. The form of the tall vase is slender and even feminine in design with a gentle flare at top and base. The Steuben vase is unusual, with a stylish form that is rather chunky by comparison. Each is in good condition and is marked on the base in the proper manner: "Steuben Aurene 1647" and "L.C. Tiffany Favrile 1065-984M," suggesting but not guaranteeing authenticity. Neither is a great rarity, but the value of the Tiffany is higher than the Steuben. Why? Two main factors explain the discrepancy: size and demand. Like it or not, value tends to increase with size, and there is more popular demand for Tiffany art glass in the global collectibles marketplace.

Notice the five pieces of cameo glass on the table. Two are French, three are English. Most English cameo glass is white cased to colored glass, as are **#4, 7,** and **8.** The others are French cameo glass, both scenic, **#1** and **10.** Considering the form of the examples and the design of the decoration, the three English pieces are light, delicate, and elegant. By comparison, the French pieces are strong, with forceful graphic impact. All are in fine condition. The British pieces have added value because of their form. The red vase **#4** is a diminutive sphere and skillfully decorated with a bird, giving it special value. Birds, animals, fish, and people add value to art glass. The red bottle **#7** has extra value as a perfume, called a lay-down teardrop scent bottle. Perfume collectors are legion. And the miniature lamp has special appeal to that specialty area in which collectors tend to be avid. All three English cameo items enjoy collectibility factors in more than one idiom, thereby increasing their treasure status.

Back to the French cameo glass. Number **1** is an especially well-detailed De Vez scenic vase with two layers of glass acid-etched with floral design above a scene with deer (!) in a forest. The animals increase the value here, but there is no comparing its collectibility factors with those of the Gallé example **#10.** Even though this vase was made after his death in 1904, Gallé glass is still more highly regarded than most of the contemporary glassworks of this period and method. A hands-on examination of the vase would show a grand vista through the trees of a magnificent mountain range and a distant lake. At least

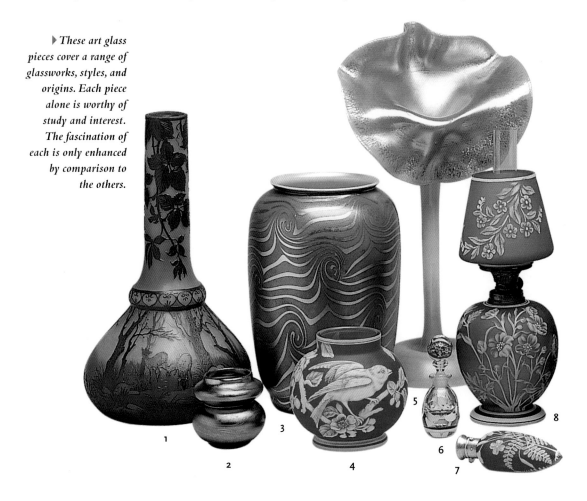

▶ *These art glass pieces cover a range of glassworks, styles, and origins. Each piece alone is worthy of study and interest. The fascination of each is only enhanced by comparison to the others.*

four layers of glass are etched as opposed to one or two in our other cameo examples. The Gallé vase is appraised higher than three of the other cameo pieces, but the most valuable of the group is the Stevens & Williams English cameo miniature lamp **#8.** It is a rare item, a survivor from the relatively few produced in the late 19th century, and it shows why rarity is one of our guiding appraisal factors. Still, the most valuable item remains on the table.

Two of the art glass vases are decorated with pulled and coiled designs with an iridescent art glass surface. The green vase **#3** is Durand art glass, made by the Vineland, NJ, company, and decorated in their most famous pattern. The decoration, called King Tut, was named in response to American interest in all things Egyptian during the relatively few years of Durand's production, 1924–1931. They used a limited number of forms during that time; advanced collectors can recognize their shapes easily. Note that the pulled coils of decoration are symmetrically placed and skillfully executed on this example, and the color and lustre are especially vivid. It is a fine example of Durand art glass. Compare this to the iridescent vase with pulled feather decoration that is accented with ten complex and colorful peacock eyes, **#13.** This Tiffany Studios vase is a classic in American Art Nouveau-style, form, and decoration, and it is difficult for the Durand piece, fine as it is, to complete with that. Even the peacock decoration is quintessential Tiffany, increasing its collectibility greatly.

While we are considering the iridescent pieces, **#5** is a fine gold flower-form vase also made by Tiffany Studios and usually called a jack-in-the-pulpit vase. At just under 14in/35.5cm tall, this blossom vase is only average for Tiffany; some are perilously taller and proportionately more valuable. Be aware that when you check the rim on iridescent pieces like this, you may feel some textural roughness. Not to worry, the stretched edges will often feel that way. Just check to be sure there are no breaks or chips in the glass, quite different from texture. This Tiffany floriform has one of the company's simplistic marks, "L.C.T.W6679," but it is as good as gold, and so indeed is the vase. In appraisal value, though, the two most important vases are still on the table.

The little silver flower pot **#12** is a Tiffany & Co. decoration. Charles Lewis Tiffany, who owned Tiffany & Co., was the father of Louis Comfort Tiffany, who produced the Tiffany Studios art glass we collect today. Although they sometimes sold Louis Comfort's glass, Tiffany & Co. did not produce glass and should in no way be confused with Tiffany Studios. This decorative little sterling silver vase is worth about $900. It is a nice collectible; not glass.

Another little trinket **#6** is a diminutive paperweight perfume bottle made by Charles Kaziun in the 1980s, a piece of contemporary studio art glass. It was made in the warm glass technique of flameworking (also called

9   10   11   12   13   14   15

lampwork), combined with the paperweight method of casing the decoration within colorless molten glass. Kaziun added a "K" signature cane inside his work that assures identification for collectors and appraisers. This bottle is unusual for its matching double decoration in the base and stopper, and will attract both perfume and paperweight collectors. This piece is worth about the same as the Webb perfume **#7**, despite the difference in their ages. Relative age does not necessarily affect appraisal value, but appealing to collectors in more than one venue does.

Among Tiffany's rarest and most coveted art glass achievements is **#11**. The paperweight vases were created by trapping the decoration within two layers of transparent glass, sometimes lightly colored, sometimes iridized. This example is a "morning glory" vase, skillfully assembled, highly prized, and rarer than rare. The signature mark reads "Louis C. Tiffany—Special Exhibit 1293N" and is accompanied by an original Tiffany label, both of which increase the inherent value. This is one of the most important and valued art glass examples shown here.

Two pieces remain to be identified, and both score high on all value factors. The little Tiffany vase **#14** has great form and color. Red is rare in Tiffany, and this one is made more brilliant because it is cased to opal white, adding depth and vibrancy. The tiny handles were created by a master glassmaker, who pulled them from the vessel at the fire. The tactile quality of this gem cannot be adequately explained. It has to be experienced. It would be hard to turn this one down, whatever the asking price.

At the center, **#9** is the only molded piece of art glass on the table. René Lalique named it "Courges" (French for "gourds"), and it shows why some consider him a master of 20th-century design. Consider the form: the squat round shape of the vessel is itself a pumpkin gourd. The chosen color is purple/aubergine, the color of an eggplant or gourd. The vegetable is likewise portrayed in the design of the molded decoration, repeating the shape/form. Notice that in the execution of the decoration, the background is textured and frosted; the vines and tendrils are raised and polished. Lalique collectors see the design occasionally, but seldom in a color that does what this does, narrating the form and the decorative design chromatically. This is the most valuable item on the table, an absolute treasure.

Looking at art glass, of course, is always subjective and judgmental. Everyone brings his or her own preferences and experiences to each display of art glass he or she encounters. This exercise in "looking" is meant to sharpen your observations, broaden your focus, and suggest alternatives to your usual viewpoints. Looking at art glass can enrich your life.

The photograph below presents another group of assorted art glass—the tallest, approximately 18 inches (45.7cm)—that includes the makers Gallé, Daum, Loetz, Lalique, Barovier, Venini, Tiffany, Steuben, and Chihuly. These pieces are both American and European and range from the late 19th century (Gallé) to the late 20th century (Chihuly).

▼ *The tallest piece at center, an Artisti Barovier vase, is alone worth about $40,000. The collection as a whole is worth roughly $150,000.*

Looking at contemporary art glass requires a slightly different vision than that for earlier work. Dale Chihuly is one of a new generation of art glass artists who are part of the Contemporary Studio Glass Movement. He stands among those whose work is the best of today's art glass, largely being sold in private galleries and art studios, gift shops, and department stores with whom the artists have arrangements or contacts. Searching for contemporary studio glass art in the usual collectibles marketplace is not particularly productive, because the work has not had time to reach a second-hand, or used, marketplace. Occasional discoveries in auctions and shows, especially those focused on modern decorative arts, are fortunate exceptions. Every so often they do provide wonderful surprises for the persistent and tenacious treasure hunter. Be assured, as you are looking at and for art glass, that more pieces will come to light for collectors and serious seekers of contemporary studio glass art. In the meantime, exciting and potentially important glass art is available in small studio shops operated by the artists themselves.

Some of the art glass pieces you have seen in the preceding pages you will encounter again in the series of two-page comparisons that are the heart of this book. Some could even come your way at the most unexpected time or place—at an antique shop, show, auction, garage sale, on the web, even in your own attic. What you find in these pages will help you determine whether you have found a treasure and how you should value it.

▲ *Venini monumental art glass flowering plant, designed by Napoleone Martinuzzi, c.1930. $15,000–25,000. 7ft/2.1m tall.*

◄ *Durand candlesticks, c.1928. Note the pulled and coiled King Tut decoration on gold iridescent glass. $1,800–2,000.*

▶ Quezal Decanter,
c.1912. This iridescent
decanter has double-hooked
and pulled-feather
decoration. $4,500–6,000.
11in/27.9cm tall.

American Art Glass

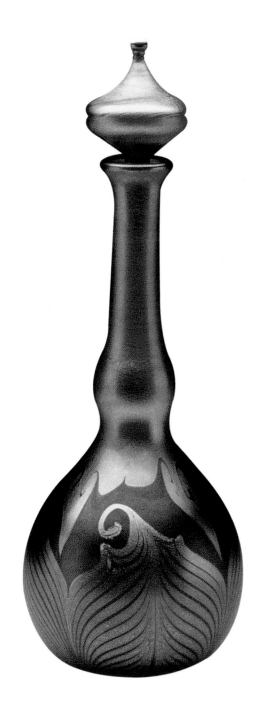

Alton Glass Works— Trevaise Glass

Cardenio F. King founded his Alton Glass Works on the bankrupt shoulders of the Sandwich Glass Co. early in the 20th century. The Trevaise glass he produced continues to be valued 100 years later, not only for its iridescent surface and distinctive coloration, but also for its historical significance as the final flowering of art glass in Sandwich, MA. Because Alton, too, went bankrupt within a year of its start-up, Trevaise vases are valued as well for their relative scarcity in the marketplace.

Although clearly Art Nouveau in style, which tends to be highly perishable, Trevaise pieces are not particularly vulnerable to breakage. They have a transitional Arts and Crafts flavor, allowing them a comfortable fit in both stylistic settings, a plus for collectors.

Trevaise glass is best known by its color and telltale wafer base. Produced almost exclusively as opaque, thickly walled vases, it appeared in shades of green or, less often, in amethyst or purple. Iridescent golden swirls and organic leaf forms ornamented the freeblown and essentially oval vase forms. The rims were sometimes tooled into triangular or squared-top openings. The glassmakers reinforced the base at the pontil mark with a glass wafer—a characteristic that helps collectors identify the often unsigned and unmarked ware. The added blob of glass can be as small as a dime or as large as a quarter, and is smoothed or polished so that the vase can stand straight.

The cost of Trevaise ware is conservative compared to much of the other iridescent art glass. This may be due to the regional nature of demand, the infrequent inclusion of the line in reference books, or its scarcity. The line could, however, prove to be a good investment. Demand seems to be rising, and the supply will always be limited.

Trevaise Green-Amber Vase, c. 1908

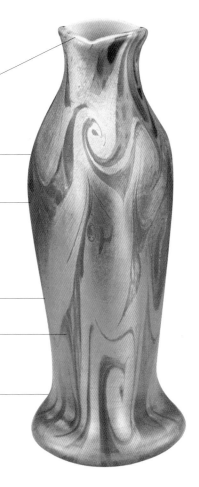

The rim opening is well-articulated and complements the triangular design.

The glassmaker created this triangular form using hardwood paddles while the piece was still in its molten state.

The height is average for Trevaise vases and is pleasingly proportional to the design.

The green-amber color is also typical of Trevaise ware, not quite green, but too dark to be called amber. The glass itself is thick and opaque, centering attention on the form, color, and decoration.

The decoration is extensive and well-executed.

The base's glass wafer was engraved with an "L.C.T."—an attempt to label it as Tiffany. This defaces and devalues the vase.

Height: 8½ in/21.6cm
Value: $1,000–1,200

Trevaise Purple Vase, *c.*1907

The baluster body of this vase, like the example opposite, is triangular—especially unusual for Trevaise ware.

The vase's height, considered tall, adds to its value.

The deep purple color of the piece is unusual—purple examples are considered rare and therefore more valuable.

The iridescent decoration is especially well-defined. The swirls and coils are of lustrous silver-blue and symmetrically cover the entire body.

The technical challenge of crafting the unusual pedestal foot was not quite met, as the vase is slightly off-center.

The foot makes the vase more graceful, but the tilt has to be considered a flaw that detracts from value.

Height: 10½ in/25.4cm
Value: $1,200–1,400

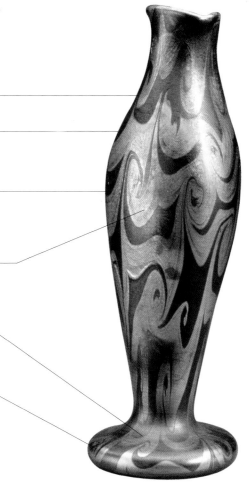

• *The Alton Glass Works's only line of art glass, produced in 1907 and 1908, replicated the iridescent glass being made at that time by Tiffany, Quezal, and Steuben in the United States, and by Loetz and Webb in Europe.*
• *Occasionally, the oval bodies were shaped into artful designs with swelled curving sides, a raised pedestal-style foot, or an elongated neck.*
• *Alton glassblowers had trouble with more complicated designs. Examples of Trevaise glass are frequently found in less-than-perfect condition.*
• *Because total output of Trevaise glass was so limited, serious collectors tend to be somewhat accepting of flaws.*

The End of a Glassmaking Era

The Alton Glass Works was established by Cardenio F. King in 1907 from the remnants of the Sandwich (MA) Glass Co. The latter had declared bankruptcy, after a period of bad accounting and labor disputes made financial recovery impossible. Essentially a financier and businessman, Cardenio King assumed the bankrupt company's debts, took over its land and buildings, and wisely hired experienced and forward-looking craftsmen, many of them former Sandwich Glass employees.

Although the main thrust of glass production at Alton was utilitarian and/or industrial in nature, King launched an iridescent art glass line he called "Trevaise." Developed by workers said to have come from Tiffany and other major art glass studios, the "Trevaise" line became a significant part of the company's output.

Unfortunately, the effort proved to be too little, too late. Undermined by the same financial difficulties that had plagued its predecessors, the Alton Glass Works failed after only a year. King absconded with company funds, was found, tried, and fined—a sad ending to a viable, engaging enterprise.

Glass-making had enjoyed a long chapter in Sandwich, MA. The failure of the Alton Glass Works marked its end. The legacy endures, however, in the distinctive, and sometimes quite beautiful, Trevaise glass that is sought today by historians and collectors alike.

Brilliant Period Cut Glass

The 35-year period from 1880 to 1915 is considered to be the epitome of the Brilliant Period of cut glass. The phenomenon was primarily American but originated in Europe. So popular was the glass produced, and so prolific were the factories involved, that the subject warrants its own treatment here.

The significance of the Brilliant Period of cut glass is evident in every antique shop, flea market, and appraisal program throughout the country. The glass appears everywhere; it is, or has been, in virtually every home, on every table, and in every china cabinet in the United States. People bought it, loved it, took good care of it, and passed it on to subsequent generations.

Most cut glass originally sold to relatively wealthy people, the so-called "carriage trade." Expensive both to manufacture and to buy, cut glass nevertheless enjoyed a remarkable popularity and sold well, especially in times of economic prosperity. By the time of World War I, however, its popularity had waned. The Victorian style of cut glass lost favor in homes that inclined toward the Arts and Crafts movement, and it was deemed inappropriate with Art

Deco furnishings and accessories. People relegated their cut glass to the backs of cabinets and attics for a time.

Over the years, the market value of cut glass, like that of most antiques and collectibles, has fluctuated in cycles. In the late 1950s, a renewed appreciation of traditional handcrafted decorations rekindled interest in American Brilliant Period cut glass. As the art glass spurred a series of articles, books, museum exhibitions, and auctions of private collections, demand increased and market prices escalated. American Brilliant Period cut glass came out of hiding and was restored to its original lustre for a new generation of collectors.

Again in the 1990s, when many "gay '90s" Victorian homes were restored and numerous large, many-gabled neo-Gothic houses built, a new generation of decorators sought the original cut glass decorations from the turn of the 20th century. The momentum of that revival has continued into the 21st, manifested in websites, seminars, and clubs throughout the United States. As a matter of course, the market value of Brilliant Period cut glass has risen in response to this burgeoning demand.

Brilliant Colorless Cut Glass Bowl, c.1900

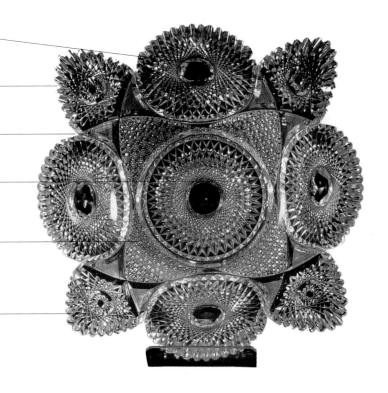

Four-side and four-corner hobstars around the raised, curved sides increase complexity.

The scalloped rim cuts deeply into the bowl to allow the cutting of the hobstar pattern.

The glass blank's high lead content shows in its weight and thickness, clarity, and brilliance.

The central hobstar pattern matching the corners gives added continuity to the design.

The central square is fine-cut overall (the plate opposite has double decorated squares). Less complexity means less value.

Brilliant cut glass bowls are often marked at center; this one is not. Similarities to the piece opposite, however, suggest the same maker.

Size: 3¹/₄ x 11¹/₂in/
8.3 x 29.2cm
Value: $2,000–3,000

Brilliant Colorless Cut Glass Plate, *c.*1900

This serving plate has eight hobstars around its scalloped rim. Compare with the bowl opposite, which has oval stars at the corners.

The blank is thick and heavy, indicating high lead content and allowance for extra depth in cutting.

Two superimposed squares within the hobstar border surround the central hobstar festoon pattern.

The diameter is impressive and allows more than usual artistic freedom of design in the pattern.

A diminutive cane pattern inside the squares, with small hobstars at angles, results in extra graphic impact.

This piece might increase in market value with a mark; but knowledgeable collectors attribute it to Hawkes.

Size: 14in/35.5cm diameter
Value: $4,000–5,000

• *Market value depends now, as always, on literal brilliance —the quality of the blank and precision of the cutting.*
• *Quality blanks resulted from good ingredients: high lead content for the heavy glass and fine sand for clarity.*
• *Cracks and chips decrease value drastically. Even in rare pieces, prices decline with professional restoration.*
• *Color in cut glass is rare and increases market value greatly. Overlaid American patterns, a rarity, are favored by collectors.*
• *Collectors should beware of reproductions, especially of color-overlaid pieces. German, Bohemian, and Chinese reproductions are known to exist.*

American Cut Glass

American Brilliant Period cut glass had its origins in Europe, especially in Victorian Britain, where glass cutting and carving defined the financial success of many glass companies. Immigration of workers to the United States in the mid-to-late 19th century imported glass-working techniques and skills to new and expanding factories, especially to New England, the central Eastern states, and the Ohio River Valley. With bountiful natural resources and financial capital available, the glass industries throughout the country welcomed the influx of skilled labor.

From the 1880s, cut glass evolved into a two-pronged industry: the production of "blanks" for bowls, plates, vases, and other forms; and the the actual cutting shops where the blanks were decorated. For the first, the factories necessarily cooperated with one another, buying and selling as blanks were needed. Among the cutting shops, however, competition developed over possession of the cutting patterns. Each company registered its own designs with the U.S. patent office, seeking a period of protection. Eventually, designs became fair game for competitors.

Signatures on cut glass pieces came into use because of fierce competition between firms. These acid-stamped marks are often difficult to locate or see, so collectors need to search diligently. The Brilliant Period companies producing and marking their cut glass include: Clark, Corning, Dorflinger, Eggington, Fry, Hawkes, Hoare, Libbey, Maple City, Sinclaire, Strauss, Tuthill, Unger, and more.

Cambridge Glass Company

The Cambridge Glass Co. provided the American public with elegant, stylish, and, above all, colorful home glassware at affordable prices. The company introduced pressed glass products in new colors with exotic and descriptive names for its tableware, vases, service pieces, crystal stems, tumblers, and novelties. Even in the late 1920s and '30s, during the Great Depression, Cambridge managed to thrive. It maintained showrooms in New York City, Pittsburgh, Los Angeles, and Chicago, as well as displays in department stores and shops throughout numerous smaller cities and towns of the United States.

Special decorating shops were part of the Cambridge Glass Co. operation. There the workers offered gilt and hand-painted polychrome designs, etched and wheel-cut decorations, and special-order work with monograms or personalized motifs. The costs remained stable. In addition, the quality of the products and the artistic merit of patterns and designs served to fuel ongoing popularity.

The collectibility of Cambridge glass was built into the original concept. Patterns—with the original colors and decorations—remained available through the years. A single wedding gift could create a lifelong commitment to a given pattern, encouraging later additions. Today, as well, for the current collector, a pattern, color, or particular decoration often inspires an entire collection, requiring multiple forays to shops, flea markets, trunk sales, and online auctions.

The Cambridge Glass Co. products continue to be desirable for the same reasons they were 75 years ago. The collector will often find pieces marked with the Cambridge "C" in a triangle-molded trademark. Books and catalog reprints are available for identifying pieces, and collectors can contact the organization of National Cambridge Collectors for information and advice. Because the company was so successful over such an extended period of time, an abundance of the collectible glass exists in the current marketplace. Prices for unusual patterns, colors, or novelties run higher than for the more abundant pieces. As always, rarity, condition, and design will influence value and motivate collectors.

Amber Buffalo Centerbowl, *c.*1940

This shallow bowl with molded relief design and rim curved inward was designed as a serving platter or floral display.

The diameter gives ample room for the well-designed Western scene at center and edge.

The golden amber color, accented by frosted etching, accentuates the piece's impact.

This raised pattern, misnamed "Everglades," adds value on the market.

Background art, including cactus plants and weapons, gives graphic impact to the buffalo-hunting scene.

Scratches and wear inside the bowl decrease value for collectors; condition problems always lower price.

Size: 3 x 16in/7.6 x 40.6cm
Value: $150–250

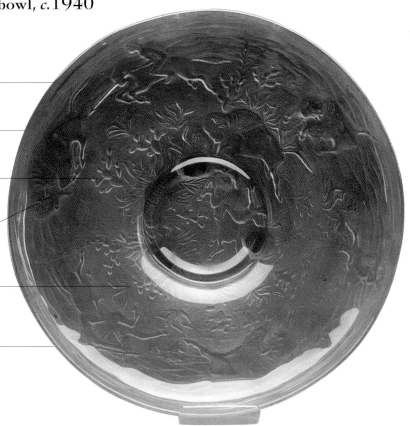

Crown Tuscan Decorated Flying Nude, *c.* 1940

This molded figurehead of a nude woman at the bowl's "helm" is the best recognized Cambridge symbol.

The Flying Nude bowl came in different sizes. This model is of median height.

The shell-form molded bowl is in an opaque pink color, part of the ever-popular Crown Tuscan line.

Gold and enamel decoration of pink roses, purple violets, and green leaves, such as seen here, add color and value in the collectible marketplace.

The raised ball-and-pedestal foot sets off the bowl with a sculptural effect, adding to artistic impact and value.

Decoration around the disk foot matches the floral motif above and adds similarly to the value.

Size: 9 x 12in/22.9 x 30.5cm
Value: $250–400

- *Cambridge Glass Co. added 35 new colors to their line between 1922 and 1938.*
- *Patterns for the pressed stemware involved etching on transparent or colorless crystal; most pieces were marked with the "C-in-a-triangle" trademark.*
- *Crown Tuscan was created by founding president Arthur J. Bennett in 1932, becoming a bestseller in production until the closing in 1958.*
- *Cambridge Glass was one of the first to embrace industrial changes—a serious conflict between art and industry for some art glassmakers.*
- *Pressed glass reproductions rarely appear, because they don't offer much profit. Some Cambridge replications do exist, however, so collectors need to be careful.*

The Arrival of Pressed Glass

Early in the 20th century, William McKinley began his second term as U.S. president amid prosperity. Big businesses flourished, including a conglomerate called the National Glass Co., made up of 19 glass companies in five states. The group developed plans to add another plant—the biggest and most productive of all—in Cambridge, OH. The plant was built and incorporated by 1901, but a major change in the economy led to its sale and reorganization. Thus emerged the Cambridge Glass Co. in 1907.

Under its president, Arthur J. Bennett, the new Cambridge Glass Co. became a major producer of glass tableware, home accessories, and crystal stemware. The firm employed thousands of people and supplied gift shops and upscale department stores all across the nation, through economic upswings and downturns, from the 1920s until the late 1950s.

The burgeoning of the Cambridge Glass Co. coincided with the demise of the American Brilliant Period of cut glass, at the time when World War I depleted the supply of lead required for cut glass. This left an opening for easily produced glass products to enter the marketplace. New technology allowed just the needed impetus to the pressed glass industry when Cambridge was expanding and developing new colors, forms, and customers.

Cambridge Glass Co. produced quantities of varicolored and decorated glassware through the Depression years and continued, with adjustments, through World War II and into the 1950s. Only after the American taste for this famous glassware had waned did the company finally close in 1958.

Consolidated Glass Company

Glass designer Reuben Haley's most important claim to fame was his design for Ruba Rhombic, the Consolidated Glass Co.'s innovative glass line designed in 1928. He could not have chosen a worse time. As Ruba Rhombic was arriving in U.S. stores, the stock market crash of 1929 knocked Wall Street into panic. Soon there was no interest in a startling new design of art glass that did not match the popular notion of "quality" glassware. Geometric and linear, Ruba Rhombic came in colors such as jungle green, lilac, smoky topaz, sunshine yellow, opal, black, and silver. Production slowed as the Depression settled in, and, by 1933, Consolidated halted production of the design. Sadly, Reuben Haley died long before his design came into its own some 60 years later.

Even though the Ruba Rhombic line had not found its era, Consolidated continued as a highly productive and largely profitable glass company through much of its history. The "Martele" series included many other successful models of decorative art glass that have also become collectible in the marketplace today. Molded glass

vases called Martele Fairy, Catalonia, Foxglove, Peonies, Sea Gulls, Swallows, Pine Cone, Olives, Owls on Reeds, Dogwood, Katydid, Tropical Fish, Screech Owls, Dancing Nymphs, and more, were often produced in white or custard glass with the raised designs overpainted in color. Pieces appear in colored glass, some of it frosted, and some left clear. Collectors seek the rare pieces and/or those that match their various collecting preferences.

The Phoenix Glass Co. in Monaca, PA, developed a strong link to Consolidated. Kenneth Haley, Reuben's son, designed for Phoenix, and the similarity between the collectible glass made by the two companies created considerable confusion for identification purposes. To make things worse, Phoenix took over Consolidated's molds and produced its art glass line from 1933 until 1936, when the latter company re-opened. Collectors are fortunate to have available a comprehensive research book by Jack Wilson, *Phoenix and Consolidated Art Glass 1926–1980.* Wilson's book provides a great resource for dispelling the confusion between the two companies.

Catalonia Nasturtium Vase, *c.*1931

The central flared rim is slightly out of round, in keeping with the free-form effect of the design.

Three openings at the piece's shoulder allow use as a vase for flower arranging; the collectible form increases its value.

The vessel is of a tripartite lobed design—named for a Spanish coastal region near Monaco—an exotic collectible then and now.

Horizontal ridges add to the flowing, free-form artistic image, difficult to capture in molded glass and a plus-value factor.

The name "Nasturtium" and the color "honey amber"—both used for promotional purposes— added popularity and value.

While not marked or labeled, the vase is certainly Consolidated, number 1170 in the 1931 catalog.

Height: 4¾in/12cm
Value: $300–400

Ruba Rhombic Lilac Dresser Set, *c.* 1928

The tray—a rhomboid form with oblique angles and irregular faceting—is a great rarity when it appears with matching bottles.

The tray is long and flat on top to hold the accessories. Total value of the set greatly exceeds the sum of its individual items.

Lilac color adds another dimension to the rarity of the set and its value; the color is seldom found in Ruba Rhombic.

The angular lines and asymmetrical dimensions go beyond Art Deco into Cubist and Moderne, both in great demand.

Ruba Rhombic's angularity often creates condition problems; it is rarely found without some chipping. This set is perfect.

The set is not marked or labeled, but collectors would not care. A label would not add appreciable value to the set.

Size: 11 x 10 x 7³/₄in/
28 x 25.4 x 19.7cm
Value: $6,000–7,000

• *Less than 1,500 pieces of Ruba Rhombic art glass are believed to exist, due to limited production and brittleness.*
• *The only Ruba Rhombic item produced by Phoenix Glass Co. was a large fishbowl on metal stand, designed by K. Haley. Only four are known, all in a clear Vaseline glass color. Keep an eye out for number five—incredible value.*
• *The Catalonia line appeared in many colors and forms. Expect Catalonia prices to increase over time.*
• *Consolidated's Martele line and Phoenix's sculptured line have greatly increased in value and are expected to continue. Rare forms and unusual colors are best bets.*

From Lamp Parts to Art Glass

The Consolidated Lamp and Glass Co. was established in 1894, in the town of Coropolis, PA. As the name implies, Consolidated's main business involved the production of glass for lamps: shades, fonts, globes, chimneys, and bases. The company thrived and expanded with the electrification of the United States. Its success thrust Consolidated into the art glass and tableware industry.

In the mid 1920s, Consolidated's chief designer, Reuben Haley, caught on to the new style of art glass spreading across Europe. Introduced in 1926, the Martele series imitated the molded vases made by René Lalique, especially Haley's grasshopper and lovebird models. The glass was less fine and the work of different quality from Lalique, but the designs were virtually the same. Consolidated sold its glass in stores such as Woolworth's and Kresges.

Two years later, in 1928, Reuben Haley designed and introduced a new line that would become Consolidated's most famous and celebrated, Ruba Rhombic. The series consisted of tableware, vases, dresser sets, pitchers, tumblers, and trays—altogether about 40 different pieces in a broad range of colors. At the time, the company touted the line as "An Epic in Modern Art." It was made for about five years.

In 1933, the Consolidated Co. closed down briefly to weather the Depression. In the same year, designer Reuben Haley died at the age of 61.

Durand Art Glass—
Vineland Flint Glass Works

The Vineland Flint Glass Works of Vineland, NJ, produced Durand Art Glass from late 1924 through 1931, a period associated with Art Deco, the "Jazz Age," and the "Roaring 20s." But the art glass made at Vineland was more expressive of earlier styles. Victor Durand Jr.'s art glass reflected the traditions of the New Jersey glass makers of the 19th century. When, in 1924, Victor Durand Jr. hired workers who were experienced in the Art Nouveau tradition, they combined forces to create glass in the styles they knew best.

Significantly, the designs of Durand Art Glass were popular with American buyers of the time. In spite of the many new styles, people bought the old for their homes. The art glass division held its own admirably for its seven years of production, especially considering the challenges of the Depression years. In fact, Victor Durand Jr. was planning expansion and merger at the time of his death.

A paradox exists in Durand Art Glass: while it resembles art glass produced elsewhere at the same time, it remains relatively easy to identify as Durand. For example, Durand's King Tut decoration uses pulled coils and swirls of color that resemble vases by Quezal or Tiffany. Yet the best Durand examples—like the vase shown here—have tight, crisp coils with regimented spaces and repeats of the motif. Collectors pay a premium for such quality.

In the late 1920s, when fashionable homes adopted ceiling lamps, chandeliers, and wall sconces, Durand Art Glass produced thousands of light shades for them. Many were made of the same iridescent glass as the vases, using the same decorations and colors. Some were signed at the top rim, but most were not. These have become important collectibles, regardless of the maker. Prices seldom exceed $500, except for great rarities, and many can be found for less than $200. Condition always affects market value.

Spanish Yellow Pulled Feather Centerbowl, *c.*1930

Note the unusual form with its double-flared rim over a conical body and cupped pedestal base.

This piece is in brilliant yellow transparent glass with white pulled feathers outlined in blue; the motif repeats at the base.

The exceptional clarity of the glass shows no flaws or blemishes; scratches would lower the value significantly.

Note the pale, fuzzy feathers on upper bowl. These show less skill than the foot's crisp design.

Matching patterned pieces are hard to find, as production was so limited. Collectors seeking a pattern tend to drive prices up.

The bowl is not marked or signed, but the "signature" is the unique Durand design.

Height: 9in/22.9cm
Value: $1,500–1,800

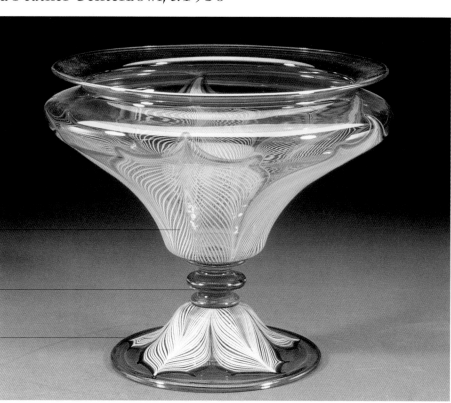

Green on Gold King Tut Vase, *c.*1929

This piece is a real beauty, with its raised rim on a broad shouldered, bulbous body of well-proportioned classic form.

Note the three layers of glass with four colors—green decor on gold glass over an opal white layer, and lined with gold inside. This gives great depth and vibrancy to the whole.

The tightness and symmetry of the swirled coils requires great skill with hot glass and hooks. Difficulty is reflected in increased demand and high price.

Compare the precision on the King Tut with the pulled feather bowl opposite. Both are typical Durand Art Glass ornaments.

Condition here is pristine, both in form and in decoration. The overall iridescence is the icing on the cake. Buyers will pay more for perfect pieces—if they can find them.

The base is marked with "Durand 1964-10"— the model number (not the date), and the height. Some collectors will not buy unsigned pieces; many will.

Height: 10in/25.4cm
Value: $2,500–3,500

• *Transparent "Spanish yellow" glass with pulled feathers was popular, sold as vases, candlesticks, plaques, and stemware. Collectors actively seek these.*
• *Durand's crackled glass and threaded pieces were difficult to make, but easy to damage. Perfect items are expensive.*
• *Marks include an engraved script "Durand" or a silvered "Durand" inside a large "V." The design number and height might be included. But many pieces are not marked, so wise collectors will make themselves familiar with the unique properties of the work.*

Victor Durand Jr.

Established in the late 19th century by Victor Durand Sr. and his son, the Vineland Flint Glass Works originally produced utilitarian glass and bottles. After World War I, Victor Jr. became director of the company and expanded into handcrafted art glass vases and lampshades. In 1924, he persuaded qualified glass workers such as Emil Larson, Martin Bach Jr., and others from the defunct Quezal Co. to join him, thereby establishing an experienced team for the newly formed art glass division.

The glass produced by Victor Durand Jr. compared favorably to that produced at Tiffany, Steuben, Quezal, Imperial, and Kew Blas, thanks to the combined talents of skilled master glass workers. Durand's glass teams blended many of the techniques and designs from competitors, and developed new, innovative forms and procedures in the process.

Victor Durand's plans to further develop the Durand Art Glass division ended abruptly with his death in 1931. The story goes that no one cared to keep the business going without the man whose dreams had built and sustained it. In 1932, Durand was bought by the Kimball Glass Co.

Durand Art Glass— Typical Lines

Today's collectors easily recognize many of the Durand Art Glass lines introduced at the Vineland Flint Glass Works from 1924-1931 as "typical" of Durand. Most notable among these is the "King Tut" design that graced hundreds of vases, lamps, and shades in all variations of color. Other examples include Durand's experimental cameo glass, intaglio-cut cased pieces, and the clear engraved items. Unusual forms unique to Durand include the genie and ginger jars, plaques, and certain of the mantel, chandelier, and torchère lampshades.

As color was so much a part of the art glass mix, Durand chemists were always attempting new shades and variations. The most significant of Durand's new colors was called Lady Gay Rose, which produced a lush opaque pink glass when cased to white and lined in iridescent gold. It was most frequently decorated with the King Tut decoration and is today one of the most popular of Durand collectibles, no matter what the form. It is interesting that this color, much in demand by today's collectors, did not enjoy much popularity at the time of production. Buyers and homemakers thought it a bit garish or ostentatious. Because it did not sell especially well, production was limited. Today, of course, that contributes both to its scarcity in the marketplace and to its value.

Another well-recognized Durand decoration involved a hot glass application known as "threading." Glassmakers took very narrow glass threads in matching or complementary colors and randomly wrapped them around an item while in the molten state so they adhered to the body of the piece. This proved to be a very vulnerable/breakable decoration, and perfect pieces are consequently rare. In shops—actual or virtual—damaged threaded items sell for less than half of the price as for those in good condition.

Crackled Glass Covered Ginger Jar, c. 1930

Covered jars such as this are rarities, and this integrated cover is original and perfect. It even has its berry-form finial on top.

Quasi-Oriental forms had great appeal in the 1920s. The ginger jar was popular then, and collectors look for it today.

Crackled glass in three colors— in this case white, green, and red—is rare. Collectors will expect a higher price for this.

The jar is oversized. Durand made smaller models in many kinds of glass.

See how the glass splits and splinters in the cooling process. Many attempts resulted in cracked or broken pieces, making successful pieces rare.

Height: 10in/25.4cm
Value: $1,200–1,500

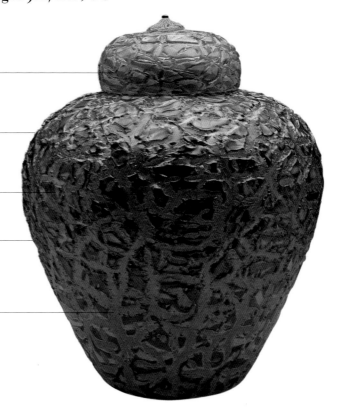

Lady Gay Rose Vase, *c.*1925

The raised flared rim displays the bright orange-gold iridescent interior of this oval cased-glass body.

This simple, basic Durand form is taller than average, which makes for an impressive display of the better-than-average decoration.

Lady Gay Rose was Durand's tour de force, especially with this bright red-rose color and silvery-gold luster—a high-ticket item.

The King Tut swirls and coils are secondary to the color; but together with the height, they increase the value.

Contrast this smooth, tactile, and blemish-free surface with the rough-textured jar opposite. Each is top of its line.

The vase is not marked underneath. Market valuation would not be reduced for most collectors: the vase is "above reproach."

Height: 9³/₄in/24.8cm
Value: $1,500–2,000

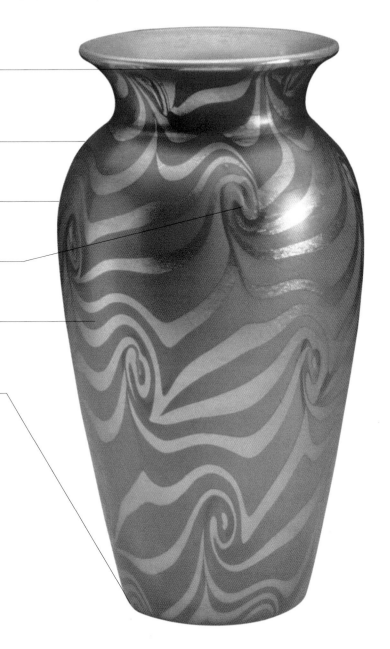

• *Handcrafting covers to match glass items is technically difficult. A perfect match has more value, because it is rare.*
• *A berry prunt is a small, berry-form blob of glass formed or molded to cover a pontil or ornament an object. Its presence adds value; its absence would decrease value.*
• *Many Durand pieces were sold as lamps, drilled at the factory, and fitted with electric fixtures. Collectors must realize that such pieces are considered damaged.*
• *Durand's best iridescent glass has an especially deep color and luster. Collectors seek pieces with unblemished surface and even distribution of color.*

The Museum of American Glass

The Museum of American Glass at Wheaton Village is located in Millville, NJ. This unique venue offers an outstanding display of Durand Art Glass for collectors who would like to expand their knowledge and familiarity with Durand's production. According to the museum's information, its collection includes more than 6,500 items on display, all part of a comprehensive overview of American glass-making, presented both at the museum and at the Creative Glass Center located in the Village.

H.C. Fry Glass Company

Aside from superior Brilliant Period cut glass, the American art glass most closely associated with Henry Clay Fry's Rochester, PA, glass company was the "Fry Foval" glass. Produced briefly from about 1925–1926, it was a delicate translucent material formed into many shapes and completed with colored glass handles, rims, prunts, threads, finials, and/or bases applied or added as decoration. The contrasting colors included blue or green, and occasionally black, lavender, or pink. The resulting item was elegant and understated, artfully designed, and skillfully executed.

Considering the timing of its introduction, Foval received a strong popular welcome. However, the Depression economy did not sustain the market for art glass, and Fry was forced to discontinue the Foval line rather quickly.

The Fry Glass Co. also made art glass that was similar to some of Frederick Carder's glass at Steuben in Corning, NY. Both companies produced colorless glass pieces, many with optic diamond patterns and decorated with threading in either random designs or in controlled stripes. Collectors often find these pieces difficult to attribute, especially since the shapes of record for Fry and Steuben are also similar—for example, the console sets of centerbowls with candlesticks.

The Fry Foval ware made a significant impact in the marketplace of the period, in spite of the limited time and quantity of production. The publication in the 1960s of several books on art glass revived interest in the form, an interest that was further encouraged with the growth of collectible art forms in the 1990s. That interest clearly continues unabated in the 21st century.

Pattern-Molded Diamond Optic Vase, *c.* 1926

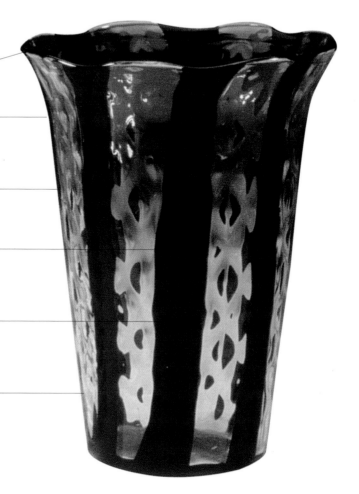

The flared rim above the cylindrical, colorless glass body is a classic form used by art glass craftsmen, past and present.

Of average size for this design, the piece gives appropriate space for both pattern and decoration.

The glass was blown into a diamond pattern mold, creating an optical illusion of multi-diamonds viewed through transparent glass.

This example of colorless crystal decorated with eight broad, integrated stripes (not applied) of opaque black glass is rare.

The decoration here lends verticality to the form, skillfully tooling the stripes with symmetrical spacing; this strong design element adds value.

The piece bears no mark or label, making identification difficult; advanced collectors recognize Fry ware by studying available books and catalogs.

Height: 8in/20.3cm
Value: $500–700

Fry Foval Opal Candlesticks, c.1927

This classic design has an integrated flat bobeche to catch melted wax above the oval candle cup.

A jade-green glass connecting wafer holds the candle cup to the shaft; green jade is popular on opal Foval and is rarer than the blue.

The height of this piece is average—not the tallest Fry produced, but very collectible.

The jade green spiral threading is symmetrically spaced here and gives the illusion of a twisted glass shaft.

The pair match exactly, probably made at the same time and from the same batch. This greatly increases the value over an assembled pair.

Note the jade green wafer-knop that holds the shaft to the disk foot and matches the wafer at top, enhancing the artistic impact of the design.

Height: 12in/30.5cm
Value: $1,500–2,000

• *Although Fry Foval glass was made only from 1925 to 1926, it has acquired a competitive group of collectors. The prices jumped with art glass in general in the 1990s.*
• *Although other Fry art glass was more skillfully designed or executed, the easily-recognized Foval advanced most in price.*
• *Fry Foval opal ware with pink or lavender trim is extremely rare and valuable in today's marketplace.*
• *Fry's Foval art glass always has a white-opal body with colored trim, while Steuben's jades have colored bodies with opal or alabaster trim. A collector should learn not to confuse these two.*

Changing Production with the Times

Henry Clay Fry established the H.C. Fry Glass Co. of Rochester, PA, early in the 20th century, after operating the Rochester Tumbler Co., a huge business in glass tumblers and canning jars. Fry's new company focused on Brilliant Period cut glassware that is widely known for fine quality and superior craftsmanship. Sadly, changing times affected Fry no less than others. By the end of World War I in 1919, the interest of the American buying public had drastically declined. Fry was forced to end cut glass production.

In the 1920s, Fry moved on to pressed and blown glass items with etched, hand-painted, and enameled decoration. Employing techniques used for canning jars, he produced heat resistant ovenware. The Fry Glass Co. then introduced an opal glass similar to Carder's straw opal at Steuben and Tiffany's pastel glass. Fry called his opalescent glassware "Pearl art glass" and, later, "Foval." His most popular offering to the art glass field, it was produced in great quantity, although only for a brief period of time.

Handel & Company

Philip Handel is well known for his company's glass lampshades, produced from 1893 to about 1936. Less familiar is the large number of collectible glass items the company produced during the same period. Handel had perfected a unique outer surface on glass, achieved by heating it after applying a specific kind of glue. When the glue dried and flaked off, the surface of the glass was left with a frosted "chipped ice" appearance. Handel patented this technique in 1904, and used it on vases, covered jars, glass chimneys, and mantel ornaments, as well as on his lampshades. Handel added to this unique feature of his work the "reverse painted" method of decorating glass on the inside surface. This technique resulted in dramatic effect when a piece was lighted from within. The American public loved it from the start.

Handel decorated a line of opal glass items stamped "Handelware" on the base. Decidedly masculine in style, the line included tobacco jars and cigar humidors with hand-painted American Indians, monks, horses, or dogs. These pieces show up at flea markets, shows, and on websites with some frequency, usually subject to paint wear or flaking. The value of perfect ones is escalating, largely due to wider appeal and declining availability.

Handel's leading art glass line was known as "Teroma ware." Artists applied enamel-painted decoration to the obverse, or outside, of the glassware, then heated the piece to give strength and permanence to the design. These vases fetch high prices on the antiques and collectibles market.

Handel & Co. also produced cased glass blanks with etched decoration. The Dorflinger Co. supplied delicate colorless glass vases cased with a layer or two of transparent glass in color. Then Handel would acid-etch designs through the top layer of glass. The resulting "cameo glass" vases became popular additions to the sales offerings of decorating shops, and especially so at the Handel studio.

In the 1990s, the market value of Handel lamps increased dramatically. As awareness and knowledge of the company grew through the publication of pamphlets and books, the value of Handel's art glass products increased accordingly. This trend continues into the 21st century.

Hand-Painted Teroma Scenic Vase, *c.*1910

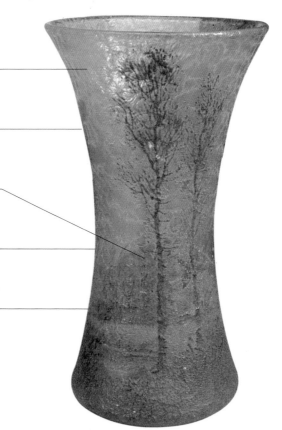

The cylindrical form shows a textured and frosted "Teroma" background—the primary attraction for collectors.

The height of this piece provides a background for the landscape; however, taller would be more effective and more valuable.

Muted colors give the scene an impressionistic aura; the owner of a similar lampshade would pay a premium for this vase.

Glass for Teroma vases is heavy and thick-walled to withstand the technique, so the condition is usually good—a plus for value.

Many Teroma vases are artist-signed, as are Handel shades; this vase is unsigned, decreasing the value for collectors.

Height: 8in/20.3cm
Value: $1,000–1,500

Etched Cameo Glass Vase, *c.*1910

The baluster form in curving Art Nouveau style has a graceful, blossom-like flaring rim with etched cameo border design.

The colorless glass body is cased in a transparent golden-amber. Acid etching creates a frosted texture behind the floral motif.

The artistic presentation of the stylized flowers and leafy fern-like bouquet circling the vase enhances the piece's value.

Both form and decoration reflect a feminine Nouveau style in the European representational manner, for which market demand fluctuates.

The vase is signed "Palme" in etched design at the side and inscribed "Handel 4258" on the base. Both increase value significantly for collectors.

Elaborate stylistic design on the pedestal foot shows skillful mastery of etching technique on a highly detailed motif.

Height: 11in/27.9cm
Value: $1,800–2,500

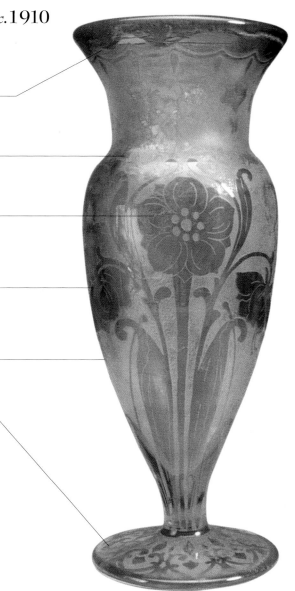

• *Handel gathered a studio of artists to provide images, including Palme, Bedigie, Parlow, Gubisch, and others.*
• *Cameo etching is seldom found in Handel work because of the technique's expense. For this reason, the vase decorated and signed by George Palme (above) is a rare item.*
• *Designs with birds, butterflies, animals, and fish, or scenes with waterfalls, canyons, and mountains are especially valuable in the marketplace today.*
• *Any damage on Handel pieces decreases value greatly. Look for ground out or epoxy filled chips or paint touch-ups, all of which detract from appraisal estimates.*

Glass Decorator

In the latter part of the 19th century, decorating of glass and chinaware to be sold in gift shops and department stores became a common occupation in the United States. Philip J. Handel apprenticed in this work at the Meriden (CT) Flint Glass Co. until he and a friend were able to set up their own business.

Then, at the age of 27, Philip Handel opened his own decorating shop, Handel & Co. Although Handel was never a glassmaker, he became an important lamp maker. He expanded manufacturing to metal lamp bases and fittings so the firm could sell complete lamps, and produced other glass and metal decorations as well.

Philip Handel died in 1914, but the company continued under family management through World War I and the 1920s. Finally, in about 1936, Handel & Co. closed, a victim of the changing times.

A.H. Heisey Glass Company

At the height of A.H. Heisey Glass Co. production, more than 700 workers were employed in the several factories that comprised the Heisey plant in Newark, OH. Augustus Heisey himself and each of his sons were among the designers of patterns and pieces, many of which were patented designs. During the 63 years the company operated, they produced thousands of pieces of colorless crystal and colored glassware in all manner of form and function, decorated and undecorated, some press-molded by a technique they patented as "plunger cut" in 1905, and some freeblown.

The Heisey Collectors of America, a group established for the enjoyment and edification of its members, has attracted a large following due to the numbers of enthusiastic people who have become collectors of the glass through the years. The enormous quantities and great variety of items created by Heisey have made collecting Heisey both easy and affordable for the interested public. The glass can be found in all facets of the marketplace, and prices run the gamut from cheap to dear. Expectations for continued popularity are excellent.

According to the available literature, the Heisey Co. had a business relationship with the Holophane Co. in France, a firm that produced glass lenses and lighting devices. Some of Holophane's work was produced at Heisey's Newark, OH, plant, including Holophane ribbed glass shades and certain auto headlights.

After World War I, Holophane expanded into art glass at their Verrerie D'Andelys factory, naming the product "Verlys," a contraction of the factory name. Again, the Heisey Co. eventually produced some of the "Verlys" glass at the Ohio glass factory, in addition to its own colored glassware and, later, figural forms.

According to Viola N. Cuddy's book, *Heisey Glassware*, the Heisey Co. promoted the Verlys art glass with illustrations in the Heisey 1956 catalog, including the phrase "now hand made in America by Heisey." These pieces are especially prized by Heisey collectors, as well as by the collectors of the French glass made by the Verrerie D'Andelys (Verlys) Co. The prices have escalated in the marketplace and show every indication of continuing as demand exceeds supply.

Verlys Spring-Autumn Vase, c.1955

The slight flare at the top of the cylindrical form allowed mass production with Heisey's patented press-molded method.

Brilliantly clear, colorless glass has an amber color "patine" for accent in the European style.

The depictions of a woman dancing in springtime and another harvesting in autumn are well-defined and expressively drawn, adding value.

Two-season vases were highly collectible and much in demand when made, and continue to be popular items today.

The script signature "Verlys" on the underside of this piece indicates the use of an original mold, increasing the value.

Height: 8in/20.3cm
Value: $500–700

Verlys Mandarin Vase, c.1955

This ovoid cylindrical vessel is straight-sided for the most efficient press-molded technique, a Heisey specialty.

The piece's greater-than-average height shows the figure with parasol to full advantage; the overall raised Oriental motif uses the vertical space.

The colorless glass—with typical Heisey clarity—is colored in gray "patine" in the French manner to accent the decoration.

Skillfully sculpted detail, which shows the Chinese mandarin with umbrella, button hat, and flowing robes, enhances value.

The raised platform base with simulated teakwood fretwork adds to the Oriental motif, a popular theme that further increases value.

The vase is inscribed "Verlys" on its base in script signature; marks tend to raise value for collectors.

Height: 9in/22.8cm
Value: $700–900

• *In 63 years, Heisey made tens of thousands of items that are now highly collectible. They were not expensive originally, and all but rarities are not wildly expensive now.*
• *Heisey whimsies and figurals are in demand, especially in color. They are usually marked and can be identified using the excellent books available.*
• *When Heisey closed, the Imperial Glass Co. acquired some Heisey molds with the trademark. New pieces are less valuable.*
• *Chips and cracks decrease value but can readily be seen. Check for polished rims, restored damage, altered figurals, or other tampering.*

Innovations

Early on, the Heisey Co. initiated the "H-in-a-diamond" mark that was impressed or raised on many items and/or embossed on labels affixed to the wares. Heisey patented the trademark in 1901, and used it most effectively. Collectors have learned, however, that unmarked pieces are found with some frequency.

The addition of colored glassware in the 1920s gave new impetus to the Heisey Co. In 1933, Heisey introduced the novelties and whimsies that became so popular with the American public at the time. Glass animals, fish, birds, and other unusual figural forms were produced in every achievable color. Added to the rest of Heisey's output, these gems have multiplied the number of Heisey collectors, and generated swap-clubs, books, newsletters, and chat rooms around the globe.

Hobbs, Brockunier & Company

Hobbs, Brockunier & Co. of Wheeling, WV, was established by experienced men trained in their craft by the best of the New England Glass Co. master workers. Many were sons of men who apprenticed them in the factory in Cambridge, MA. There, Joseph Locke worked his trade and introduced unique new glass designs, technical innovations, and advancements.

It was Locke who patented the process for making Amberina, the art glass of transparent fuchsia-red shaded to amber. Locke's process led to Hobbs, Brockunier's most famous glass, "Coral," later known as Wheeling Peachblow. The Wheeling product was smooth rather than ribbed, but was also of clear dark red blending into amber glass and cased with opaque white on the interior. The most famous Wheeling Peachblow shape was a replica of the "Morgan" vase, a Chinese porcelain vessel of considerable renown. The Peachblow vase was sold with an exotic amber glass pedestal base, comprised of five dragonheads, and became the 19th-century signature product of Hobbs, Brockunier.

In addition to its popular Wheeling Peachblow art glass, Hobbs, Brockunier & Company developed a number of product lines that were later copied by other glass companies. William Leighton Jr. and a co-worker, William F. Russell, were responsible for the patent on opalescent Hobnail glass, also known as "Dewdrop." Leighton also introduced spangled glass, a process that suspended silvery bits of mica in glass. These artistic innovations at the end of the 19th century made significant contributions to the art glass industry.

For collectors, the glass products of Hobbs, Brockunier & Co. are relics of another time and place. They experienced a surge in popularity in the 1960s—when art glass books by Albert Revi and Ray & Lee Grover were published—and again in the 1980s and '90s.

Wheeling Peachblow Claret Pitcher, *c.*1890

The cased opal white inside gives added depth to the Amberina color and accentuates the graceful pouring lip.

An applied rigoree collar at the neckline is an artistic design feature that may add value.

The narrow body creates the mahogany-red depth most desired by collectors.

The slim angular form of this elegant carafe adds value.

Note the dark amber handle with its deeply ribbed surface, skillfully applied to the body.

The base flares out in a statuesque conical form, increasing value.

Height: 9³/₄in/24.7cm
Value: $900–1,200

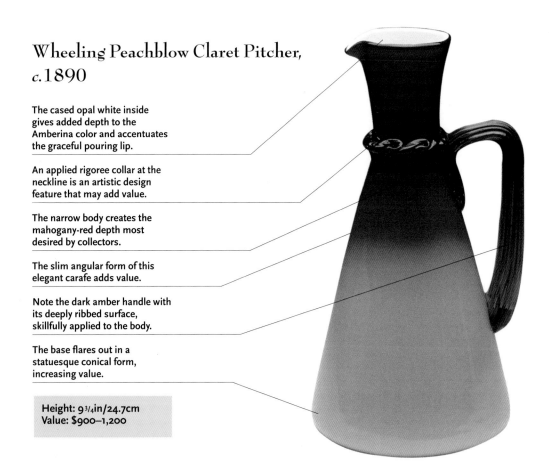

Wheeling Peachblow Drape Pitcher, *c.*1890

Opal white lining shows at the tooled rim; the opaque interior accents the design and deepens the outer color.

The squared form at top adds artistic impact to the functional pouring lip of the pitcher, increasing value.

An added feature for collectors, the applied reeded handle of colorless glass is frosted by acid finish-work.

The pattern mold in a drape design—always scarce and valuable—is the major feature of the pitcher.

Faint vertical ribbing shows through the amber drape area, accenting the design and exhibiting the mold maker's skill.

A raised, round disk foot adds an artful element to the pitcher that increases its value and desirability.

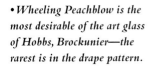

Height: 6in/15.2cm
Value: $1,200–1,500

• *Wheeling Peachblow is the most desirable of the art glass of Hobbs, Brockunier—the rarest is in the drape pattern.*
• *When heating Amberina to achieve the red/amber hues, narrow designs turn a rare and valuable mahogany, or "chocolate," color.*
• *Technical issues of casing glass can cause stress cracks, and may also trap impurities between the glass layers. Collectors often tolerate such blemishes in light of rarity, but condition still matters.*
• *Figural fruits of Wheeling Peachblow glass were sold as whimsies in the late 1880s. These were hollow, shaded red to amber outside, and cased to white. They are scarce treasures worth finding.*

Wheeling Peachblow

John L. Hobbs and James B. Barnes established the business that became Hobbs, Brockunier & Co. in 1863, in the midst of the Civil War. In the following year, William Leighton discovered an inexpensive way to make lime glass without the disadvantages of the previous techniques. Leighton's patented formula was adopted throughout the glass industry and was responsible for the immediate success of Hobbs, Brockunier & Co. At the Philadelphia Centennial Celebration of 1876, the company received awards for Leighton's achievements.

In the prosperous years of the 1880s and 1890s, Hobbs, Brockunier & Co. produced late Victorian "fancy glass"— what came to be known as American art glass. Previous experience with Joseph Locke at New England, and new experimentation with Ruby and Amberina glass led to the development of the company's most famous art glass, Wheeling Peachblow, originally named "Coral" by Hobbs, Brockunier & Co., apparently to distinguish it from similar patented glass. The plated glass was highly regarded and financially successful, as were the company's other exclusive, innovative items.

As the U.S. art glass success of the early 1900s was peaking, the Bohemian glass factories were exporting their own less expensive glassware into the United States. Competition from abroad and the Depression arising from the panic of 1901 pushed U.S. glass companies into hard times. Hobbs, Brockunier & Co. closed. Yet it left a legacy that spans the differences between the "old" 19th-century and the "new" 20th-century styles in design, composition, and technique.

Honesdale Decorating Company

Typical of many U.S. glassmakers, Honesdale Decorating Co. tended toward conservatism in regard to changing styles. Under the direction of Carl Prosch, the company focused on adorning glass with modified Art Nouveau and early Arts and Crafts style decorations, as popular taste demanded. The success of the company suggests that Prosch's strategy suited his era.

Honesdale artists most often used a decorating technique that alternated the use of acid with acid-resistant materials to selectively etch layers of glass. Their addition of enameling and gold embellishment created the character for which Honesdale became widely known. The decoration continues to be recognized for its design and quality, as well as Prosch's distinctive style.

Prosch no doubt brought his Viennese background to bear on the flowing lines and idealized images of nature he used in his decorations. He was certainly exposed to the Secessionist movement and the parallel growth of Arts and Crafts in Europe. It is a measure of his artistic talent that he was able to adjust his designs at Honesdale to appeal to the American art glass market—ornamental glass sold in department stores and gift shops. Honesdale's glass achieved enough popularity to maintain fiscal stability when larger and better-positioned businesses folded. Its longevity reflects its artistic impact in the United States.

The market for Honesdale pieces has remained fairly consistent throughout recent years. No great influx of pieces has occurred; indeed, relatively few show up in shops, shows, or sites. This owes to its scarcity rather than the lack of buyers' interest. When pieces have appeared on the market, prices have reflected inflation. That trend is expected to continue. Early European Arts and Crafts ware is popular now, and it is expected that Honesdale work in that style in particular will escalate in market value.

Cameo Etched Art Glass Vase, *c.*1905

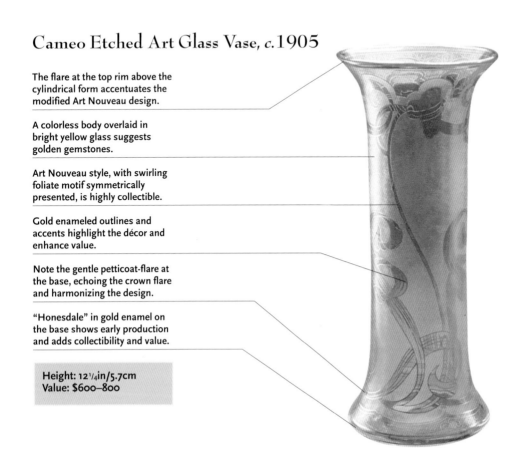

The flare at the top rim above the cylindrical form accentuates the modified Art Nouveau design.

A colorless body overlaid in bright yellow glass suggests golden gemstones.

Art Nouveau style, with swirling foliate motif symmetrically presented, is highly collectible.

Gold enameled outlines and accents highlight the décor and enhance value.

Note the gentle petticoat-flare at the base, echoing the crown flare and harmonizing the design.

"Honesdale" in gold enamel on the base shows early production and adds collectibility and value.

Height: 12¼in/5.7cm
Value: $600–800

Double Etched Art Glass Vase, *c.*1910

This bulbed top with flared rim offers a suitable placement for a wide, stylized floral border—a case of flora following form.

Two layers of amber glass over the colorless body provide added depth to the piece and allow more inventive use of the motif.

The vertical ornamentation on the frosted etched middle area was inspired by the Bohemian Secessionist movement.

The height of this vessel, required for the decorating technique, is about average for Honesdale vases.

The graceful flare at the foot artfully draws the eye to the integrated lower border design.

The underside bears the gold script "Honesdale" mark, indicating early production. This feature increases market value.

Height: 12¼in/5.7cm
Value: $900–1,200

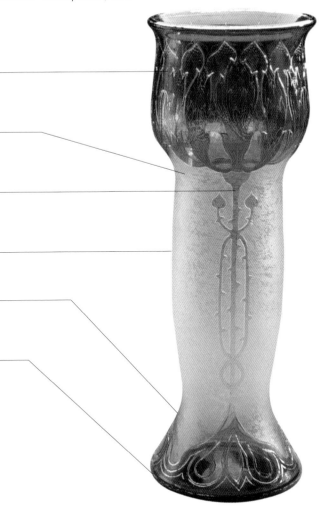

• *Honesdale vases often appear in forms similar to the pieces shown here—tall, slender, unadorned, and elegant—to allow for vertical decoration.*
• *Dorflinger blanks are thinly walled and delicate, with as many as four layers of clear, colored glass. Some later blanks from Heisey bear the "H-in-a-diamond" mark.*
• *Honesdale decorations borrow from Art Nouveau, Arts and Crafts, Secessionist, and Art Deco styles. Still, the work is recognizable.*
• *Quality control was such that flawed pieces were rejected, so damage is a result of chips, flakes, or wear to the decoration. Collectors should watch out for retouched gold or enameling.*

Carl Prosch

The Honesdale Decorating Co. was originally established by the Dorflinger Co. (PA), the distinguished American Brilliant Period cut glass company. The decorating shop was operated by Carl Prosch, a respected European immigrant glass craftsman.

The highly regarded work of the Honesdale Decorating Co. soon found its place among the elite of American art glass production. The work consisted mostly of cameo etched and engraved designs on glass blanks provided by Dorflinger and, eventually, other glass companies. The blanks were typically composed of colorless lead crystal cased with transparent colored glass layers. Honesdale focused on the transitional Art Nouveau style, with elaborate ornamentation on vases, tazzas, candlesticks, garnitures, and centerpiece consoles, as well as table settings designed to the popular tastes.

Carl Prosch was able to purchase the Honesdale Co. in 1916. Production slowed during World War I, but soon thereafter, in the 1920s, Prosch introduced successful designs in the Art Deco style. Otherwise, he relied on more traditional European styles. The company continued until 1932, when Prosch retired at the age of 68.

Imperial Glass Company

The Imperial Glass Co. is perhaps best known for its Carnival glass, the popular iridescent U.S. glassware produced in the early 20th century. The name "Carnival glass" derives from its original promotional use at carnivals, movies, and even grocery stores. Imperial made early—and lucrative—deals with such companies as Woolworth's and Quaker Oats to produce giveaway pieces that are far more valuable now than when first made.

The collectibility of Carnival glass cannot be overestimated. Clubs, conventions, newsletters, websites, books, and catalogs abound. The glass can be found in antique shops and auctions as well as at flea markets and estate sales. Other glass companies that produced Carnival glass include Northwood, Fenton, Millersburg, and others.

In the 1920s, the Imperial Glass Co. made a successful effort to enter the high-end art glass market, competing against the makers of freeblown art glass in the United States and abroad. Imperial's first "Free-Hand" pieces appeared in 1923 and apparently were well received. Unfortunately, the "Roaring '20s" was not the best era for introducing new iridescent art glass. The Great Depression was at the door. Nonetheless, Imperial's new glass was technically and artistically a success and has become a favorite of collectors in the last few years, although little is available due to the short period of production.

In the mid 1930s, the Imperial Glass Co. developed another popular glassware line that has also become collectible. Called Candlewick, the pattern consists of a colorless glass decorated by a border of spaced beading. All sorts of table service pieces were made, in addition to purely decorative objects, totaling over 700 different items. Because of the quantity, Candlewick pieces show up with some frequency.

Although it has undergone restructuring several times over the years, the Imperial Co. remains in business today. It reproduces some of its early patterns, as well as some by other companies from whom it purchased early molds. Fortunately for today's collectors, Imperial marks the new pieces with a superimposed "IG" to distinguish them from the earlier glassware.

Blue and White "Free-Hand" Vase, c. 1927

The freeblown conical form with conforming rim opening is accented by applied glass wrap.

Stark white on bright cobalt blue makes a dramatic statement in the Art Deco style, in contrast to the Art Nouveau vase opposite.

Note the similar heart and vine decoration on these two vases, despite their different styles.

Even so short a vase is imposing because of its squat sloping form and dramatic accent color.

The interior shows some water stain, which lessens value, even though it is not visible.

The original "Free-Hand" label on the base adds value and helps identify the vase as Imperial.

Height: 4⅝ x 6in/
11.7 x 15.2cm
Value: $850–950

Handled "Free-Hand" Vase, *c.*1925

The handles are the crowning glory of this vase—artfully crafted and skillfully applied.

With elegant curving lines, this unusually tall form is pure Art Nouveau style. Collectors would expect to pay a high price for this scarce example.

Unusual "black amethyst" coloring sets off the decoration. This very dark purple color is collectible itself and adds value to the piece.

Brilliant orange hearts and trailing vines swirl with an iridescent lustre that decorates the entire body.

The round pedestal foot with ball stem of "black amethyst" matches the handles above. This integrated design feature distinguishes this vase above the vase opposite.

The Imperial Glass Co. "Free-Hand" label underneath is original—another plus feature for a collector.

Height: 11in/28cm
Value: $2,500–3,000

• *Vases were often embellished with such elements as the hand-crafted handles and raised pedestal foot of the vase shown above and the white rim wrap of the piece at right.*
• *Imperial's "Free-Hand" pieces bore labels with the company name and product line. Lost labels make identification a challenge.*
• *Many Imperial "Free-Hand" items are cased, with a bright orange glass interior—a helpful clue when the original label is gone.*
• *Imperial also made pressed glass vases called "Imperial Jewel," which were mold-initialed. Value has increased, and more for "Free-Hand."*

Responding to Popular Demand

Originally manufacturing utilitarian products, the Imperial Glass Co. responded in the early 20th century to a demand for artful glass. It produced numerous diverse lines of glassware, including a successful line of cut and engraved glass. When the popularity of cut glass declined, the firm shifted to making more pressed glasswares. It later produced a line called "Nu-cut," which simulated the hand-crafted Brilliant Period cut glass.

The Imperial Co. also responded to America's love affair with the iridescent glass of Tiffany, Steuben, Quezal, and others by producing several lines of its own pressed iridescent glassware. These included Carnival glass in its many patterns, stretch glass, opalescent glass, iridized milk glass, and more. In a further attempt to capture a piece of the decorative glass market, Imperial introduced an art glass line called "Free-Hand Ware." This was produced for about five years, beginning in 1923, and has become a highly sought after collectible glass in today's market.

Kew Blas Art Glass

Kew Blas art glass was produced in Somerville, MA, by the Union Glass Co. in the early years of the 20th century. Although similar to other art glass, Kew Blas also had its own distinctive features in two quite different kinds of art glass. One was a single-layer, freeblown amber glass, as seen on the 1912 flower-form vase illustrated on the opposite page. The other was an opaque, cased style with iridescent decoration, produced mostly in the form of vases and shades, as seen on the 1910 piece below. Naturalistic green leaf forms highlighted in amber-gold with iridescent lustre—either selectively or overall—enhanced most of the Kew Blas opal white pieces. Kew Blas specialized in precise symmetry of that decoration, and often evidenced an unusual flow and rhythm to individual design elements. However, not all pieces were equally well-executed.

Apparently the supervision at Kew Blas allowed work to pass through that contained flaws, inferior color, or poorly executed decoration. For this reason, collectors should look carefully at any Kew Blas on the market. Prices should reflect inconsistencies in workmanship, but unfortunately, they may not.

Interestingly, the market value of Kew Blas has fluctuated over the years as more top-quality items have surfaced, and certain collections have focused on it. A well-promoted exhibition in the 1990s at the DeCordova Museum outside of Boston in Lincoln, MA, commemorated the centennial of Kew Blas. In its wake came increased awareness of Kew Blas's desirability and availability, along with higher prices—especially for the superior pieces. As always, design, condition, and rarity influence appraisal and market value.

Green-on-Opal Pulled Leaf Vase, *c.* 1910

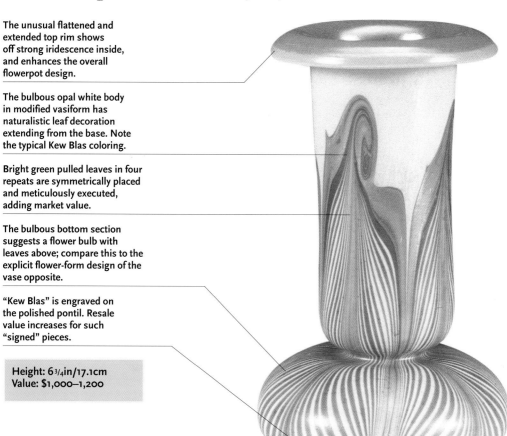

The unusual flattened and extended top rim shows off strong iridescence inside, and enhances the overall flowerpot design.

The bulbous opal white body in modified vasiform has naturalistic leaf decoration extending from the base. Note the typical Kew Blas coloring.

Bright green pulled leaves in four repeats are symmetrically placed and meticulously executed, adding market value.

The bulbous bottom section suggests a flower bulb with leaves above; compare this to the explicit flower-form design of the vase opposite.

"Kew Blas" is engraved on the polished pontil. Resale value increases for such "signed" pieces.

Height: 6¾in/17.1cm
Value: $1,000–1,200

Gold Iridescent Flower Form Vase, *c.* 1912

Note the wide stretched texture on the crimped rim; iridescence adheres unevenly and catches light nicely. Collectors look for such fine examples.

The Art Nouveau jack-in-the-pulpit vase is of iridized golden amber glass, with pink and lavender lustre on the flared "blossom."

The blossom on this rare flower form appears in full bloom. Collectors compete to acquire such a piece.

While the "stem" appears too short for the blossom and vase height, rarity of form keeps market value high.

The foot of vase is well crafted; the skillful execution of its natural bulb shape adds to appraisal value.

There is an engraved "Kew Blas" underneath, a boon to identification and market value.

Height: 12in/30.5cm
Value: $1,500–2,000

• *Kew Blas pieces were often heavier than those made by competitors. When they were good, they were excellent, but delicacy was not a priority.*
• *Kew Blas made tableware in typical colors, but with wonderful reeded handles on sugar bowls, creamers, and pitchers. Collectors seek perfect pieces and expect to pay in the $300–900 range.*
• *Prices are generally lower than comparable art glass houses, partly because of the wide variation in quality. Bargains can be found.*
• *Many pieces were marked with the engraved printed name, usually across the polished pontil. Occasional forged marks have been seen, so it is well to be cautious.*

A New Art Glass

Union Glass Works produced Kew Blas art glass from the late 1890s to about 1924. (William S. Blake, the Union Glass Works superintendent, named Kew Blas by rearranging the letters of his initials and last name.) Kew Blas diverged from much earlier New England glass production. Glass factories had generally focused on functional items such as window glass, containers, lamps, and tableware. Their art glass had been Victorian, Brilliant cut, or engraved.

Kew Blas art glass, however, was influenced by Tiffany's Art Nouveau work in both style and design, as well as by Quezal, Steuben, and Trevaise. Some of this similarity, of course, owed to the popularity of Americanized Art Nouveau styles—companies do respond to "best sellers." In addition, glass workers moved from company to company, and often brought their secrets as well as their skills with them.

One William Johnson, for example, worked briefly for Tiffany, then shifted to Martin Bach Sr. at Quezal for a while, and finally moved to the Union Glass Works and, within it, Kew Blas. No wonder, then, that today's collectible Kew Blas pieces can be hard to distinguish from the others.

Kimball Glass Company

When Col. Evan E. Kimball took over the Vineland Flint Glass Works after Victor Durand's death in 1931, he was loathe to produce art glass, despite the apparent popularity of Durand wares between 1924 and 1931. He did not view the Depression years as a good time to expand into and experiment with art glass while other art glass ventures were failing. Quezal had closed by the mid 1920s. Tiffany had retired and sold his company to Nash in 1928. Nash had folded within two years. Steuben was changing over to colorless crystal. Kimball continued the Durand shapes, designs, and molds only halfheartedly, but he produced enough art glass to make a long-term impact on the art glass market.

Kimball's glass of choice was Cluthra—the heavy, swirled, and mottled glassware named by Frederick Carder at Steuben, and produced by Moncreiff as "Monart" ware. Kimball's Cluthra production differed from each of these by minimizing the bubbles in the glassware and focusing instead on the swirling, cloud-like impact, and on colors in new and innovative combinations.

Kimball continued the classic forms and designs that previously had been successful at Durand. As a result, collectors of Durand art glass generally form the core group of Kimball art glass collectors. The market value of Kimball increased with the 1960 art glass revival, driven by a number of books published at that time and by museums aggressively entering the marketplace. Because Kimball art glass was produced for only a two-year period, relatively little appears in today's market. When demand exceeds supply, competition intensifies and prices rise.

Swirled Cluthra Beehive Vase, *c.*1931

The ridged oval "beehive" body with raised rim is popular as both a Durand and a Kimball collectible.

Average in height by art glass standards, this vase is valued not for size but for the hive form— rarely found in any art glass.

The piece exhibits an unusual combination of striated color within layers of transparent green glass outside, cloudy white inside.

Reddish-brown powders of color in splotches and swirls appear artfully metallic—uncommon for Kimball Cluthra.

Stylistically modern, this vase would attract Art Deco collectors for its form and coloration.

The base "signature" marks of "K" and "Dec 30" with factory shape numbers increase value.

Height: 6¼in/15.9cm
Value: $600–800

Salmon Orange Cluthra Vase, *c.*1932

The long, slender neck flaring at the rim emphasizes the internal decoration.

This taller than average classic shape is bulbed, then flared to extend upward; height is a definite asset.

Kimball's salmon color is accentuated by swirling clouds of white in the glass wall, a very effective use of color.

The vase's modernistic style and verticality are useful decorative features.

An addition like this unusual applied disk foot of amber glass adds both sculptural profile and value.

The base is marked "K Dec. 7/20169 15" for Kimball, decoration, color, and height; the silver tone of the mark is valued as a clue to authenticity.

Height: 15in/38.1cm
Value: $900–1,200

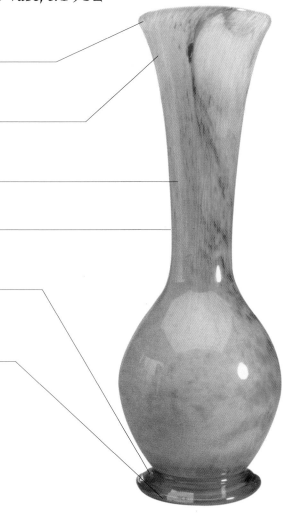

• *Kimball's hallmark art glass, Cluthra, complements a variety of styles, including Art Deco and modernism.*
• *An unforeseen benefit of Kimball's use of Durand shapes and designs is the pleasure of finding Durand patterns in Kimball art glass.*
• *Kimball Cluthra was made by two methods: color enclosed in two surrounding layers of glass; and color swirled into glass without blending it.*
• *Silvered Kimball marks appeared on the pontil: "K," "Dec," and numbers for color and height. View any deviations with skepticism.*
• *Kimball art glass was relatively simple and had few flaws or problems. Any blemishes or scratches would decrease value substantially.*

Col. Evan E. Kimball

Early in the 20th century, Col. Evan E. Kimball produced vast amounts of glass materials that directly competed with Victor Durand's Vineland Co.— one of the largest single-owner glass works in the country. From about 1911 until after World War I, though, the two businesses allied themselves to make, among other products, glass tubing and laboratory accessory glassware.

In 1919, the Durand–Kimball alliance reverted to separate and autonomous operations. Durand's financial success allowed him to promote his "fancy shop," which eventually became the Durand Art Glass Co. Col. Kimball, a more pragmatic man, continued production of functional glass items.

In the late 1920s, Evan Kimball and Victor Durand again considered an alliance in order to combat hard economic times. Before they could act, Durand was killed in an auto crash, and Kimball purchased the complete Vineland Flint Glass Works. Col. Kimball reluctantly adopted certain Durand techniques and produced a limited quantity of vases, lamps, and decorative glassware. When they proved unprofitable, he ended the art glass production altogether.

Libbey Glass Company

Edward Drummond Libbey moved his existing glass company from Boston to Toledo in 1890, bringing more than 100 loyal employees with him. The new Libbey Glass Co. produced Brilliant Period cut glass, for which Libbey's Boston firm had been famous, as well as art glass lines that still interest collectors today. Such Libbey items as Agata, Amberina, Pomona, Green Opaque, Maize glass, and more, regularly appear in most art glass venues.

Relatively unaffected by World War I, Libbey reissued the Amberina art glass line in 1917, publishing a catalog of 40 available designs. The Amberina line, stamped with an acid mark of the Libbey signature or "L" in a circle, is avidly collected as "Revival" art glass today. In the 1920s, Libbey introduced modern industrial techniques and designs for his art glass and tableware. Cut glass was phased out as the Art Deco style caught American awareness. In 1931, the Libbey Glass Co. employed A. Douglas Nash, whose experience with Tiffany and his own studios led to a four-year stint at Libbey and some new designs. Collectors find his whimsical "Silhouette" line of crystal tableware, for which he designed pieces with animal stems, among the most desirable.

Libbey also employed designers Edwin W. Fuerst and Walter Dorwin Teague in the 1930s. Together they designed "Embassy" crystal for the 1939 World's Fair in New York, while Teague designed "Federal" stemware on his own. Both lines of crystal are highly prized by collectors today, bringing unusually high prices because of their quality, beauty, and rarity.

Today, Libbey glass is found in unexpected forms and places: Coca-Cola glasses and souvenirs, novelties, tumblers by the thousands, light bulbs and signs, and on and on. The significance of Libbey Glass Co. to the glass industry and the world of collectibles is incalculable.

Libbey–Nash Series Zipper Vase, c.1933

This smooth, flared rim with chip-resistant edge above a tapered oval body is identified as the K-542 shape in the series.

Height is above average for Libbey–Nash vases, which adds some value as a collectible item.

The so-called zipper design of vertical parallel lines recalls Nash's chintz pattern—a boon to collectors.

The pastel green pattern of dashes is a well executed, rather subtle decoration.

Integrated colorless glass connecting the wafer and round foot holds the oval vasiform aloft with simple design elegance.

The base is stamped with "Libbey" in a circle, adding value for collectors who want signed pieces.

Height: 10in/25.4cm
Value: $500–600

Morning Glory Compote, *c.*1920

The wide, flattened, flared rim is scalloped gently to represent an actual blossom.

The compote's size creates a strong artistic impact, and its form is especially desirable to collectors.

The blossom's underside is "veined" realistically with opalescent vertical ribs, accenting the flower form.

A vivid purple-blue color enhances the flower form; opal white on the raised ribbing highlights the design, increasing value.

The connecting stem, which further suggests a morning glory blossom in nature, increases interest and value.

An acid stamp with the "Libbey" script signature in a circle on the applied round foot assures identity and value for collectors.

Height: 7in/17.8cm
Value: $1,200–1,500

• *Edward Libbey's experimental spirit, coupled with a willingness to mass produce, led to enormous glass output, much of which is available and collectible today.*
• *Edwin Fuerst's designs in the Art Deco style are valuable collectibles.*
• *Collectors identify Libbey creations and designs by the "L" or "Libbey" stamped on the base, often in a circle. Labels—usually lost—add value when found.*
• *Typical Nash designs have not appreciated greatly as collectibles. There is room for value to increase in the future.*
• *Libbey's freeblown art glass from the inter-war period, 1919–1940, is especially collectible because of quality, design, and relative rarity.*

Coming of Age

The Libbey Co. came of age at the Columbian Exposition in Chicago (1892–1893), where it competed with such companies as Tiffany and won numerous awards. At the St. Louis World's Fair (1904), Libbey displayed a replica of the Brilliant cut glass "MacKinley" punchbowl, touted as the largest known single cut-glass piece and evaluated at over $20,000—an enormous amount at the time.

In the 1920s and 1930s, Libbey concentrated production on tableware for home, hotel, and restaurant use.

At one point, they claimed to handle 52 percent of the U. S. tableware produced annually. At the same time, they were producing freeblown art glass for gift shops and department stores all across the country.

In 1935, the Libbey Glass Co. became part of the Owens-Illinois Corp. The Libbey division continued to produce glassware, as well as to make significant contributions to the development of experimental industrial techniques used in glass manufacturing.

Mount Washington Glassworks

Mount Washington Glassworks produced some of the best-loved art glass in the collectible field. The company devoted much production to non-utilitarian glass, with imaginative designers and craftsmen creating glass in innovative, experimental styles, as well as glass that was reminiscent of the past.

One of Mount Washington's most popular freeblown glass lines was Amberina, or Rose Amber, a heat reactive glass shading from deep ruby red to clear amber. Another, named Burmese, resembled British "Queen's Burmese" made by Thomas Webb, with translucent pink shading to pastel yellow. These two lines draw collectors of vases, rose bowls, toothpick holders, salt dishes and shakers, muffineers, pitchers, creamers, syrups, cruets, candle holders and chamber sticks, dresser jars, hair receivers, powder boxes, match holders, and pin trays, to mention only some. Many pieces were mounted with silver-plated holders or handles. Theses were often stamped with "MW" or "Pairpoint Mfg. Co." and identify the source of both glass and metal fittings.

Crown Milano and Royal Flemish lines also thrived during the factory's heyday. Crown Milano, preceded by the Albertine line, was opal-white glass colored and decorated by hand in enamels, as seen on the vase below. Royal Flemish, illustrated at right, was transparent colorless glass decorated in the same manner but usually with a background grid-work in gilt enameling. Royal Flemish is the rarest and most collectible Mount Washington glass, bringing ever higher prices at shows and auctions.

Market value of Mount Washington glass in general continues to be stable in the ever-changing world of styles and crazes. Prices do not seem to surge when the economy surges, nor to decline as it ebbs. Collectors' ongoing fervor attests to the glass's significance and vitality.

Early Crown Milano Egyptian Vase, c.1888

Three spaced handles accent the flared rim over a broad opaque opal-white glass body with glossy finish.

The elaborate gold-enameled frame in Middle Eastern style accents the central scene effectively.

This piece's wider body creates a better canvas for scenes than does the one at right.

Details suggest that both vases were painted from the same reference, or by the same hand.

This vase compares well with the piece at right, but Royal Flemish commands higher prices.

The Red Albertine mark on the base dates to the earliest Crown Milano work; later pieces show a crown and "CM."

Height: 12¼in/31.1cm
Value: $7,000–9,000

Royal Flemish Egyptian-Style Vase, c.1894

Note the raised rim and collar and applied angular handles on the characteristic Royal Flemish frosted, transparent glass.

Gold-enameled scrolls at top and on the handles integrate well with the frame around the scene.

The unusually detailed landscape exquisitely depicts a camel rider with accompanying guard, crossing the desert near pyramids under a star-filled sky.

Compare the painterly detail work with the similar scene at left, both imaginatively rendered.

The height of this slender oval body emphasizes the artful technicality of the painting.

The base is unsigned, but typical Royal Flemish characteristics authenticate the vase.

Height: 13in/33cm
Value: $14,000–18,000

- *Royal Flemish, patented in 1894, was regarded as top-of-the-line. Always expensive, it brings highest market prices.*
- *The most desirable vases—rare and highly collectible—depict nautical scenes, people, landscapes, animals, or birds.*
- *Mount Washington often produced glass with an Egyptian motif—Middle Eastern designs were considered exotic and sold especially well. They remain in high demand.*
- *While Mount Washington products are susceptible to chips and breakage, value more often decreases because of wear to enamels, especially the gold accents.*
- *Vases decorated completely, front and back, have better market value and artistic impact.*

A Complex Business

No glass factory in New England has a more convoluted history than does Mount Washington Glassworks. Yet its ongoing saga of interrelationships and employee exchanges typifies the glass industry in the United States.

Deming Jarves of the Boston & Sandwich Glass Co. established Mount Washington in 1836 to produce such utilitarian glass for the home as fluid lamp fonts, shades, and chimneys. In 1866, W.L. Libbey of the New England Glass Co. bought out Mount Washington. Three years later, Libbey moved the company to New Bedford, MA, near the Pairpoint Metalworking Co. Libbey sold the glassworks in 1870, and in 1894, Mount Washington became part of the Pairpoint Manufacturing Co. The firm produced Brilliant cut glass, lamps, glass decorations, and metal fittings for such items. By 1900, Pairpoint had overshadowed Mount Washington but continued to produce many of its glass lines into the 20th century.

Mount Washington Glassworks—Variations

The Mount Washington Glassworks was among the most prolific of the American glass companies, despite innumerable business problems that eventually resulted in its takeover by Pairpoint. The firm created many different product lines, each one comprising a wide variety of forms: pitchers, bowls, sugar bowls and creamers, lamps and lanterns, trays, biscuit and tobacco jars, dresser sets, and others. In fact, Mount Washington was able, more than most, to make form follow function. The items sold well, partly because American buyers could perceive utility in their "art" purchases—an important incentive for the pragmatic and conservative New England market.

The most important Mount Washington art glass product line was the Royal Flemish *(pages 62-63)*,

sometimes bearing the Mount Washington winged dragon, or griffin, with which the company was so closely associated. The main characteristic of the Royal Flemish line is a body of colorless, clear glass. Other Mount Washington lines, such as Napoli and Verona, also used clear glass.

One may question whether the punch bowl seen opposite is part of the Royal Flemish line, or if it is a one-of-a-kind item, simply using Palmer Cox's Brownies *(see feature on page 65)* to decorate a colorless glass blank item. The consensus among collectors seems to be that the punch bowl is unique, but decorated in the typical Mount Washington manner. Unquestionably of Mount Washington origin, this rare piece probably will not be found again in the collectibles marketplace.

Royal Flemish Flying Griffin Vase, *c.* 1900

The raised rim has a classical scrolling, gilt-enameled, repeating motif—an elegant British Victorian-style touch.

The graphic impact of this restrained and perfect oval form increases the value of the piece.

Note the background that simulates "stained glass" in amber, russet, and ochre.

This piece skillfully presents the full menace of the griffin: the horns and ruff, the scowl, beak and tongue, sharp claws, scaly body, and long tail.

When found intact, early labels showing the flying griffin motif increase the value of a piece.

Although there is no mark or label on this example, collectors would not be deterred.

Height: 7in/17.8cm
Value: $5,000–7,000

Punch Bowl with Palmer Cox Brownies, *c.*1894

Note the rim, crimped in 12 evenly spaced notches; a dozen such punch cups would be a treasure.

The wear on the gold rim and base decoration does not detract from its accent value or the piece's overall desirability.

An elaborate pink framework separates three vignettes of Brownies in humorous postures.

Each scene includes several broad-bellied Brownies with long, spindly legs, wearing odd hats and carrying strange tools.

Characters in the droll scenes are in recognizable roles, such as the policeman and the Irishman.

The punch bowl is inserted into the matching base, with typical Mount Washington scrolling devices, outlined in gold accents.

Neither bowl nor stand is signed or marked, but collectors would still be happy to find this rarity.

Size: 13 x 16in/33 x 40.6cm
Value: $25,000–35,000

• *Design, condition, and rarity affect appraisal. These pieces score high on all.*
• *Color is another major value factor; the multicolor Brownie decoration above adds impact, value, and collectibility.*
• *The rarity of both pieces here increases their value. As the punch bowl is extremely rare, value is extremely high.*
• *The "trademark" Mount Washington vase is rare, but not one of a kind, and not as important in terms of size. Dragon/griffin collectors of the 21st century could drive the price higher.*

Palmer Cox and His Brownies

Palmer Cox was born in 1840 in Granby, Quebec, a small town settled originally by immigrants from the Grampian Mountains of Scotland. Cox grew up with stories from the old country, including the much-embroidered folk tales about "little people," or "Brownies."

Palmer Cox set out from his Canadian home in 1857 to seek fame and fortune in New York. Minimally successful, he sailed for California in 1863. There he sought work as a writer, adding to it his talent for illustration and drawing. In 1874, he appeared in print for the first time in *Squibs of*

California, but response was weak. Two years later, he returned to New York.

When he began working with children's books and magazines, he found the acceptance for which he had hoped. In 1880, the highly regarded *St. Nicholas Magazine* published his stories. Searching for inspiration to create a book series, Cox recalled the Scottish tales from his childhood. He first introduced the popular Brownies, named for their coloring, in 1883 in a story published in *St. Nicholas*; they were an immediate hit. Cox's first book, *The Brownies, Their Book*, was published in 1887.

A. Douglas Nash Corporation

In its three short years of existence, the A. Douglas Nash Corp. had a significant impact on the history of art glass. The Nash company was essentially a reorganization of Louis Comfort Tiffany's company at a time when that business was already doomed. It was 1929, the year of the stock market crash, and Nash would find his real success in innovations, rather than in longevity. He was most fortunate to retain the services of Jimmy Stewart, one of Tiffany's key glass workers. With Stewart as head gaffer, Nash could, in his firm's short life, experiment and develop significant additions to the corporation's product line. He produced art glass and fine metalwork using several wholly new concepts that were not only successful in those hard times, but were also imitated by others in later years.

Nash's most notable achievement during this period was the development of "Chintz" glass, a kind of striped ware with internal patterning. He also produced a ribbed polka dot line and expanded his popular pastel table crystal, "Phantom Luster." At the opposite end of the color spectrum, Nash produced an inordinate amount and variety of red glass. For technical reasons having to do with coefficients of expansion and chemical affinities, true red is difficult to achieve, especially when aligned with other colors in the same piece of glass. Nash was able to attain a variety of reds, and he made the most of their artistic impact. The reds proved to be the most popular and marketable product for A. Douglas Nash Corp. Not surprisingly, in today's antique and collectible marketplace, it is the reds that attract the most attention and value.

Brilliant Red and Striped Chintz Vase, *c.*1930

This broad oval form with raised rim is a quintessential classic design.

The basic brilliant red color was manipulated in rib mold to achieve the contrasting stripes.

The varied spacing of the stripes adds complexity and graphic impact to the vase.

The piece's height is average for Nash's Chintz and manageable for this complicated technique.

Contrasting color and the metallic shimmer of the stripes makes for Art Deco drama.

Inscribed on the base is "Nash RD 66," the number designation for shape and/or color combination; its presence increases value.

Height: 5in/12.7cm
Value: $1,000–1,500

Ribbed Red Polka Dot Vase, *c.*1930

The extended collar here gives added height and space for integrated ornamentation.

The oval form has strong, raised, symmetrical ribbing achieved in a mold blown technique.

Artful placement of stark white polka dots in the graduated spiral decoration contrasts with the vertical ribs.

Brilliant crimson red gives artistic impact to this vase, while dots add a surprisingly modern element.

With dots on the unusually high ribs, the vase is a rarity.

The inscription, "Nash GD 154" on the underside, identifies and dates the vase, increasing its value.

Height: 9in/22.9cm
Value: $1,500–2,000

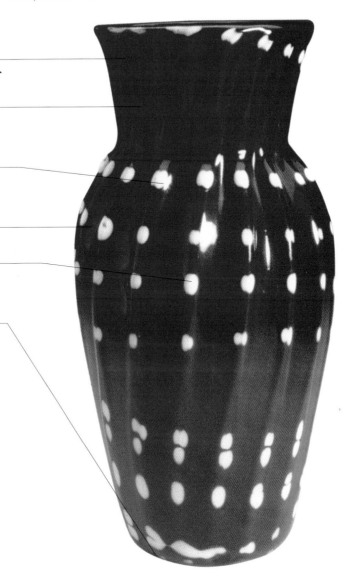

- *The Paris Exhibition of Decorative and Industrial Arts that celebrated the Art Deco style greatly influenced Nash's design and marketing.*
- *Nash "Polka Dot" art glass required great skill to achieve ribbing and ridges on which dots were aligned, limiting the number of pieces produced.*
- *Examples of Polka Dot art glass are rare and popular among collectors, with rising market value.*
- *Alternating wide and narrow stripes give Chintz glass a linear Art Deco look; monochromatic or metallic stripes on brilliant red glass accentuate the style.*
- *The Chintz vase is a perfect piece; in contrast, the dots are not precisely executed on the Polka Dot vase. In this case, the rarity of the latter is a major factor in the higher market value.*

The Tiffany Connection

Both Louis Comfort Tiffany and his vice president—long-time friend and associate, Arthur J. Nash—retired in 1919. Although Tiffany continued to back the firm financially, management of Louis C. Tiffany Furnaces Inc. passed to Nash's son, A. Douglas, who remained in charge until 1928, when he acquired the company.

During the younger Nash's nine years as manager, Tiffany Furnaces continued to produce the glassware for which it had become famous. While much smaller, the business remained reasonably successful. Times changed, however, and eventually Louis Tiffany withdrew his support. Nash purchased Tiffany Furnaces with the proviso that the Tiffany name would not be used.

The A. Douglas Nash Corp. ceased operation in 1931, and Nash accepted a position with the Libbey Glass Co. in Toledo, OH. There he created the popular Silhouette line of table crystal.

New England Glass Company

In the late 19th century, the New England Glass Co. (NEGC) of Cambridge, MA, created art glass items known at the time as "fancy glass" or "art ware." Although the style was late Victorian, the technical processes were decidedly American versions of techniques from abroad. Edward Drummond Libbey succeeded his father as owner of the New England Glass Co. in 1833. On the company's staff was Joseph Locke—chemist, artist, and designer. It was Locke who, in 1883, patented the process for the heat reactive glass called Amberina, one of New England Co.'s most successful lines. Locke then took Amberina a step farther, creating the rib-molded cased glass known as "plated Amberina."

In 1885, New England produced its own variation of Peachblow glass, a glass made by various glass companies in the United States and Britain. New England Glass agreed to call its version "Wild Rose" to distinguish it from competitors' lush rose pink to creamy white glass. Again, Joseph Locke took Wild Rose, and from it developed Agata glass, patented in 1886. This art glass surpassed the original from which it was derived, then and now.

New England Glass Co. continued to be a significant and prolific business at the end of the 1880s. Locke helped to develop Green Opaque glass, the Maize pattern, and the delicate etched glass called Pomona, all of which were popular lines in the New England Co.'s sales catalog. The artistic impact of Locke's work continues to be felt a century later. The art glass that New England Glass Co. produced is admired and pursued by enthusiastic glass buyers today. This glass appeared in many forms and relatively large quantities, making a real "find" an exciting possibility for collectors.

Scalloped Agata Vase, c.1887

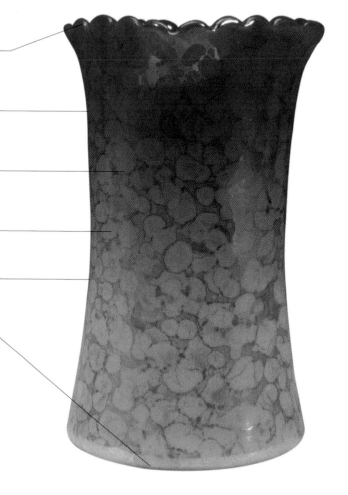

The top rim is both squared and scalloped, over a cylindrical body that flares gently at top and base.

This form is known as a "celery" vase; compare the subtle differences in shape from the piece opposite.

Peachblow "Wild Rose" shades to pale pink-white below; note that this glass is not lined with white.

The Agata is decorated overall with evenly-distributed golden amber and blue/purple splotches.

The height allows a graceful presentation, which accentuates the spotted ornamentation.

The vase was freeblown—the pontil on the center base was polished smooth.

Height: 6in/15.2cm
Value: $1,000–1,200

Plated Amberina Vase, *c.*1888

The flared rim on the oval body of this Amberina creates an elegant balanced design.

The piece is fully lined with opal white glass; note that this is creamy, not stark white.

Twelve raised vertical ribs protrude from the body, the defining characteristic of NEGC plated Amberina.

Dark fuchsia-red shades to clear amber; the white showing through adds depth, richness, and a stronger, striped effect.

This is an outstanding example of the dramatic contrast of deep raspberry with pale transparent amber.

Compare this bright "wet" look with the pastel opposite.

No signature appears on the base. Pieces rarely have the original paper label, which would increase value.

Height: 6¼in/15.9cm
Value: $4,500–5,000

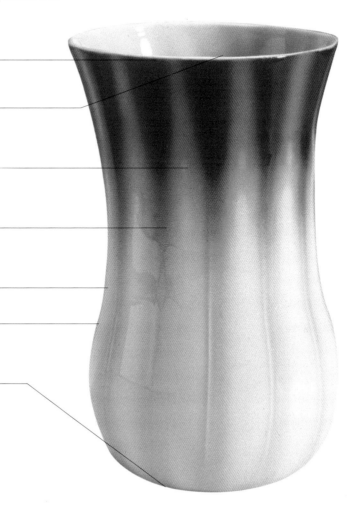

• *NEGC Amberina is identified by the deep fuchsia color at top graded to amber. When the amber is on top, it is called "reverse Amberina."*
• *Plated Amberina is always lined with creamy white glass, which accents the surface ribs.*
• *Only NEGC made plated Amberina with ribbing—most rare and valuable to collectors. Wheeling Peachblow— Amberina lined in white— was never ribbed.*
• *Agata is one layer of glass with the outer surface decorated in splotches—more splotches means higher value.*
• *The color of Peachblow and Agata is often called raspberry.*
• *Neither plated Amberina nor Agata was signed, but each type's uniqueness makes marks unnecessary.*

Glassmakers in New England

In New England, a triumvirate of glassmakers arose in the 19th century that included the New England Glass Co.(1818), the Boston & Sandwich Glass Co. (1826), and the Mount Washington Glass Works (1836). Each company manufactured functional glassware such as window glass, bottles, and lighting devices, and also produced blown and pressed glass. Many of their workers emigrated from overseas with a knowledge of glass-making; a substantial number were master craftsmen. The businesses prospered mid century, enjoying a relationship both cooperative and competitive.

In the late 1880s, Midwestern competition in the glass business, coupled with labor problems in New England, led to the demise of the triumvirate. Boston & Sandwich closed in 1888. Mount Washington became part of Pairpoint in 1894. The New England Glass Co. was reorganized in 1890. Edward Drummond Libbey, then sole owner, moved the business to Toledo, OH, and incorporated as the Libbey Glass Co. Libbey continued to make the best examples of New England art glass, developing more modern and innovative designs as public demands and styles changed.

Pairpoint Glass Company

The Pairpoint Company, despite reorganizing and relocating, has been a stable entity in the glass manufacturing world for well over a century. It has always maintained that consolidating artistic glass and metal products can support a successful business. The many and varied Pairpoint items in the antique and collectibles marketplace today attest to the truth of that premise.

The Pairpoint Co.'s most significant accomplishment grew out of marketing table lamps with mold-blown, reverse-painted shades. Other glass companies nationwide also found the lamp industry a welcome panacea for the financial stresses associated with art glass production. Although electricity reached private homes slowly, new electrified lamps inexorably replaced the old gas and fluid lamps of the 19th century. The manufacture of glass-shaded lamps was undertaken by Handel, Phoenix, Jefferson, Miller, Bradley & Hubbard, Moe Bridges, and Pittsburgh.

That collectors have included their lamp products in any art glass category raises the ever-present form-versus-function conundrum. Yet no one denies that many of the lamps and shades of the period successfully added aesthetic impact to the function of lighting a room.

The Pairpoint Co., together with the Mount Washington Glass Works that joined it, resolved the ongoing conflict between art and industry. While capturing the industrial advantages available in the factories—mass-producing the portions of work conducive to such techniques—the company preserved artistic integrity by incorporating as much handcrafting and innovative design as possible. In later years, the company introduced art glass lines that honored the older styles, while meeting the new demands of the public. The examples illustrated here represent items available in the market that show allegiance to both concerns.

Cobalt and Colorless Swirl Centerbowl, *c.*1939

This shallow dished-bowl form is larger than average for freeblown disks manipulated at the fire.

The diameter allows use as a centerpiece arrangement or a decorative piece for serving hors d'oeuvres.

The vivid contrast between the brilliant cobalt blue and the colorless crystal twirl attracts collectors.

This spiral design required a master glassblower's work.

The strong artistic impact of this modern, Art Deco style is much in demand.

The optic technique of the graphic pinwheel element is seldom rendered with precision; it is a highly collectible style.

No mark appears, but collectors know the design.

Size: 3 x 11in/7.6 x 27.9cm
Value: $700–900

Pair of Gunderson Period Mantel Vases, *c.*1945

Flame shaped, spiral-turned finials match the spiral-turned balls below; these Pairpoint revival elements increase value.

Value is much lower if matching covers are missing; collectors beware!

The height of these pieces accentuates the striking color-and-clear glass combination.

The brilliant ruby-red rosaria color coupled with colorless crystal accent glass is a popular and valuable combination.

Collectors consider paired mantel vases as a unit; the paired value exceeds the sum of two singles.

The goblet-form vases connected to crystal clear, spiral-turned ball stems and raised pedestals illustrates the 19th-century style.

Height: 17in/43.1cm
Value: $900–1,200

• *Late designs of Pairpoint glass, such as the red-on-black Art Deco martini sets, are prized collectibles that have been copied abroad.*
• *Demand and rising prices for older Mount Washington glass such as Peachblow and Burmese led to revival of that ware, often bearing enamel decoration and "P-in-a-diamond" mark on the base.*
• *Value is increasing for studio glass work with such innovative designs as the spiral swirl illustrated at left, which is made in other colors and forms as well.*
• *Collectible perfume bottles and cup plates produced at the Sagamore studio appeal to a growing group of collectors.*
• *While lamps are the most valuable Pairpoint collectibles, early and late art glass is both available and affordable.*

Form and Function

The Pairpoint Manufacturing Co. was established in New Bedford, MA, in 1880 primarily as a metal-work producer. In 1894, Pairpoint joined with the Mount Washington Glass Works *(see pages 62–65)* to produce "fancy glass" and metal works. They continued to make the well-established Mount Washington art glass, often using Pairpoint metal handles, covers, and holders.

As electricity became available, the company converted many of its fluid and gas lamp designs to electric lighting devices. The lamp industry became pivotal to the Pairpoint firm in the 20th century. Glass lampshades in general, and the reverse-painted shades made at the New Bedford factory, were much in demand. Today these mold-blown, hand-painted glass shades, sold with their original Pairpoint bases, are 100-year-old antiques. They sell for thousands of dollars and are widely regarded as good investments at that. Meanwhile, continuing the tradition at the Sagamore studio, Pairpoint uses old formulas and techniques to reproduce art glass for collectors and an appreciative public.

Quezal Art Glass and Decorating Company

Quezal glass was named for a beautiful and elusive Central American bird named the "quetzal," which has feathers similar to, but more vibrant than, those of the more common peacock. It was the dream of Martin Bach Sr. to incorporate the quetzal's colors into ornamental glassware for the home market. Bach's company, the Quezal Art Glass and Decorating Co., produced his glass for only 22 years, from 1902 until 1924. This period saw the decline of Art Nouveau, the birth of Art Deco, and the merging of many styles to serve a culture too diverse in its tastes for any single one of them. The significance of Quezal art glass in this maelstrom of artistic activity is difficult to assess. In fact, the company manufactured beautiful glass, enjoyed by thousands, collected by hundreds, and coveted by many more as time goes by.

The marketplace for Quezal art glass has changed as more Americans have become aware of its special properties. Certainly the demand has increased while the available supply has decreased, simply due to attrition. Glass breaks, and it also disappears permanently into public or private collections.

Whatever the financial problems within the company, the quality of the glass and decoration never faltered. The products benefited greatly from itinerant workers who brought skills and techniques with them. Technical flaws are virtually nonexistent in Quezal, and its appraisal and fair market pricing reflects this. Condition—except for chips, scratches, and the like—is seldom a problem. Value has consistently increased for Quezal art glass and will surely continue as exhibitions ensue and reference books appear. Quezal appears to be a good investment.

Pastel Yellow Rose Bowl, *c.*1905

This "rose bowl" without Victorian crimped top is a hard-to-find, simple vase that appeals to many collectors.

The small body is squat instead of round; this raises its value for Quezal buyers, but detracts for rose-bowl collectors.

The vase has a pleasing tactile satin finish on cased yellow surface, a color rarely found in American Art Nouveau glass.

Note the regimented and symmetrical decoration; lily pads are aligned rather than random.

The market would favor the romanticized style of the vase opposite over this prim decor.

The engraved "Quezal" with scroll underline on the base indicates early production and increases value somewhat.

Height: 4in/10.2cm
Value: $2,000–2,500

"Black" Glass Teardrop Vase, c. 1910

Note the smoothed rim, rounded at the fire, of this freeblown oval body in teardrop form.

Like the bowl opposite, this vase's average size, by Quezal standards, does not detract from its artistic stature.

The deep purple here appears black; cased with colorless glass, it has depth and a rich opaque quality.

Silvery-gold, heart-shaped leaves seem to float on the dark surface, similar to the lily pad ornament opposite.

Note the iridescence here that is especially effective on the darker background. Quezal collectors would expect to pay more for this quality.

An unusual mark underneath includes the location of manufacture: "Quezal N.Y."— collectors like unique elements and will pay for them.

Height: 5¼in/13.3cm
Value: $5,000–6,000

• *Quezal art glass was always freeblown, frequently cased, and usually decorated with pulled or tooled organic motifs in the Art Nouveau manner.*
• *Some Quezal art glass was ornamented with applied forms, such as reeded handles, pedestal or platform bases, threading, or prunts.*
• *No two flower-form vases were exactly alike; they are especially sought after by collectors.*
• *Quezal art glass was generally symmetrical in form and decor, lending a decided classicism to the designs.*
• *The prosperity of the 1990s has raised value and awareness of American art glass as a collectible, leading to escalating prices for Quezal.*

Old Ways in a New World

Martin Bach Sr. and others began the Quezal Art Glass and Decorating Co. in 1902 in Queens, NY. Bach had worked at Tiffany's Corona Glassworks for eight years and left with hopes of establishing his own glass company. After finding funds and supporters, he began art glass production of his own.

Bach combined old and new styles so successfully that his company grew and prospered. In 1914, Bach was joined by his son, Martin Jr., who served briefly in World War I, then returned to Quezal, and became a craftsman in his own right. Martin Sr. died in 1921, leaving the company in major financial difficulties that were the prelude to the end of its art glass production. Martin Bach Jr. accepted a position at the Vineland Glassworks in 1924 as Victor Durand started his own Durand Art Glass.

Quezal Art Glass—Iridescent

T he Quezal Art Glass and Decorating Co. actively produced freeblown and handcrafted art glass for 22 years. Historically speaking, the years between 1902 and 1924 were turbulent and filled with exciting progress and change. In companies such as that of Martin Bach and his son, the old handcrafting ways of the past became a springboard for the future. They embraced technological change and used new methods to develop their own techniques. In the process, they created styles of glass they loved and believed in.

Quezal continued making art glass in the American Art Nouveau tradition even after World War I and into the "Roaring '20s," when the new Art Deco style was emerging in Europe. It is this very consistency in Quezal art glass that appeals to those who seek to collect it. Within its consistency lies Quezal's most significant legacy, that the artistic integrity of the Quezal product was never compromised. Because little variety of style, form, or design exists, the collector stands a better chance of finding multiple pieces that suit a particular collection.

Flower-Form Vase, *c.*1908

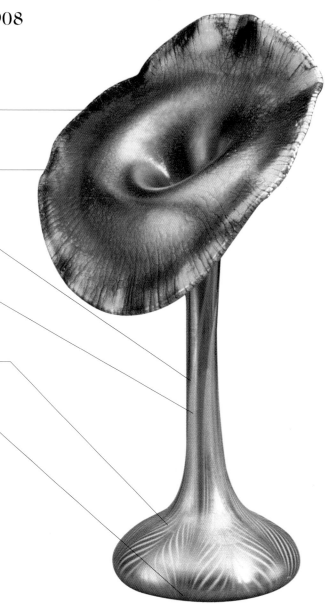

This jack-in-the-pulpit vase with broad open "blossom" uses a Tiffany form to excellent advantage. Figurals are always in demand.

Color as strong as the bright blue iridescent luster on the blossom edge increases the value significantly.

Notice the two layers of glass color, both vibrant with iridescence—an interior ambergris clear glass and an exterior opal-white with green.

In an impressive size, the long slender stem emphasizes the artful flower-form design.

Two ornamental decorations also enhance the vase: outside, green and gold pulled feathers; inside, an extraordinary iridescence on the blossom.

Many flower forms were not marked; this piece's signature "Quezal /M/3" increases its market value.

Height: 11in/27.9cm
Value: $3,500–4,500

Green Iridescent Decanter, *c.* 1912

This bottle form has an elongated neck, bulbed gracefully at mid-point and capped by an integrated stopper with ball finial.

Because this rare form is a desirable size for aperitif or liqueur, market price escalates.

The rare bronze iridescence over dark green glass gives distinction to this vessel; brilliant metallic highlights add value.

Both examples illustrated here are in excellent condition; a chip to the edge or a lost stopper would cut value by at least half.

Compare these double-hooked feather elements—executed by a master craftsman—with the less difficult pulled decor opposite.

An engraved "Quezal" appears underneath on the polished pontil; marks increase value because of the demand for "signed" pieces.

Height: 11in/27.9cm
Value: $4,500–6,000

• *Quezal was produced by master craftsmen who compare well to competitors. As a result, Quezal pieces are valued very favorably in relation to other art glass.*
• *Collectors seek items with unique or unusual features. The Middle Eastern style of the decanter at right is favored on the market and adds value.*
• *The jack-in-the-pulpit piece at left illustrates an early 20th-century update of a design that British workers brought to the United States.*
• *Vases with two-sided decoration invariably have more value than those with decor on one side only.*
• *Quezal used many marks over 22 years. Collectors can learn Quezal shapes to help identify unmarked items.*

Publicity and Value

In January 1998, the magazine *Antiques* published an essay about the Quezal Art Glass and Decorating Co. Written by Malcolm MacNeil, collector and glass expert, the article has raised awareness of art glass in general, and of Quezal in particular. MacNeil's upcoming book is eagerly anticipated in the glass world. In the meantime, his work has given Quezal a shot in the arm in terms of market value.

An unintentional result of many articles, books, and exhibitions in the antiques and collectibles community is the subsequent increase in value of whatever items they cover. Because overall attention has increased, expectations are high for art glass.

Steuben Glass Works

Established in 1903, the renowned Steuben Glass Co. continues today as one of the leading producers of art glass in the United States. As a result, collectors of Steuben glass have an enormous selection from which to choose, including a wide array of styles, forms, functions, and especially colors. Steuben's founding director, Frederick Carder, was schooled in the design and production of British cameo and Victorian art glass. He considered himself to be a classicist, and focused throughout his career at Steuben on color in all possible shades, variations, and combinations.

The techno-chemical research and development initiated by Carder has led to a century of innovation in new types and colors of glassware. Just a sampling of early Steuben lines and colors includes: Verre de Soie; gold, blue, red, green and brown Aurene; Tyrian, Florentia, Intarsia, Rouge Flambé, Mandarin Orange, Cluthra, and Silverina; jades in green, yellow, rosaline, blues, and plum; Oriental Poppy, Selenium, Moss Agate, Quartz, Ivory, and Ivrene; Mat-su-no-ke, Cintra, Lace, and many more.

Collectors can focus on a particular category, color, or type of design. Steuben's etched glass in the Art Deco style is widely available, as are items in Art Nouveau and classical styles. Steuben provides a variety of art objects for the home, including lighting devices and architectural elements. Most helpful of all for the collector, there exist line drawings of all of Steuben's glassware. The book, *The Glass of Frederick Carder*, written by Carder's apprentice and longtime associate Paul Vickers Gardner, includes most of the line drawings and has recently been reissued.

As in all collecting, the Steuben collector needs to become acquainted with the look and feel of the glass and the different marks used through the years. Tom Dimitroff's excellent reference book, *Frederick Carder and Steuben Glass,* is a must in every collector's library.

Demand for the Carder Steuben colorful, pre-1933 pieces is increasing. It is quite likely that Steuben art glass will continue to appreciate in value in the future, with prices, as always, reflecting the design, condition, and rarity of each particular item.

Alabaster Vase with Red and Gold Aurene Decoration, *c.*1910

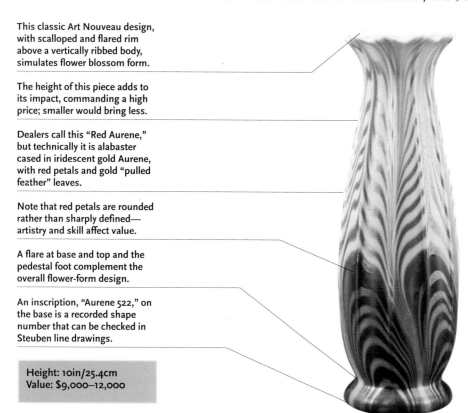

This classic Art Nouveau design, with scalloped and flared rim above a vertically ribbed body, simulates flower blossom form.

The height of this piece adds to its impact, commanding a high price; smaller would bring less.

Dealers call this "Red Aurene," but technically it is alabaster cased in iridescent gold Aurene, with red petals and gold "pulled feather" leaves.

Note that red petals are rounded rather than sharply defined—artistry and skill affect value.

A flare at base and top and the pedestal foot complement the overall flower-form design.

An inscription, "Aurene 522," on the base is a recorded shape number that can be checked in Steuben line drawings.

Height: 10in/25.4cm
Value: $9,000–12,000

Blue Vase with Intarsia Collar, *c.*1915

Angularity of design suggests the Egyptian revival, Art Deco style of the 1920s. This vase shows Steuben's innovative work.

Applied gold Aurene bands frame the flared collar with Intarsia decoration; design increases value and desirability.

The vase's height allows the gold Aurene leaf and vine decoration around the shoulder to draw attention up to the border.

A brilliant blue glass layer cased in opaque white gives depth, vitality, and contrast to the gold—details that add value.

The decoration here is more random than the decor of the vase at left. Both blue and red are rare in these designs, and much coveted by art glass collectors.

The inscribed "Aurene" on the base enhances value slightly. Collectors would be hard-pressed to find a similar vase on the market because of its rarity.

Height: 10in/25.4cm
Value: $18,000–20,000

• *"Carder Steuben" art glass commands the most attention from advanced collectors, with the possible exception of post World War II Steuben crystal masterworks.*
• *Steuben glass color is a major value factor. Oddly, some of the rarest colors were used in lampshades and bases. Alert buyers may find treasures among such pieces.*
• *Carder was known as a "hard taskmaster"; few Steuben pieces appear with flaws or blemishes.*
• *Collectors will buy Steuben pieces in poor condition only if they are great rarities. They tolerate inherent flaws, caused during production, and reject condition flaws, caused after production.*

England's Loss, America's Gain

Steuben Glass Co., in Corning, NY, had its roots in England in the early 1900s. There Frederick Carder, 37, became a highly respected designer, carver, and engraver of cameo glass at the Stevens & Williams Co. His associates included John Northwood, legendary glass master, and Carder's mentor and friend. After Northwood died in 1902, Carder was passed over for a promotion at Stevens & Williams.

Soon after, in 1903, two visiting businessmen from Corning, NY— Alanson Houghton and T.J. Hawkes— made Carder a job offer he could not refuse. Carder became cofounder, superintendent, and manager of the newly created Steuben Glass Works.

Hawkes hoped to provide lead glass "blanks" for the Hawkes Cut Glass Engraving Co. Carder soon expanded the company's operations, acquiring new furnaces and hiring more workers. Thus he set the stage for the rapid development of the Steuben art glass department. So successful was he that Steuben Glass became known worldwide for its quality and design.

Steuben Glass Works— Evolving Styles

Between 1918 and 1933, the glass produced at Steuben continued to be of high quality and innovative design. The classical influence of Frederick Carder's early training never deserted him, but his business acumen led him to accept and perfect new ideas and trends, including, but not limited, to Arts and Crafts, Art Deco, and modern design. As other glass companies succumbed to the Great Depression, Steuben, under the wing of the Corning Glass Works, continued to create and incorporate new techniques and styles.

The market for Steuben ware was affected by world changes involving tariffs and labor, in addition to the general economic decline culminating in the U.S. stock market crash of 1929. Fluctuation in prices followed general trends, but sales of decorations, architectural elements, lighting, and home accessories continued. The public responded to the new Steuben ware as they had to

the old; pieces purchased then have steadily increased in value as they have been treasured and passed along in families. They have become more prominent in private collections and art museums.

The vases shown here represent the body of work called acid-etched decoration. Such pieces were freeblown and often cased with a second and even a third layer of glass. The pattern designs were then etched, or cut back, by acid to show the underlayer of glass and achieve the pattern decoration. Collectors especially prize the acid-etched glass pieces that Carder designed in the emerging Art Deco style, such as those seen here.

Art glass of this type has continued to be as popular now as it was originally. Prices have more than kept pace with inflation and have proven to be excellent investments. Despite market changes, collectors continue to buy at ever-increasing prices as more competitive buyers appear.

Dragon Vase, c. 1925

This Steuben shape and its green jade glass suggest the classical form of Far Eastern ginger jars.

Collectors pay more for people or animals such as this, as both are scarce.

Double decoration raises the value level here. Note how the etched scrolls cover the alabaster body around the jade glass layer.

The dragon design is well positioned. Stylized puffs of smoke add interest and value.

The lack of motif repetition can decrease the piece's value.

This alabaster has less artistic impact than does the rare two-color Cluthra seen opposite.

Collectors would note that the jade is pale, a devaluer.

Height: 9in/23cm
Value: $1,500–1,800

Art Deco Vase, c.1927

A raised, flared rim complements the oval, neo-classical form; the spiked border with graduated dots adds to the Art Deco style.

The two-color Cluthra of bubbled and mottled glass, shading from yellow into pink-rose, makes this a rare and costly example.

Dramatic and collectible, this gold-ruby glass was acid-etched with Art Deco elements in the Steuben "Clifftwood" pattern.

Heavy and wide, the vase exhibits an elegant graphic impact. Both its size and decoration increase its collectibility and market value.

Appraised according to design, condition, and rarity, this piece scores high on all counts. The difficult technical processes increase its value.

Compare the vibrant color and skillful technique of this vase with the one opposite; this Cluthra vase is a top-of-the-line example of Steuben's work.

Height: 10in/25.4cm
Value: $4,000–5,000

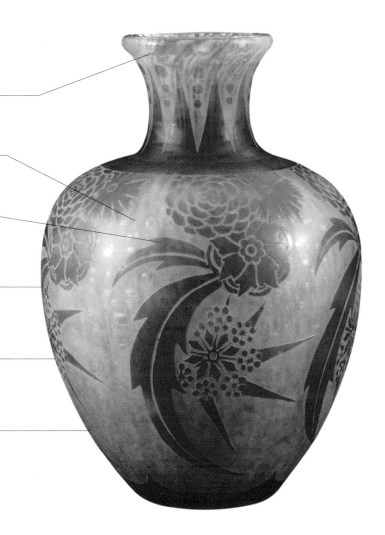

• *Acid-etched vases were among the most popular Steuben products, sold in fine stores and produced for lamp companies to use as bases.*
• *Even in the 1920s, Carder showed his classical preferences in designs such as the two examples shown here. Value depends here on decoration.*
• *Especially rare are pieces produced with a Cluthra background glass. The medium adds interest and value.*
• *A double-etched feature is found often in such Oriental designs as the dragon at left. The overall scrolling elements appeal to collectors.*
• *Dragon, Chinese, and Canton are popular Carder designs among collectors.*

The Works of Frederick Carder

Major changes occurred at Steuben during World War I as the company met requirements to produce glass-related war materials and conserve certain chemicals. In 1918, the Corning Glass Works acquired Steuben, which continued with Frederick Carder as director. This rocky alliance produced some of the most interesting art glass to emerge from the "Roaring '20s."

After the United States entered the Depression, profit margins declined in the Steuben division of Corning. Carder was replaced as director and "promoted" to art director. He continued to contribute, however, and

his success led him to experiment and produce some of his and Steuben's most artistic works.

Carder worked with the *pâte de verre*—literally "paste of glass"—process. He also experimented with the "lost wax" technique called *cire perdue*, and still later with a process he called Diatreta. These pieces seldom come to market; but, over time, Carder sold or gave away many pieces that do occasionally appear. A *cire perdue* dolphin sculpture *(see page 164)*, signed "F. Carder 1947," sold for $12,000 in 1993 and has more than doubled in value since that time.

Steuben Glass Works— Masterworks

During Arthur Amory Houghton Jr.'s tenure as president at Steuben, head designer and art director Sidney Waugh hired well-known artists, architects, and sculptors to design for Steuben masterworks. Some produced single prototypes; others worked with the company for years. Among them were Walter Dorwin Teague, Paul Schulze, David Dowler, Donald Pollard, George Thompson, Peter Aldridge, Bernard X. Wolff, Jane Osborn-Smith, Joel Smith, Lloyd Atkins, Robert Cassetti, James Houston, Don Wier, John Dreves, Irene Benton, and, more recently, James Carpenter and Lino Tagliapietra. Their works have represented U.S. art glass in numerous international celebrations and exhibitions, including presidential tributes, world fairs, royal weddings, and diplomatic presentations, not to mention sports awards and historical mementos.

The masterworks, as well as lesser Steuben creations, are well-recorded for collectors and students in Mary Jean Madigan's *Steuben: An American Tradition in Crystal.* Recently revised and updated, the Madigan book includes most Steuben designs and identifies designer, engraver, and other pertinent information. With help from the Steuben research department, this book can supply any information needed by a recipient, inheritor, or insurance company.

Colorless Steuben crystal is frequently found where antiques and collectibles are offered for sale. Estate sales and Internet venues occasionally offer pieces with the characteristic engraved squiggle that sharp eyes can read as "Steuben." Barring chips or scratches, Steuben has increased in value steadily, in proportion with the economy, and is expected to continue that trend into the foreseeable future.

Commemorative "Paul Revere" Vase, *c.* 1976

This commemoration of the Revolutionary War, "One if by Land, Two if by Sea" narrative was designed by Sidney Waugh, significantly increasing the value.

The exhibition piece is listed as extremely scarce in Madigan's book, which increases the value.

The vasiform is unusual, skillfully designed so each vignette can be seen front-on or through the crystal-clear glass, from any angle.

The Old North Church steeple is engraved with the single light announcing the British troops in the distance; note details of cross, bell, and light beams.

The vase, inscribed "Steuben," comes in its fitted, velvet-lined box with original papers, adding to collectibility and value.

Height: 12in/30.5cm
Value: $7,500–9,000

"Ladder Of Dreams" Sculpture, c.1971

This angular, prismatic tablet was designed by George Thompson as an exhibition piece, then presented for sale and special order.

The height, thickness, and asymmetrical form allow ample space for the engraved decoration.

Freeform staging suggests a wooden playground area, in stark contrast to the intaglio rendering of the children.

Engraver Tom Vincent skillfully executed the appealing design; such desirable subject matter and skill adds to collectibility and value.

Collectors appreciate that the solid crystal tablet, while heavy and unwieldy, is stable and secure when placed.

The sculpture is accompanied by the original velvet-lined presentation box, an added value factor, as is the "Steuben" signature on base.

A black glass light stand accompanies the sculpture for illumination when desired.

Height: 11³/₄in/29.8cm
Value: $12,000–15,000

• *Sidney Waugh is best known for his Art Deco-style "Gazelle Bowl," which retails for over $25,000, and for his masterpiece "Atlantica," a huge cast-glass sculpture.*
• *George Thompson designed such pieces as the "Ladder of Dreams." His "Cathedral," designed in 1955, retails for $15,750.*
• *Exhibition pieces, like these two, were conceived and executed with special care and creativity and are frequently among the rare examples collectors especially seek.*
• *The Steuben series of "Hand Coolers" can become rarities through attrition.*

Arthur Amory Houghton Jr.

Arthur Amory Houghton Jr. took over as president of Steuben in 1933. When he did, he named Sidney Waugh to Frederick Carder's position, moving Fred "upstairs." During this changeover of men and styles, several sales of Steuben factory leftovers were held, although important pieces were saved. The remaining Carder Steuben art glass was destroyed in a dramatic management move dubbed locally as "The Smashing." It signaled a major new beginning for Steuben.

Noting the popularity of Scandinavian colorless glass, Houghton set the chemists to work on a formula for the clearest, purest, most refractive glass possible. The result was coded "G10M," a recipe for the high-lead crystal glass that came to be synonymous with Steuben. Houghton then undertook a massive campaign to establish a new image for the company based on its new product material. Sidney Waugh, as artistic director, put his weight behind the campaign.

Tiffany Glass and Decorating Company

Louis Comfort Tiffany is considered by many to be the single most influential person in the history of American 20th-century glass. His work included leaded glass windows, leaded glass lighting devices, and art glass. His work in bronze, enameling, mosaics, pottery, and, of course, his paintings are further examples of his formidable artistic achievements.

Tiffany's most characteristic art glass is gold iridescent glass—best known as "Tiffany glass." Glass artisans had long been attracted to the luster and shimmer of ancient iridescent glass. They attempted to reproduce its attributes in the factories of Europe. A well-traveled American abroad, Louis Tiffany had seen the iridescent glass of Ludwig Lobmeyer and of the Loetz Glassworks in Austria. Tiffany soon produced some of his own in his U.S.

glassworks (with considerable competition from Carder at Steuben and others). He made the gold iridescent pieces in great quantity and many forms, and he made them affordable. Their impact was such that they became recognized and replicated throughout the country.

Tiffany paperweight vases are among the most complex of his art glass. Simulated glass blossoms were sandwiched between two thick layers of transparent glass, a feat deemed challenging by any master glass worker, since it is manipulated in the molten state. For Tiffany, such a challenge was simply another hurdle to overcome. By the turn of the century, he had exhibited and sold his own paperweights to great acclaim. Tiffany hired the best people available and worked closely with them. He expected them to succeed, and they did.

Blossom-Decorated Paperweight Vase, *c.*1908

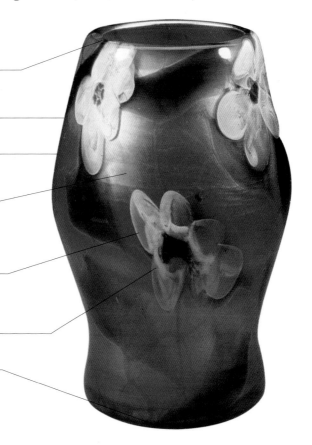

This Art Nouveau curved organic form with open rim gives ample size and space for artistic decoration.

The vase's smaller-than-average size does not decrease its value, except by comparison.

Clear aqua-color glass encases the decoration.

The interior has an iridescent gold sheen, giving the vase a golden-orange hue key to value.

Red-centered, white blossoms and green leafy stems appear free-floating against the bright red-orange iridescent background.

The decoration evokes Impressionist paintings with undefined images and ethereal quality.

The vase is inscribed underneath "L.C. Tiffany Favrile 5779 C."

Height: 7in/17.7cm
Value: $6,000–8,000

Narcissus Paperweight Vase, *c.*1910

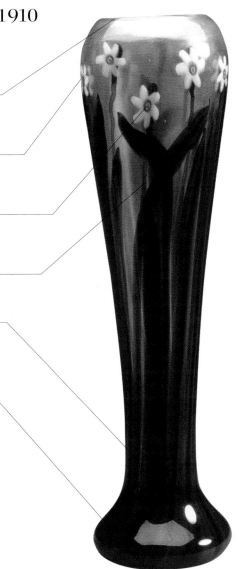

This elongated, slender ovoid form bulbs at the top with a rim folded inward to accentuate the floral border design.

Transparent colorless glass surrounds the decoration of ten brilliant, full-white narcissus blossoms.

Colorful Millefiori glass canes are inserted realistically into each blossom center, adding significantly to beauty and value.

Natural-looking brown stems and green spiked leaves give verticality to the motif, accenting vase height and elegance.

Exceptional clarity of the Tiffany glass shows the vivid detail of the image, even toward the base.

Inscribed on the polished base rim is "L.C. Tiffany Favrile 2731G," a "signature" that increases value for many collectors.

Height: 16in/40.6cm
Value: $18,000–25,000

• *Adding glass Millefiori canes to paperweight vases was difficult; perfect ones are rare and expensive; flawed ones are acceptable to some collectors.*
• *Aquamarine paperweight vases and bowls are the rarest of the rare, seldom seen outside of museums.*
• *Tiffany's love for flowers led to experiments with floral decorations in glass.*
• *Fluctuations in the Tiffany market have occurred ever since President Teddy Roosevelt first threw Tiffany pieces out of the White House in 1904. Today, expensive pieces bring more than ever.*
• *As a rule, large pieces are more valuable. Intense, precise, and well-defined decoration influences value as well.*

The Man Behind the Business

As a painter, Louis Comfort Tiffany was fascinated by glass's artistic potential, and he established the Tiffany Glass Co. in 1885 to explore such uses. Seven years later, he began commercial production of art glass with the start-up of Tiffany Glass and Decorating Co.

Tiffany hired Arthur J. Nash, newly arrived from England, as vice-president and manager of the factory in Corona, NY. Nash stayed with Tiffany until they both retired in 1919, by which time the company had become a foremost producer of art glass and lamps, making "Tiffany" a household word.

Tiffany's work spanned a half century of changing styles and times. He employed thousands of people and beautified tens of thousands of homes with his creations. His art glass went out of style eventually, but Tiffany went on producing his famous Art Nouveau designs. Even after retirement, he continued to back his company financially until 1928, when it was taken over by Nash's son.

Tiffany Glass and Decorating Company—Tiffany Studios

The Louis C. Tiffany studios employed thousands of people. For his leaded glass windows, he hired designers, glassmakers, workers who leaded the windows, and transportation teams. The heavy windows would be assembled on-site in churches, cathedrals, mausoleums, synagogues, private homes, corporate headquarters, banks, museums, theaters, and opera houses—all requiring full-time employees. Meanwhile, popularity and demand soared.

Tiffany's lamp designers included men and women, whom he invited to his gardens to choose flowers and match colors. Other workers cut glass segments, affixed patterns, and leaded the glass. In the foundry, workers created bronze lamp bases from design through completion. Critics suggested that the lamps were made

from glass that was left over from window production. But Tiffany demanded exactly the right glass for every lampshade. Pieces would literally be struck out of a shade if Tiffany disapproved. Leftovers would not do.

And so with art glass. Tiffany strove to create the world's best art glass. With the help of his master glassmakers, he created decorations as strikingly beautiful as the Gallé he saw in Paris, the Webb in England, the Loetz in Vienna, and the ancient glass of Rome and Africa. The artistic impact of Tiffany's glass went far beyond those who first loved it. It greatly affected the work of artisans who were Tiffany's contemporaries and continues to influence artists in today's art glass studios. Beyond that, it commands great attention in the antiques and collectibles marketplace right up to the present.

Egyptian Revival Vase, *c.* 1910

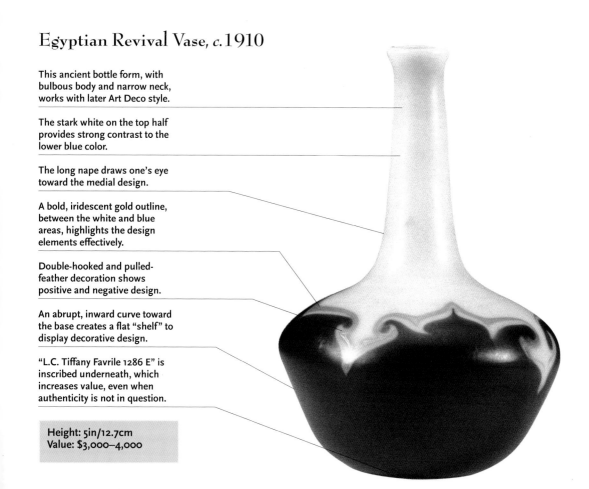

This ancient bottle form, with bulbous body and narrow neck, works with later Art Deco style.

The stark white on the top half provides strong contrast to the lower blue color.

The long nape draws one's eye toward the medial design.

A bold, iridescent gold outline, between the white and blue areas, highlights the design elements effectively.

Double-hooked and pulled-feather decoration shows positive and negative design.

An abrupt, inward curve toward the base creates a flat "shelf" to display decorative design.

"L.C. Tiffany Favrile 1286 E" is inscribed underneath, which increases value, even when authenticity is not in question.

Height: 5in/12.7cm
Value: $3,000–4,000

Brown and Stretched Gold Vase, *c.* 1912

This oval form was ornamented with an elevated and flared collar.

The top has been tooled and widened while hot, giving the "stretch" effect and a rough-textured, irregular edge.

The gold iridescent top shows dimpled marks of tooling where it was applied to the brown base, a rare and tricky maneuver.

The dark honey-colored brown body is cased to an opal-white interior, giving it weight and enhancing its color.

The flat-disk, pedestal foot was formed and applied to the base at the furnace, a fine finishing touch.

The "L.C. Tiffany Favrile 8719 G" inscribed on the underside of the base adds to value.

Height: 5in/12.7cm
Value: $4,500–6,000

• *Two-toned vases are scarce in freeblown art glass, because two "batches" means two rates of expansion at the fire, decreasing the success rate.*
• *Tiffany vases that are 5in/12.7cm tall decorate well, please the eye, display easily, and are relatively affordable.*
• *The mahogany-brown color, seen on the vase above, was popular in Arts and Crafts style and early 20th-century designs.*
• *Freeblown stretch glass achieved great success at Tiffany in the 1910s. It was copied inexpensively as Depression glass, which is also collectible today.*
• *Fluctuations in market value for collectible art glass are inevitable; ups and downs follow the economy. Tiffany pieces of good design, and in excellent condition, are A-1 investments.*

Charles Hosmer Morse Museum

One of the most important collections of the works of Louis Comfort Tiffany is that of the Charles Hosmer Morse Museum in Winter Park, FL. The museum was established in 1942 by Jeanette Genius McKean and her husband Hugh F. McKean, the latter a friend of Tiffany's and director of the museum until 1995.

A visit to the extensive Morse collection offers insight into Tiffany Studios' scope. The museum brochure states: "At its peak the Tiffany furnaces produced 30,000 items annually—most of them lampshades, which reached a production rate of four per hour from each of five 'shops,' or 1,000 per week. There were 200–300 tons of glass stored at the plant and it was classified into 5,000 different colors and varieties. Distributed by the Shreve Co. in San Francisco, Neiman Marcus in Dallas, and, of course, Tiffany & Co. in New York [and] . . . Tiffany Studios, his blown glass was as commercially successful as it was artistically superb."

▶ *August Jean Vase, late 19th century. This art glass piece was decorated with applied and enameled ornamentation. $900–1,200. 11in/27.9cm tall.*

European Art Glass

Gabriel Argy-Rousseau

Gabriel Argy-Rousseau became fascinated with the *pâte de verre* technique as a young student in Sèvres, where the glass master Henri Cros was producing major works in the ancient art. Cros had rediscovered the process in 1884, first exhibiting a plaque in the Greco-Roman style at the Paris Salon in 1885. He went on to create huge panels of glass, was decorated with the French Legion of Honor, and eventually established his workshop at Sèvres, where he died in 1907. He left marvelous masterworks, but few collectible pieces for future admirers.

Albert Dammouse and Georges Despret, Cros's contemporaries, also worked in *pâte de verre* late in the 19th century. They exhibited at the Paris salons and were considered masters. François-Émile Decorchemont and Almeric Walter came on the scene a bit later and were also highly successful in *pâte de verre*. Both artists produced highly collectible works during the years when Argy-Rousseau was most prolific.

Of these five highly regarded masters in *pâte de verre* art glass, Gabriel Argy-Rousseau is considered to have created the most significant body of work in the collectible field. His extraordinary use of color, variety of form, ingenuity in design, and mastery of the technique allowed him to produce art glass that defined the medium and left its impact on the Art Deco style.

Knowledge and availability drive the collectibles market in the 21st century. Through the boom years in antiques and collectibles, the public has come to admire the work of Gabriel Argy-Rousseau and has learned of his work through the publication of books and articles about him, most especially *G. Argy-Rousseau: Glassware as Art,* by Janine Bloch-Dermant. Reported auction prices and the rise in his popularity in the Japanese market have contributed to public awareness. Add to that the availability of the work in antique shops and shows, upscale markets, and the ubiquitous Internet, and you have a highly collectible body of work.

Pâte de Verre Flowering Sprig Vase, c.1920

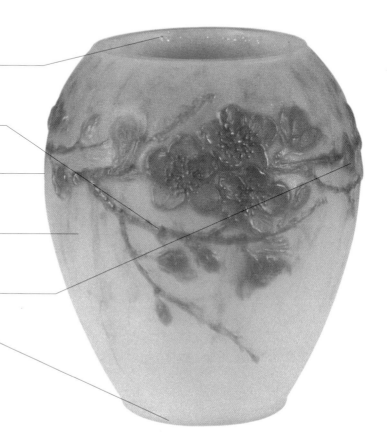

The rim opening permits glass paste to be tamped into crevasses of the mold, giving crisp, well-detailed decoration.

Naturalistic curving branches drift gracefully below the main design around the shoulder; a painterly motif raises price level.

Height—typical of Argy-Rousseau—and oval body allow a good area for decoration.

The mottled white background, in which many subtle colors appear, accents red blossoms and adds to market value.

Flowering blossoms continue all around the vase, presenting an elegance that appeals to collectors.

"G. Argy-Rousseau," indented at the lower edge, is designed into the mold.

Height: 5³/₄in/14.6cm
Value: $5,000–7,000

Spiders and Brambles *Pâte de Verre* Vase, *c.*1920

The wide opening allows paste of glass to be pressed tightly into the mold, making excellent detail on the vase.

The ovoid form offers a broad expanse for decoration; the smaller-than-average size does not lower value.

Colorful bushes make the black spiders and white webs stand out; subject and color enhance the beauty and value.

The design is repeated on both sides—an important feature. The more spiders, the greater the market value.

White spider webs are raised and intricately designed, a masterpiece of workmanship in the mold.

A recessed, molded "G. Argy-Rousseau" appears at the lower side, as well as "France" underneath.

Height: 4¾in/12.1cm
Value: $6,000–8,000

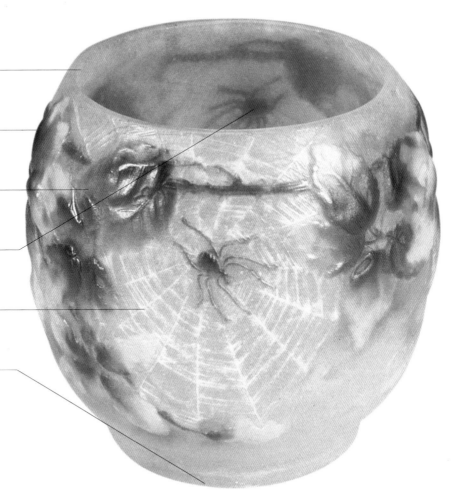

- *Argy-Rousseau's most popular designs were animals, birds, insects, butterflies, and people. His florals did not command the higher prices.*
- *Many designs featured angular shapes and geometric motifs, attracting Art Deco collectors.*
- *A group of Egyptian/Art Deco pieces, inspired by King Tutankhamen's tomb, were well received. Collectors expect high prices today.*
- *A mark does not increase market value, because his work was virtually always signed in the mold. If it is missing, collectors should ask why.*
- *Large Argy-Rousseau pieces bring high prices. Many were drilled for lamp bases, so look carefully for damage or repairs such as filled holes.*

Pâte de Verre

The *pâte de verre* technique translates in English as "paste of glass." Essentially, glass was ground to a fine powder and mixed with water, adhesives, and color to create a paste. This was then heated in an artfully designed mold until the material melted and vitrified into the desired form.

Argy-Rousseau became a master of the process, opening his first workshop in Paris in 1906. After serving in World War I, Argy-Rousseau entered into a partnership with the owner of a Parisian decorative arts gallery, thereby forming "La Societé des Pâtes de Verre d'Argy-Rousseau" and selling his wares. This arrangement continued for a decade and included the most productive years of Argy-Rousseau's life. He was the recipient of countless awards and accolades.

The period of Gabriel Argy-Rousseau's most successful production coincided almost exactly with the growth and fruition of the Art Deco style. However, tastes change and styles come and go. In the latter 1930s, Argy-Rousseau found himself and his work out of fashion. After World War II, he was never able to reestablish himself in the art glass world. He died in 1953, at the age of 67.

Burgun, Schverer & Cie

In the late 19th century, experimentation and innovation prevailed in art glass production. A seeming conflict arose between the Art Nouveau style, with its focus on nature in design and decoration, and the techniques evolving from new, industrialized methods. Yet businesses needed to be financially viable, then as now. Burgun, Schverer & Cie, in operation since the early 18th century, had found ways to remain in business and profitable for nearly two centuries. In the 1890s, the company continued to find ways to make handcrafted art glass profitable without resorting to new technology.

Burgun, Schverer & Cie, with the help of designer Désiré Christian, devised a complex, multicolor cameo glass that did not require several separate layers of colored glass. The technique involved the hand painting of decoration on the inner layer of glass, then the covering of the painting with a single transparent layer. This outer layer could then be etched and wheel-carved, using much less time and effort than in the cameo process to achieve a similar effect. The result, in fact, appealed to many as a quite different kind of glass, collected and enjoyed for its own qualities. This *intercalaire* art glass does not seem to have been reproduced or replicated, unlike the French cameo glass of Gallé and others.

In the 21st century, collectors seek the Burgun, Schverer art glass for the same reasons as the original buyers. The glass is beautiful, well-designed, and well-executed. It is also available, if scarce. In the midst of the information age, collectors have become aware of how and where to find it. Certainly it is available in antique auctions, shows, and markets. International chat rooms and websites may be able to locate pieces for online collectors. One needs to remain alert to the possibility of fraud, however, and the best protection is knowledge.

Cameo Cut and Etched *Intercalaire* Vase, c.1900

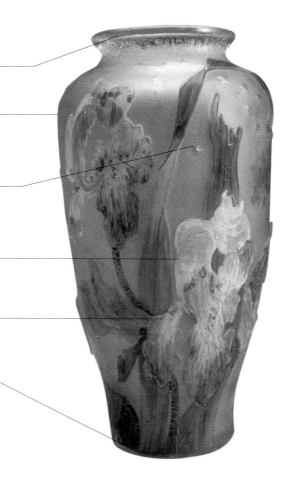

This translucent vase with etched surface has a raised rim and a border accented by gold enameling.

The above-average height allows space for an intricate decorating procedure and increases value.

The background glass is etched with stars and shows Martele carving marks; both enhance the motif and increase complexity and value.

The *intercalaire* decoration of iris blossoms and green foliage is painted between layers of glass, a rare technique that is much in demand.

The ethereal quality of decoration recalls Impressionist works, adding to the glass's popularity.

The BS&C trademark etched on the base identifies the work and increases its value.

Height: 9¼in/23.5cm
Value: $8,000–10,000

Cameo Etched and Enameled Vase, *c.*1895

This neo-classical urn-shaped vessel has three ornamental handles applied at the shoulder to add interest and value.

The unusual fiery-opalescent amber color accentuates the painted mural design.

Wide medial border and medallion cartouches contain figures of apparent Middle Eastern origin, a valuable motif for many collectors.

Decoration is both acid-etched and enamel-painted; extensive detailing on handles and borders adds value.

The round platform foot has a valuable, repeating enamel-painted border design that contrasts with the rim border.

The base is etched with the elaborate Burgun trademark highlighted in gold that collectors seek.

Height: 7¹/₄in/18.4cm
Value: $9,000–12,000

• *Dichroic glass (glass that changes color when light passes through it) was used both as decoration and to accentuate decoration.*
• *Amber glass that sparkles like fire when lighted was used very effectively by BS&C.*
• *Decor with scenes and people always increases value, as does decoration that tells a story. Biblical references are a plus.*
• *Burgun & Schverer pieces frequently have silver mounts, often applied as a pedestal, sometimes partly over the mark. Original mounts increase value.*
• *Burgun's trademark is a medallion with banners and "Verrerie d'art de Lorraine" entwined with thistle, leaf, and cross bearing "BS&CIE," all etched on the base.*

Surviving the Art Glass Industry

The history of Burgun, Schverer & Cie was inextricably linked to the artists Émile Gallé and Désiré Christian. Mathias Burgun and his son Antoine operated the company in Meisenthal, with Christian as their artistic director and head designer. The company had originated in France, but became part of Germany after the restructuring of Alsace–Lorraine. Burgun, Schverer's business contacts in France, were disrupted by the relocation, but were restored through an arrangement to provide glass for the Gallé Glassworks and to complete certain work for Gallé under the guidance of Christian. This agreement continued until 1895, when Antoine succeeded his father as director, and Burgun, Schverer & Cie became an independent company.

The reorganized Burgun, Schverer & Cie soon established its own style, creating art glass of distinctive design and artistic merit. Its specialty, *intercalaire* art glass, offered a finished item with a shimmering quality and an illusion of depth that became BS&C's characteristic image.

Czechoslovakian Art Glass—1920s

The early years of Czechoslovakia's existence as an independent republic were transitional years stylistically. In the early 1920s, Art Nouveau designs were still popular and cameo glass was still selling well. Arts and Crafts decorations played well in American cities, Secessionist designs were current in Europe, and Art Deco styles were catching on. Czechoslovakian glassmakers sold art glass in all of these styles, designs, and categories to anyone willing to buy their wares. If some particular design, color, or form proved to be popular, the Czech factories would replicate it as quickly and effectively as possible. In order to survive, they became masterful promoters, and Czech glass was exported throughout the world during the interwar years of 1918–1938.

Considering the quantities and diversity of Czech glass exported into the United States, it is little wonder the glass is often difficult to attribute. However, while the smaller factories often produced the same kinds of glass from town to town, the larger companies, especially Loetz and Moser, continued to create innovative art glass designed by progressive individualistic artists. The work of Michael Powolny, Otto Prutscher, Josef Hoffmann, and other members of the Wiener Werkstatte contributed to an emerging Czechoslovakian style that was an amalgam of styles in vogue around the world.

Above all, Czech glass was colorful. Eclectic, it drew design elements from several schools at the same time, using angular streamlined handles and wraps on rounded curving bodies, for example, or stylized modern decorations on classic or Art Nouveau shapes and designs. While no single unified Czechoslovakian glass approach exists, collectors happily agree it has a style all its own.

Cased Art Glass Vase, *c.*1925

A flared, raised rim shows the colorful interior, adding to the artistic impact and value.

The broad-shouldered shape in squat oval form gives graphic impact to decoration; collectors like this.

This piece is taller than average, a good size for the chosen design elements; collectors seek this shape/decor/color triad.

Typical bright yellow-amber, cased to colorless glass with aubergine gridwork decoration between layers, adds value.

A narrow integrated platform base adds balance and symmetry to the design and matches the grid above.

The base is stamped underneath with "Czechoslovakia" in a semi-circular mark, a plus for value.

Height: 9in/22.8cm
Value: $500–700

Michael Powolny Compote, *c.*1925

An applied black glass rim wrap on the extended border gives angularity to the round bowl-form, an excellent design.

The functional design of the compote centerbowl, meant to display flowers or fruit, increases value.

Brilliant red-orange cased to colorless glass is typical "tango," a desirable combination.

Evenly spaced vertical lines of black glass are typical Powolny style, Czech glass collectors' number one choice.

The black glass knop/wafer between the bowl and pedestal foot matches the rim, increasing importance and value.

Although the pedestal base is unusually not stamped or marked, it does not adversely affect value in this case.

Size: 5³/₄ x 7in/14.6 x 17.7cm
Value: $900–1,200

• Michael Powolny designs are among the most collectible of Loetz/Czech production, reproduced and imitated by Czech firms and designers.
• Vertical stripes on any Czech designs tend to increase the prices and the popularity of those pieces. Not all are Powolny-quality designs.
• Vivid colors as shown here were called "tango" colors. These are great collectibles.
• The gridwork or "plaid" decoration is another collectors' favorite. Great quantities of art glass with stripes and plaids were exported to the United States.
• Rogue dealers have removed Czechoslovakian marks, "signed" the items, and sold them as earlier designs. Collectors need to beware.

Centuries of Glass-making

The 1919 Treaty of Versailles that ended World War I created the new independent Republic of Czechoslovakia. The formerly Austrian territories that made up the new country, especially Bohemia and Moravia, had a glass-making tradition that went back centuries. Many of the people of the new Czechoslovakia—a country smaller than New York State— lived in traditional small towns, centered around a factory complex.

The factory employed virtually the entire population in one capacity or another. Craftspeople often worked out of their homes, painting or enameling designs on cold-glass wares. Others engraved in their own workshops. The young boys worked in the factories, later becoming apprentices to glassblowers, training in the intricate hot-glass work as they grew older. Some became designers, learning capabilities and characteristics of the glass as they worked with it.

The creation of the new state of Czechoslovakia was an occasion for celebration and hope. In time, the economic ramifications of nationhood would also become apparent. Czechoslovak glass factories, the traditional economic barometers for the region, took the lead in developing exportable merchandise. Their glassware, designed primarily for export and reflecting many different international styles, would go on to sell in marketplaces around the world.

Czechoslovakian Art Glass—Malachite

After World War I, Czechoslovakian glass companies discovered glassware lines in France, Britain, the United States, and even at home, ones they could replicate profitably for the export trade. The Art Deco designs of Lalique or the art glass of Tiffany, Daum, and Steuben could be copied or simulated with relatively inexpensive materials and labor. The resulting art glassware was of somewhat lesser quality, but it could be produced in great quantity and sold for a fraction of the prices in Paris and New York. Far from defrauding the original makers, Czech producers established what became Czechoslovakian glass's own style—popular in its own right, recognized, and promoted worldwide.

The large and well-connected glass companies such as Loetz and Moser were able to reestablish their factories with comparative ease in the 1920s, returning to pre-war glass lines, reconnecting with designers, and renewing export businesses. But many smaller Czechoslovakian companies established themselves by specializing. For example, the pressed-glass perfume bottles popular in the 1920s and '30s became a mainstay for several glassworks.

The art glass, tableware, and crystal Czechoslovakia exported to the United States has become a firm part of America's love affair with collectibles. They are recognizable, have a meaningful history, range in price from the reasonable to the absurd, and are available. The collectors of this glass have their own websites, publications, clubs, symposiums, conventions, shows, and auctions. Thanks to researchers, further identifications of particular lines and designers are sure to emerge over time. As supply dwindles and collectors multiply, prices for Czechoslovakian glass continue to climb.

Malachite Glass Perfume Bottle, c.1935

The molded stopper matches the bottle design and style; the flared tiara form is popular in perfumes and increases value.

A raised rim on the bottle displays the stopper well and accents both top and bottom decoration.

The round, flattened form of the bottle shows the molded design to best advantage.

Czech glass and perfume collectors seek such Rococo revivalist decoration as these two cherubs flanking a grapevine.

Contrast this decor with the vase at right; this is overloaded with design elements, as perfume bottles often are.

Value is not affected by the lack of a mark on the base as the design is known to collectors.

Height: 6in/15.2
Value: $250–400

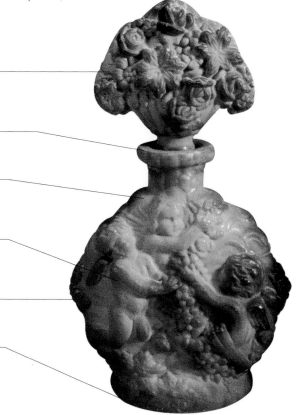

Malachite Glass "Ingrid" Vase, c. 1935

The angular octagonal rim balances this form and echoes the base—Art Deco elements that increase value.

The swirling green glass that dramatically imitates hardstone malachite is popular and valuable.

The vase's size offers an impressive background for the decoration, making height a plus-value element in this design.

The molded octagonal facets depict semi-nude women on four panels and geometric designs on the others.

Design here is similar to Lalique designs "Bacchantes" and "6 Figurines," both popular; collectors seek designs like this.

The polished base is not marked, but the Schlevogt design is well-identified in reference books.

Height: 9⅝in/24.4cm
Value: $900–1,200

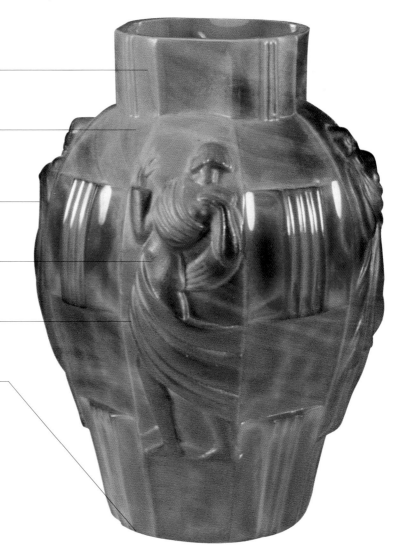

• Curt Schlevogt's "Ingrid" line included other designs and such colors as lapis blue and colorless glass, all highly collectible as Czech, Art Deco, and hardstone glassware.

• A frosted colorless style of the vase above sometimes bears a fake "R. Lalique" mark, which decreases value.

• Green malachite glass was produced by other companies, including Ludwig Moser's. The vase above has been mistaken for Moser glassware.

• An imitation lapis lazuli blue glass similar to the malachite green was made by several Czech companies. Its rarity makes it a real treasure.

• The perfume bottle is a combination of classical motif on an Art Nouveau design with an Art Deco stopper.

Politics and Production

During the 20 years leading up to World War II, Czechoslovakia was at or near the eye of the storm of European politics. The glass factories in small towns and cities struggled first to establish their success and autonomy, then later to maintain their hard-won prosperity in the face of worldwide recession and depression. Political turmoil swirled around them.

The Nazi invasion of Czechoslovakia in 1939 led to the mobilization of many of the glass factories for the German war effort, the closing of others, and conscription of the workers. Glass production for civilian purposes waited.

Czechoslovakia was reconstituted as an independent state after the end of World War II. The Communist regime that took power in 1948 nationalized the Czech glass industry. This meant that until the fall of Communism in the early 1990s, all exports of Czech glassware were handled by the state-owned export firm, Glassexport.

D'Argental & Arsall

The Saint-Louis Glassworks was part of the triumvirate of paperweight producers—Clichy, Baccarat, and Saint-Louis—and made the glass spheres, usually with internal decoration, as novelties. The objects were reasonably priced and available in great quantity, becoming highly collectible at the time they were made, again during the Victorian revival, and finally in the current paperweight market.

It was with its popular cameo glass, however, that the Saint-Louis company made its mark with buyers of the late 19th and early 20th centuries. Under the signatures of "D'Argental" and "Arsall," Saint-Louis made finely detailed cameo glass. Landscape decorations predominated, often arranged in elaborately etched and wheel-carved cartouches or frameworks. With commercial success, the company expanded their art glass production, changing techniques and styles to suit the times and customers' demands.

D'Argental and Arsall cameo glass featured landscapes, such as mountainous terrain with castles or cathedrals, riverside shores with forested hills and valleys, animals, or fishermen. Other firms replicated these motifs, as well as the deep aubergine or maroon layers of glass cased over fiery opalescent amber. Most of the Saint-Louis work is signed "D'Argental" or "Arsall" in cameo at the side of the decoration, occasionally with the cross of Lorraine below.

The market value of Saint-Louis cameo glass has fluctuated over time with economic trends. In the late 20th century, market values of cameo glass increased greatly, led by Gallé in particular, and the French glass houses in general. This owed in part to the arrival of important Asian collectors, as well as to the worldwide economic upswing. Despite the waning of the latter, there continues to be interest in D'Argental and Arsall art glass in the antiques and collectibles milieux, and there is no indication that this will end any time soon.

Floral Cameo Etched Vase, c.1910

A graceful curve tops this ovoid body in Art Nouveau manner; a border was created above the cameo etching of leaves.

The vase's size helps create the impression of natural outdoor space in a pleasant setting, appealing to collectors.

The vase is dichroic amber glass with fiery opal color, cased in subtle rosy pink and aubergine-brown layers, creating an effective contrast.

Trumpet blossoms appear in a naturalistic setting and a realistic coloration.

"D'Argental" appears at midpoint; it is raised because the glass was etched away from all but the signature.

The decoration extends to the lower edge of the vessel without being cut off, giving a painterly quality to the work and increasing its value.

Height: 9³/₄in/24.7cm
Value: $1,000–1,500

Landscape Decorated Cameo Glass Vase, *c.*1910

The raised lip on this oval form serves to complete the decoration, which would otherwise seem unfinished.

The perfect oval body provides a glass "canvas" for the expansive landscape etched overall.

The color is excellent, with translucent fiery amber, cased in layers of dark maroon over brilliant red glass—a popular color combination.

The fine details of the etched decoration—distant mountains viewed between trees along a riverbank—increase the vase's value.

Decoration is enhanced by the light showing through the colorful glass, suggesting a brilliant sunset sky.

The signature "D'Argental" with the cross of Lorraine is etched at the lower side and identifies the work.

Height: 8in/20.3cm
Value: $1,500–1,800

• *A group of Middle Eastern cameo designs with Egyptian scenes were signed "Arsall." They are scarce and expensive.*
• *The landscapes with most value include a little of everything—mountains, water, clouds, buildings, and even animals and people.*
• *Size is important with landscape pieces, allowing more creative decoration and demanding higher prices.*
• *Numerous layers of glass on cameo vases add value.*
• *Bubbles in glass or flaws in etching are rare in cameo glass. Damage decreases value significantly.*
• *Generally, D'Argental and Arsall are bargains in the collectibles field, with excellent quality and high potential.*

Compagnie de Saint-Louis

Compagnie des Verreries et Cristalleries de Saint-Louis (est. 1829) was one of the oldest and best known glassworks in the Alsace-Lorraine area of France. In the last two decades of the 19th century, Saint-Louis entered the field of art glass in the Art Nouveau style. In France alone, the firm's output joined the work of Gallé, Daum, Leveille, Burgun, Christian, and others.

Alsace-Lorraine was part of Germany from 1870 until the end of World War I in 1919, when the region was restored to France. Throughout that time, the company produced glass, primarily home decorations, tableware, crystal, windows, mirrors, lighting devices, and functional materials.

After World War I, the Saint-Louis Co. focused more on enamel decoration, working with Marcel Goupy and others. With growing acclaim, the company turned to Art Deco styles and more modernistic approaches to artistic glassmaking. The work of this period and later appears with the inscription "Compagnie des Cristalleries de Saint-Louis, S.A."

Daum Verrerie de Nancy

Relatively few important designers of art glass existed in early 20th-century France. Despite their competition, these men keenly wanted to share the secrets of their art. When Émile Gallé founded his École de Nancy (School of Nancy) in 1901, his goal was to promote various art media, including glass. Gallé was president of the school; among his vice presidents was Antonin Daum, whom Gallé admired and respected.

The Daum brothers had moved quickly into the mainstream of art glass production after 1890. They encouraged their glass masters and technicians in the use of unusual and artful processes. Antonin himself designed numerous pieces. Smart marketing led to increased demand for Daum art glass, and the Daum Verrerie de Nancy became widely known for its Art Nouveau work.

During the periods of art glass revival in the 1960s and 1990s, French art glass soared in both value and popularity. While some companies were short-lived, Daum's production at Nancy was prolific and long-lasting. As a result, collectors can gather a fine Daum collection. The current market for early 20th-century art glass made by the Daum brothers' company is strong. Prices remain high for major examples of French art glass, and experts expect prices to rise even more as the available supply declines.

Unfortunately, certain companies copied the popular glass. Reproductions have been produced in Europe, South America, and China and sold as authentic. The collector's best protection against such fraud is knowledge about the glass and its qualities. Rogue companies will not survive without a demand for their products.

Padded, Carved, and Etched Cameo Glass Vase, *c.* 1910

Note the flared top rim on the cylindrical form composed of swirled mottled purple-blue and frosted colorless and white body.

This piece is taller than the average Daum cameo vase and presents a slender, elegant background for the spring blossoms.

Dark aubergine overlaid glass is etched and carved as naturalistic spiked leaves, stems, and garden grasses in a representational style.

White pads of glass, applied hot at the furnace, are shaped and carved as snowdrop buds and blossoms in a beautiful arrangement.

Note how the background glass behind the flowers in speckled and mottled shading accentuates the floral display.

The integrated pedestal foot is inscribed underneath with "Daum / Nancy" and a cross of Lorraine, adding value.

Height: 10in/25.4cm
Value: $5,000–7,000

Mold Blown, Etched, and Wheel Carved Scenic Vase, *c.*1900

Carved leaves extend a forest scene to the top rim, increasing the graphic impact and value.

The vase's height is average for this design; while made in quantity, each example is unique.

The fiery orange body is overlaid and molded in both bright and dark greens to simulate the natural colors of the forest.

The sunset coloring of the sky is viewed through carved trees with dramatic impact. This is one of Daum's most famous vases.

On the side, the inscription "Daum / Nancy" with a cross of Lorraine between adds value and pleases collectors.

Note the careful addition of a paler green border around the base, adding to the naturalistic effect of the grassy foreground.

Height: 11in/28cm
Value: $7,000–9,000

• *The craftsmanship of the master workers allowed the Daum Verrerie de Nancy to experiment with art glass in unique ways.*
• *Daum was the first to use acid not only to etch decor, but also to manipulate the colors and selectively frost and polish surfaces.*
• *Intercalary decoration—internal decor between two or more layers of glass—was used most effectively as a shortcut to cameo carving.*
• *Scenic designs that were popular before World War I changed the glassmaker's craft forever. The intricate scene illustrated above required much time and skillful effort.*
• *The padded technique used on the vase at left effectively replicated the more complex marquetry technique.*

The Family Company

The Verrerie de Nancy was established in 1878 by Jean Daum, a lawyer. In 1879, his son, Auguste, joined him. Together they reorganized to produce functional glassware that included watch crystals and tableware. After Jean's death in 1889, his other son Antonin joined the business and sent it in a new direction, both financially and artistically. The timing was perfect. The French were buying decorative art, the Art Nouveau style was in favor, and glass making enjoyed great respect.

At the 1889 Paris Exhibition, the Daum brothers viewed impressive displays of art glass. Intrigued, they devoted a significant portion of their business to art glass. In time, the company embraced modern methods. It continues to produce high-caliber art glass under the direction of the founders' descendants.

Daum Verrerie de Nancy— Post-World War I

The Daum Verrerie de Nancy, like factories all over France, was closed during World War I, 1914–1919. When it reopened, it found a new world of ideas, tastes, and styles. Paul Daum, especially, helped the company to incorporate the new with the best of the old and economize at the same time. Innovative acid etching on "modern" designs combined well with the popular styles of the 1920s. Transparent glass, both colored and colorless, came into frequent use alone and in combination, as illustrated here. The heavily textured effect of selective acid treatment gave a rough "sandblasted" look and feel to the glass. This became especially popular when combined with smooth, polished areas on monochromatic pieces in angular and geometric designs.

The Daum Co., led by Antonin Daum, nephew Paul, and son Michel, actively participated in the world-renowned Paris Exhibition of 1925. Daum pieces, such as those illustrated here, admirably represent the Art Deco style ushered in by the event and have now become valuable examples and memorabilia of the period.

The Daum family members continued in the company until World War II. During the German occupation of France, Paul Daum was sent to a concentration camp and died there in 1944. When the glass factories reopened after the war, his cousin Michel took an active role in changing the Daum production exclusively to crystal. Immediately successful, pieces made then are popular collectibles today, especially the novelties and decorative giftware. In the 1970s, Auguste's grandson, Jacques, reintroduced *pâte de verre*, using new techniques. This line succeeded as well, especially in the United States, where it was sold in gift shops and department stores and eventually in the collectibles market. The company continues to produce art glass with international success under family directors.

Molded Lion and Lioness Vase, c. 1930

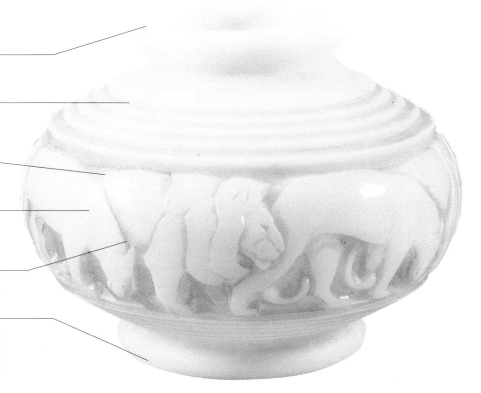

The ovoid sphere with raised flared rim above etched ring collars compares in form to the vase at left made at Nancy.

Heavy opaque white glass provides an excellent "canvas," increasing value.

The size of this piece provides for the broad medial frieze and allows crisp detail; animal decor always increases value.

The medial band of lions and mates is D'Avesn's most famous design, adding major value.

The lion decoration is accented by an amethyst "patine" wash applied in low recesses, a valuable feature.

The impressed mark on the base, "D'Avesn/Made in France," aids in authenticating and appraising.

Size: 8 x 11in/20.3 x 28cm
Value: $2,500–4,000

Etched Art Deco Vase, *c.* 1925

The perfectly molded sphere with a raised opening above etched ring collars has whimsical decoration that adds value.

Value is increased on this piece by the pleasing symmetry and balance of its dimensions.

The sphere is transparent amethyst cased to colorless crystal; rough etched texture contrasts with the polished glass layer on the exterior.

Art Deco decoration with stylized blossom-forms spaced by undulating clear amethyst-purple bands is a desirable style.

Daum exhibited vases like this at the 1925 Paris Exhibition; an award winner would be especially valuable.

The impressed mark on the base, "Daum/Nancy" with a cross of Lorraine between, will bring a higher price.

Size: 9 x 9³/₄in/
22.8 x 24.7cm dia
Value: $4,000–5,000

• Collectors seek Daum's Art Deco designs because they are compatible with other styles.
• Daum's engineers, chemists, and designers created art glass at reasonable prices that appeared handhewn and crafted by old methods.
• The vase above shows Daum's mastery with acid: such vases are truly treasures.
• Daum's work is virtually always signed, usually with the cross of Lorraine between "Daum/Nancy."
• Knowing the Daum-Croismare connection can highlight a piece undervalued in the marketplace.
• The lion vase was made by a press-molded method. The initial mold design is best; later productions may lose sharp detail elements.

New Styles and Techniques

Paul Daum, Auguste Daum's fourth son, joined the company after his father's death in 1909. He improved business practices and simplified glass-making techniques. After World War I, he relied increasingly on acid etching as he moved away from more expensive techniques. Much of the post-World War I "French cameo" glass was mass-produced, with little of it handcrafted. Cost and changing tastes required new styles and techniques.

In 1927, Paul Daum opened an additional complex of glass factories in Croismare, including "Verreries d'Art 'Lorraine,'" "Verreries Belle-Etoile," and "Verreries d'Art de M.P. D'Avesn." He hired Pierre D'Avesn as manager. D'Avesn had worked for Lalique and others, specializing in molded or press-molded glassware. Daum intended to quietly mass-produce decorative glassware at Croismare without compromising the Daum reputation for quality handcrafted art glass. Croismare used various marks and signatures, but did not, apparently, use the Daum name.

From 1926 through 1932, during D'Avesn's stay, an extraordinary amount and variety of glass was produced, much in the popular Art Deco style and much designed by D'Avesn himself. Croismare made lighting devices of all kinds in great quantity, and metal-mounted art glass decorations comprised a major portion of its successful production.

François-Émile Decorchmont

Pâte de verre, which in English means "paste of glass," was revived in France in the late 19th century to become a challenging form of art glass pursued by many, but mastered by few. François-Émile Decorchmont was one who became a master of the technique.

After much experimentation, failure, trial, error, and eventual success, Decorchmont also produced the intricate and difficult variations called *pâte de cristal* and *pâte d'email.* The former refers to transparent or translucent *pâte de verre,* the latter to glass with porcelain-like properties achieved with additives. The significance of Decorchmont's achievements in the world of art glass cannot be overestimated. He seemed to care more for the innovation than for any fame or fortune that might result.

In the period following World War I, Decorchmont produced relatively few pieces of *pâte de verre* for sale and exhibition. Frequently simple and esoteric, his work appealed to the sophisticated collector or decorator, but was not promoted or presented in the highly competitive shops, salons, or galleries of the early 1920s. However, as the Art Deco style became more prominent in the decorative arts of post-war France, Decorchmont responded with restrained changes in his glass, becoming more popular and influential as his groundbreaking genius was recognized and appreciated.

Collectors of 20th-century art glass in the 21st century market are surprised and excited to find a piece of Decorchmont's work for sale. Supply generally does not meet the demand for this art glass. On the other hand, the work is not usually "exciting" by today's standards. The nuances Decorchmont found significant and artistically important were and are of special interest to museums, advanced collectors, and galleries, which does not translate into high appraisals or price tags. One who is fortunate enough to find a Decorchmont treasure in the marketplace may also find it to be a bargain.

Pâte de Verre Decorative Bowl, *c.*1945

A wide rim on the bowl-form gives ample room for pressing glass paste into the mold.

The diminutive piece is a late example in a functional form that collectors seek and will pay for.

Mixed and swirled earth-tones of rust-red, ocher, and frosted colorless glass add value.

The bowl is decorated only by its form, use of color, and purity of design. Decorchmont collectors seek exactly this beauty.

A horseshoe-shaped molded signature at the lower side includes a cross of Lorraine used only after 1945.

The integrated solid pedestal base is characteristic of Decorchmont and adds value.

This piece is numbered "'D47" on the base, indicating it was made after July of 1945.

Size: 2⁷/₈ x 3⁷/₈in/
7.3 x 9.8cm
Value: $3,000–4,000

Pâte de Verre Molded Vase, *c.*1933

A broad open rim on the conical vessel allowed the powdered glass to be pressed into the mold for strong detail.

This is tall for Decorchmont's work in the 1930s, when he concentrated mostly on stained glass windows.

The body is a swirl of purple, aubergine, and frosted colorless powders mixed, but not blended.

Subtle decoration of spiked leaf-shapes in geometric procession around the exterior is compatible with Art Deco and Arts and Crafts styles.

Symmetrical balance of the wonderful form and decoration enhances the value of this typical Decorchmont piece.

The molded signature mark in a horseshoe shape is recessed into lower side of the vase; it increases value.

"C199" on the base indicates production between 1930 and 1939 in a complex numbering system that is helpful to collectors and curators.

Height: 5⅛in/13cm
Value: $3,500–5,000

• *Broken bubbles and skips in the surface are common in* pâte de verre *items. Collectors tolerate minor damage as part of the process.*
• *Decorchmont's numbering system is listed in the Victor Arwas book,* Glass: Art Nouveau to Art Deco.
• *The cross of Lorraine was added to Decorchmont's work after the allied defeat of Germany—a historical mark that attracts collectors.*
• *Little of Decorchmont's work was produced, and precious little survives today.*
• *Decorchmont's legacy is the* pâte de verre *revival.*

Experiments in Glass

François-Émile Decorchmont's life-work centered around *pâte de verre*, as he used his own discoveries and methods to advance the art of making glass from paste. His father, a respected professor, taught him the rudiments of sculpture, painting, and ceramics. Meanwhile, François-Émile became intrigued by the work of glass artists in the *pâte de verre* medium.

Decorchmont pursued his own experiments, primarily with glass, but also in painting and enamel work, combining the three artistically. By the age of 25 he had won awards, honors, and scholarships for both his work in the arts in general and in *pâte de verre*.

In 1907, father and son established workshops at the family home in Conches that included modernized kilns able to sustain the extended low temperatures required for *pâte de verre*, *pâte de cristal*, and *pâte d'email* (enamel). The ensuing years proved prolific.

Early in the 1920s, Decorchmont returned to *pâte de verre*, while the Art Deco style gained prominence. His exhibitions reflected the prevailing spirit and brought his art glass renewed acclaim and public demand.

Degue

The Verrerie d'Art Degue glassworks was organized in Paris in 1926 and quickly competed with the earlier established French glass companies. Owner and designer David Gueron found ready success with his line of art glass lamps, chandeliers, and half-round ceiling lampshades. These shades were composed of translucent layers of colorless glass internally decorated by swirls of color. Frosted on the exterior, the lighting devices effectively distributed light and became instant favorites with decorators and homemakers. Another of Degue's series used colorful art glass bowls or jardinieres mounted on wrought iron pedestals commissioned from Edgar Brandt. Both of these successful lines were copied and reproduced by other companies. Both are highly desirable collectibles today.

A latecomer to the world of French art glass, David Gueron was a good businessman. Although the Art Deco style was popular and profitable in France in 1926, he focused his business on the export market, especially the United States. Americans were still buying the cameo glass decorations made in the late French Nouveau manner. Signed Degue acid-etched vases, compotes, bowls, and lighting devices continued to be popular in the 1920s in department stores and gift shops across the United States. Gueron exported scenics and floral designs in large quantities that account for the many Degue pieces found in the American collectibles market. Interested collectors will find commercial Degue cameo pieces more readily than his Art Deco designs.

While Verrerie d'Art Degue exported commercial art glass, it also produced large numbers of "look-alikes" of Verrerie Schneider's Le Verre Français and Charder designs *(see page 142)*. Despite ongoing litigation against the company by Charles Schneider, the Degue copycat pieces were a success. All were vibrant imitations or variations of the Schneider work, signed with the acronym "Degue" in script. This situation caused such animosity that the two companies were nearly destroyed by it.

Now, some 70 years later, collectors select Degue pieces for their artistic quality and their significance to the Art Deco movement in the conflicted years of their production. That significance continues today during the Art Deco revival and the wave of art glass appreciation driving that revival.

Acid Etched Art Deco Centerbowl, *c.*1928

The wide opening allows for an arranged centerpiece, functional art that collectors seek.

Centerbowls are rarely found in art glass; collectors would consider this a choice example.

The opaque red background color is rare, reversing the usual order of white shading to a deep black amethyst outer layer.

Four etched blossom clusters rise above black leaves spiked in a stylized decor that adds value.

The frosted surface emphasizes the polished decoration; the red-black-white combination is popular and valuable.

The bowl is inscribed "Degue" in decor at the side, adding value.

Size: 6 x 12in/15.2 x 30.4cm
Value: $1,200–1,500

Acid Etched Art Deco Trumpet Vase, *c.*1926

The flared rim above the oval trumpet-form body is typically used as a foil for vibrant decoration.

The tall, slender shape of the piece contrasts with the abstract modernistic design and adds to the piece's value.

Brilliantly polished cobalt blue glass contrasts with a stark mottled white frosted background.

Three repeats of the abstract fern-like foliate motif increase visual interest.

A slender talus flares out to the broad pedestal foot with integrated cobalt blue color and completes the symmetry of form.

Signed "Degue" on the side and "Made in France" underneath, this was a made-for-export piece.

Height: 19in/48.2cm
Value: $1,500–2,000

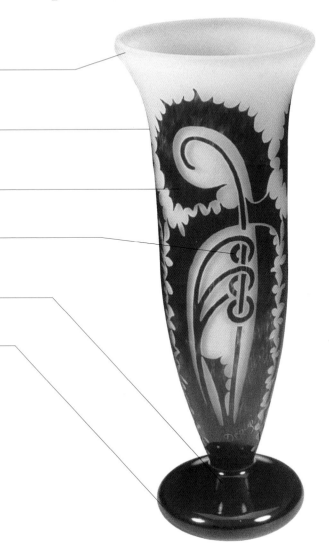

• *Comparisons of "Degue" with "Le Verre" pieces are futile. Both companies contributed to the art glass of their period; both produced wonderful collectible pieces.*
• *The blue trumpet vase is classic. Decoration is a key to style as well as to value.*
• *The red bowl is also a classic form, often called a "basket" in pottery or Indian artefacts. This form is an extraordinary blend of old and new.*
• *Degue has received good publicity in the last decade and is expected to escalate in value as it disappears into the hands of collectors.*
• *Degue art glass is remarkably free from flaws, suggesting good quality control. Collectors need to watch for ground-out chips or polished rims, which are all devaluers.*

David Gueron

Son of a Turkish family in France, Gueron established his first glassworks, Cristalleries de Compiègne, to produce tableware and other functional glass. In 1926, the year after the successful Paris Exhibition, Gueron moved into the more lucrative production of French art glass. He opened Verrerie d'Art Degue in Paris, along with a gallery to promote the art glass he named "Degue." His cameo glass designs leaned heavily toward natural motifs, but also used brilliant colors that became his signature. His internally decorated vases, lamps, and lampshades met instant success. Another Degue line used a sandblasting method to decorate monochromatic vessels with graphic devices and designs.

Not content with the success of his own designs, Gueron copied the Art Deco designs of Charles Schneider. The resultant litigation lasted for six long years, until in 1932 the case was settled out of court. Both companies were financially devastated by the process.

André Delatte

André Delatte opened his glassworks in 1921 on the outskirts of the great glass-making center at Nancy. He blatantly copied the successful styles of other glass companies, most notably of Daum, from whom he "borrowed" both techniques and designs. Nonetheless, Delatte succeeded in his own right with a number of significant art glass contributions.

Delatte embraced the Art Deco style in the 1920s when other glass artists were reluctant. As a result, Delatte found his own work imitated and reproduced. Such was the case in about 1925, when Delatte introduced deeply etched and sandblasted monochromatic vases decorated in the Art Deco style with horses, or occasionally with people. Interestingly, this design—illustrated at right in black—would fit comfortably in the most contemporary homes in the United States today. Delatte's designs were often as universal and cosmopolitan as this example.

Among collectibles today, Delatte's cameo glass is much more available than his pieces in the Art Deco aesthetic. During the period of his production, commercial success depended on reaching the broadest market, in France of course, but also in the United States. Americans did not generally accept the Art Deco style until well into the 1930s. So Delatte produced the well-designed, acid-etched cameo art glass they demanded. Bargain hunters can find these pieces at swap meets, auctions, shows, and virtual markets. The work is signed, or marked in cameo, but is not as well-known as that of other producers. It also yields comparatively low value, meaning that Delatte reproductions do not exist. Delatte prices have increased consistently through the years, but have never reached the level of Gallé, Daum, and other more prominent makers. The upward-value trend will likely continue, however, so this is a good time to look.

Cameo Glass Floral Vase, c.1923

The raised rim above an ovoid body compares with the similar form opposite; both bodies provide area for artful decor.

The vase is an average height for cameo glass, allowing plenty of smooth, egg-shaped body.

Glass is cased in a maroon-red layer, then "cut back" in floral motif, leaving borders at top and base, all value-enhancing.

This is a skillful acid-etched cameo design of graceful exotic blossoms and buds on leafy stems, without wheel cutting, but nicely polished.

On the etched signature "A. Delatte–Nancy," the "l" is extended as a cross, and the "y" underlines Nancy, features "borrowed" from Daum.

The "Made in France" stamped on the base indicates that this was made for export; value increases for items with "special" designation.

Height: 8in/20.3cm
Value: $900–1,200

Jarvil Etched and Sandblasted Vase, *c.*1925

The raised rim above a perfectly round vessel—designed for the broad medial frieze—shows excellent balance and symmetry.

The heavy-walled, solid black glass sphere makes a dramatic impact compatible with the Art Deco style decoration.

A wide band of six stylized prancing horses decorates the vase at center, increasing value.

Three horses, acid-etched on the surface, alternate with three horses deeply carved by sandblasting; this creates a dramatic positive/negative effect.

The highly polished, black surface contrasts with the acid finish on the etched and recessed horses, adding artistic clout and further value.

An etched mark on the side, "Jarvil-Nancy France," refers to the Delatte location in Jarville, a suburb of Nancy. Integral signatures add value.

Height: 6in/15.2cm
Value: $2,000–3,000

• *Delatte made a series of glass vases that were enamel-decorated in the Art Deco style with figures silhouetted in black against bright, stylized grounds; highly collectible.*
• *The black horse vase was made in many opaque colors. Signed "Jarvil," it is not always recognized as Delatte and can be a treasure-in-waiting for an astute collector.*
• *Delatte cameo glass seldom employed multiple layers of glass and wheel-carving. Virtually all are signed.*
• *French art glass from the inter-war period is widely available in the United States. Buyers can find treasures when they know more than the sellers. It pays to study!*

A Popular Glassmaker

André Delatte created acid-etched cameo glass on the production line model during the interwar period of 1918-1938. It was a time of great creativity in the decorative arts. Delatte's success depended on the support of the general public. To that end, he mass produced his art ware to be sold at reasonable prices and with identifiable functions. He produced art glass lighting devices in great quantity and popular styles.

While working with wrought iron fittings for light fixtures, Delatte developed a series of art glass items blown into wrought iron frames. This led to confrontations with Daum Glassworks, also centered in the Nancy area. Daum had been working with similar techniques before World War I and returned to them afterward. He took Delatte to court for violating his copyright, beginning a legal process that dragged on interminably. Daum, the larger business, was able to withstand the damage. The Delatte glassworks was forced to cut back, and eventually close its doors.

Émile Gallé

Much of Émile Gallé's early work resides in museums or major collections worldwide. A true genius, he translated his unbounded appreciation for nature into tangible form. His art glass is a joy to behold. Yet Gallé seldom, if ever, designed his wares. His early art glass was made at the Burgun, Schverer factories in Meisenthal. Even so, these pieces are no less "Gallé." Although not on the scene, he directed every nuance, from the thickness of the glass to the final "Gallé" signature.

Gallé's influence on the French Art Nouveau style was likewise direct and immediate. Vocal and highly regarded, he furthered his influence through the establishment of the École de Nancy (School of Nancy). He also exhibited his work at every opportunity. Well-traveled, he learned from the work of others, both contemporaries and past artists. He impressed those he met at expositions and exhibitions with his work and artistic vision.

Émile Gallé's art glass is among the most desirable of late 19th- and early 20th-century collectibles, considered a treasure wherever it is found. Although great quantities of French art glass were made for the U.S. market, relatively little appears at any given time. During the art glass revival of the 1960–1970 era, led by the publication of several books on the subject (Arwas, Blount, Grover, Revi), Gallé gained new admirers and collectors. Again in the 1990s, interest resurged, especially from the Far Eastern countries where Gallé's Japanesque and Oriental styling were especially appreciated. In the collectibles world, one major group of collectors can manipulate market prices significantly, even when they try to avoid attention. Thus, Gallé prices escalated until that market waned through economic changes. Current market values are high but stable, with especially strong prices for the finest Gallé examples, a trend expected to continue.

Morning Glory Vase with Bees, c. 1900

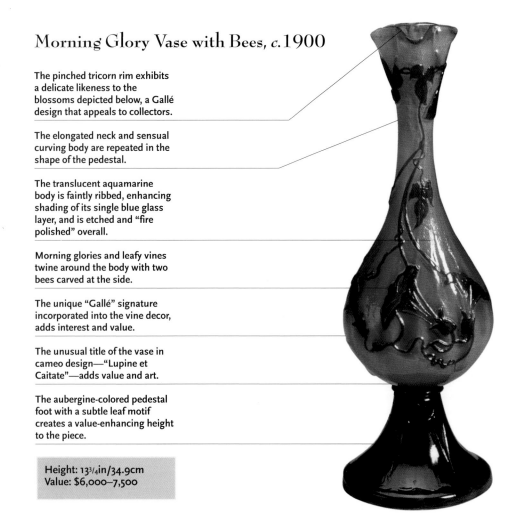

The pinched tricorn rim exhibits a delicate likeness to the blossoms depicted below, a Gallé design that appeals to collectors.

The elongated neck and sensual curving body are repeated in the shape of the pedestal.

The translucent aquamarine body is faintly ribbed, enhancing shading of its single blue glass layer, and is etched and "fire polished" overall.

Morning glories and leafy vines twine around the body with two bees carved at the side.

The unique "Gallé" signature incorporated into the vine decor, adds interest and value.

The unusual title of the vase in cameo design—"Lupine et Caitate"—adds value and art.

The aubergine-colored pedestal foot with a subtle leaf motif creates a value-enhancing height to the piece.

Height: 13³/₄in/34.9cm
Value: $6,000–7,500

Wheel-Carved and Etched Cameo Glass Vase, *c.*1894

The raised rim in the form of a flower calyx cup that holds the blossom is a typical Gallé shape-from-nature feature.

The green cup and bulbed stem graphically simulate the base of a blossom; collectors appreciate such a design.

Note the four glass layers: a colorless body cased to brilliant pink and amethyst, with avocado green at top. A complex palette adds value.

The flower-form vase invites a real blossom to complete the design—such naturalistic imagery was Gallé's specialty.

Lavender blossoms, buds, and leafy stems are acid-etched and wheel-carved to show detail, adding value.

Artistic impact is strengthened by the brilliant background color and the colorless layer that adds shimmer to the pink.

The signature "Gallé" in Japanesque style complements the design.

Height: 7³/₄in/19.6cm
Value: $8,000–10,000

• *The vase above was most likely crafted at Burgun, Schverer. With limited acid etching and great attention to detail, such an early piece commands a premium.*
• *Verrerie Parlante was the name Gallé gave to his work that "speaks in glass." Poetry, bits of literature, and phrases were written in cameo relief.*
• *Gallé studied horticulture and botany so he could replicate flowers realistically.*
• *Generally, more layers of glass mean more value.*
• *Gallé used intercalary or applied decoration. The former imbedded material between layers of glass; the latter placed the decoration on the surface.*

Development of the Artist

Émile's father, Charles Gallé, created both glass and ceramics. Émile learned under him, then was sent to work with Burgun, Schverer & Co. at Meisenthal in Alsace-Lorraine. A great friendship ensued between Gallé, Burgun, and the head designer, Désiré Christian. In 1885, the three signed a contract for Burgun to produce Gallé's work under Christian's guidance.

In the following decade, Gallé involved himself in every facet of the arts, from poetry and literature, to architecture and furniture. His work at Burgun, Schverer was unparalleled. Nonetheless, when the opportunity arrived for him to build his own verrerie at his father's estate in Nancy, he moved on it. He completed his new factory in 1894; in 1895, his contract with Burgun and Christian expired.

During the decade that followed, Émile Gallé accomplished more than many artists do in an entire lifetime. He died at the age of 58 in 1904. His exceptional glass is a tribute to his life.

Émile Gallé— Commercial Glass

A basic dichotomy exists between glass that was handcrafted under Gallé's direction and "commercial" glass that was mass-produced. Collectors find treasures among Gallé art glass from all periods of manufacture. Gallé himself eventually accepted that technology could create and enhance his product.

The "Cristallerie d'Émile Gallé" produced great quantities of art glass, including vases, tableware, plaques, bowls, lamps, and other lighting devices, compotes and tazzas, perfumes, decanters, mirrors, frames, and miniatures, virtually all signed or marked "Gallé." Pieces made after Gallé's death in 1904 were also marked with a memorial star, initiated by Gallé's wife, Henriette. This continued until after her death in 1914. These starred pieces are collectible in their own right, although not more worthy.

The glassworks was closed during World War I, from 1914 to 1918. When it reopened under family ownership, it again produced fine art glass. Most of the work tended toward the Art Nouveau style. Gallé pieces exhibited at the 1925 Paris Exhibition were characteristic of Gallé's earlier years. This glass is virtually impossible to distinguish from earlier Gallé; it is equally collectible and highly regarded.

Even in Gallé's day, there were reproductions of his glass, particularly the simpler, acid-etched commercial ware. Because it was so successful, other factories picked up the technique. They did not, however, attempt to pass off their work as Gallé; most firms signed their own name and capitalized on the successful style. Reproductions today are meant to deceive, and marks are deliberate forgeries. The best defense is a knowledgeable offense.

Etched and Enameled Middle Eastern Series Vase, c. 1885

At the flared top rim, the fiery amber translucent body shows most clearly.

The diminutive oval vasiform is average for Gallé's Persian series and quite collectible.

This series reflected Gallé's admiration for Joseph Brocard's work. It is rare and costly.

Brown enamel on amber glass creates highly desirable matching scenes in the elaborate cartouche, with Persian warrior on horseback.

Background scrolls and floral devices cover the entire piece and frame the central reserves at front and back, simulating Persian vases.

The signature "Gallé" is integral with the Middle Eastern motif, a much-admired artistic detail.

Height: 6in/15.2cm
Value: $9,000–12,000

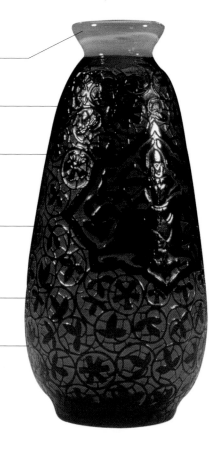

Monumental Cameo Glass Vase, *c.* 1900

The sensuous form with inward curving rim above an oval body exemplifies the French Art Nouveau style, a collector's treasure.

Statuesque height allows a full presentation of nature's beauty in a single prunus branch.

Amber-colored glass with fiery opalescence is cased with subtle shades of olive and forest green, with aubergine below.

Acid etching of decoration is skillfully, realistically executed in precise botanical realism.

"Gallé" etched as an integrated part of the decor was typical even into the 1930s; knowledgeable collectors can recognize the fakes.

Notice how the slender stem above the disk foot gives a symmetrical balance to the vase.

Height: 22in/55.8cm
Value: $9,500–12,500

• *The Persian vase* (**left**) *uses enamel to fill recesses made by acid; the vase* (**right**) *uses acid to etch through glass layers.*
• *Gallé imitated Joseph Brocard's Persians in tribute, but improved the designs by etching and gilding; this rare series brings strong prices.*
• *The vases offered here show Gallé's diversity. These differ in technique, style, and size.*
• *Note the vases' similarities: fiery amber background glass, skillful execution, and integrated signatures.*
• *The vase above is dramatic by virtue of size alone.*
• *Gallé's son-in-law reintroduced blown-out vases and lamps in the 1920s, true to earlier Gallé traditions. These command increasingly "important" prices.*

A Passion for Art Glass

From 1894 to 1904, Gallé presided over the diversified factory/studio at Nancy. He hired craftsmen to execute his furniture designs, using marquetry inlays and expressive techniques in woodcraft. His efforts were rewarded with public acclaim and recognition; he expanded the various workshops and hired more craftsmen.

Art glass remained Émile Gallé's passion. He had remodeled his father's kiln to accommodate prolific art glass production. To underwrite his artistic experiments, he introduced a less costly line of acid-etched cameo glass, maintaining high quality within the limitations of the technique.

Meanwhile, from 1901, École de Nancy provided a framework within which a variety of artists could express their ideas and techniques. Gallé himself was president until his death in 1904. His wife, Henriette, continued the business until her death in 1914.

Auguste Jean

In the decade from 1875 to 1885, Auguste Jean was among the significant European glassmakers creating decorative glass. This period marked the awakening of true art glass. Such work was not made to be used, to hold liquid, to serve food or drink, or to do anything functional. It was simply art, a revival of art that had existed in years past and was experiencing a rebirth in Europe and the United States in the late 19th and 20th centuries. Many of the techniques were new, much of the equipment had changed, but the same possibilities existed, and the same delight in the beauty of glass prevailed.

As a ceramicist, a molder of clay, Auguste Jean was accustomed to sculpting his own designs. He did the same with glass, sculpting the hot molten material to his own artistic vision. His designs were frequently asymmetrical and misaligned. He applied integral glass ornamentation to harmonize, or to clash, with the form of his vessel. His enamel decoration was more regimented and conventional, but expressed styles and arrangements that borrowed from the Orient, Egypt, Africa, and the Middle East. His pieces evoke the Aesthetic movement; his designs often suggest distinctively Secessionist characteristics. An anachronism, Jean made a significant contribution to the development of the art glass of the period and beyond.

Remarkably, Auguste Jean art glass is available here and now as collectibles. It can be found in antique auctions and shows, and occasionally in cyberspace venues. While not abundant and not always identified, the work is recognizable across a crowded room by erudite collectors. The fact that most pieces are well- and legibly marked helps in attribution. Jean adopted an oval lozenge-like mark with the script signature "A. Jean" in the center. This is usually found in the polished pontil on the base, and is sometimes incorporated in the decoration at the side.

Applied and Enameled Green Vase, *c.* 1880

The tooled oval rim, widened and squared above a flattened oval body, required hot-glass manipulation, a value factor.

Trailing prunts fall from under the rim edge artfully positioned "on" enamel decoration painted afterward; this is trompe l'oeil trickery.

Handles applied symmetrically at each side give balance to the design, accent center decoration, and add value.

The deep green transparent glass is crackled in the Rousseau manner, unusual and worthy of a museum collection.

Reflected circular reserves enameled in white and polychrome colors suggest a collectible Japanesque style.

"A. Jean" in script is marked on the footed oval base in gilt enamel; collectors expect higher prices for signed pieces.

Height: 7in/17.7cm
Value: $800–1,000

Applied and Enameled Purple Vase, *c.*1880

Architectonic elements—folded and applied rim with tooled, manipulated notches around a skewed opening—increase value.

The deep purple ovoid body is impressive in height, adding to its graphic impact.

The purple/amethyst is much in demand.

The zigzag vertical strip of glass has matching prunts/buttons applied at even intervals; this skillful work adds value.

The skillful trailing of hot blobs of matching glass applied at side adds more integrated decoration and increases prices.

Enameled medallions with gilt, regimented devices, and gold leaves accent the transparent purple cylinder.

A script signature "A. Jean" appears in gold on the oval base.

Height: 11in/27.9cm
Value: $900–1,200

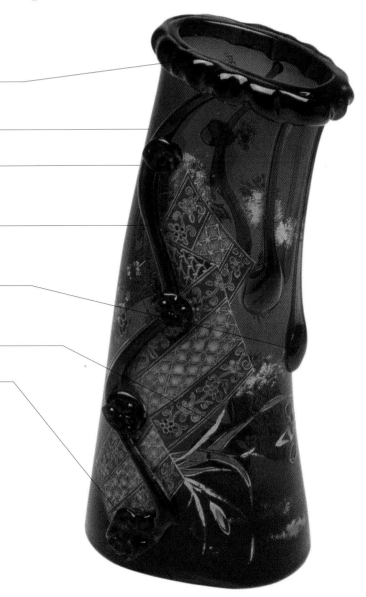

• *The forms shown here were repeated with variations and decorative changes.*
• *Auguste Jean may well have produced much more art glass than has been discovered. Astute collectors may find more if they are attuned to the characteristics of his art glass.*
• *The degree of difficulty in producing an art glass object has a direct effect on its price. Difficult pieces tend to be the expensive ones.*
• *Condition affects price; collectors should check that threads, prunts, and notches are free from chips or cracks.*
• *Auguste Jean's later work became more sculptural in design, combining his glassmaking skills with his knowledge of pottery-making.*

Evolving Styles

Auguste Jean seemingly came out of the blue to exhibit his freeblown and hand-decorated art glass vases at the 1878 Paris International Exhibition. The Arts and Crafts Museum of Paris purchased a selection of his enameled vases at that exhibition. Still retained in the museum collection, this cache of material tells more of Auguste Jean and his work than can be found elsewhere.

The art glass decorations most associated with Jean's work resemble the Persian and Japanesque genres popularized in the late 19th-century revival. International exhibitions led to an exchange of ideas among artists, colleagues, and competitors, even changing the styles of generations. Auguste Jean gave and received his share of influence in shaping art glass.

René Lalique—Early

René Lalique was the toast of the European continent in the sophisticated 1890s. He had proven himself a master in translating the Art Nouveau style into jewelry so beautiful it could be described as wearable art. His exhibitions at the 1900 Paris "Exposition Universelle" were awarded a Grand Prix and he himself a Légion d'Honneur.

Lalique's shocking use of "worthless" glass pieces in his designs, combined with daring motifs—from the nude form to the prosaic insect—attracted the kind of attention promotional experts crave. Not only was everyone talking about Lalique, many were imitating him. Dismayed by this blatant misuse of his artistic achievements, Lalique increased his glass experiments, turning to a new medium and form.

It was the perfume bottles that redirected René Lalique's life. Shifting from his incredibly successful jewelry to the intriguing world of glass, he found the sculptural properties of the medium fascinating and the promise of artistic achievements seductive. When the opportunity arose to work with the prestigious Coty perfume company, designing small gems of bottles for their product, Lalique undertook both the design of the bottles and their production. Over time, Lalique provided designs and bottles for over fifty perfume companies including D'Orsay, Roget et Gallet, Forvil, Worth, Volnay, Morabito, Houbigant, and many more. The bottle production included more than 300 different shapes and forms, many in color variations.

Collectors have much information available on how to gather a collection either of Lalique original bottles or of Lalique look-alikes. Many bottles are within the reach of the conservative pocketbook. Others are out of sight. But the information highway is open for all.

Forgeres Maison Lalique Perfume Bottle, *c.*1912

The squared, molded stopper is of green glass that matches the portrait medallions; beveled edges add a refined touch and value.

Diminutive size adds charm to the highly detailed design achieved in a limited space.

The colorless bottle in rectangular form is stained green in a molded foliate motif spaced in lappet arrangement.

The applied medallions are the glory of the design, each a beautiful nude portrait—any collector hopes to find this one.

Extraordinary sculptural molding on inserts is quintessential pre-war quality from the Combs-la-Ville factory.

Marked in the mold on base "R. Lalique" only, the bottle is catalog number 489. A tiny chip on the edge affects value slightly.

Height: 3in/7.62cm
Value: $7,000–9,000

Bouchon Fleurs de Pommier Perfume Bottle, *c.*1919

The tiara stopper with pierced crown covered in blossoms is among Lalique's most rare and valuable designs.

The height is just right for this elegant and regal piece, designed by Maison Lalique, Lalique's own line—a value factor.

The bottle is molded with a symmetrical, scalloped design that creates an optical illusion as you look through the glass.

The bottle is listed in Marcilhac 493, p. 329; this catalog listing is a must for collectors seeking authenticity—not there means not Lalique.

An unblemished ridge outlines the crown all around, and the squared ends are also in fine condition, a true rarity.

The bottle is signed on the base "R. Lalique France N. 493." All such information increases value.

Height: 5in/12.7cm
Value: $10,000–12,000

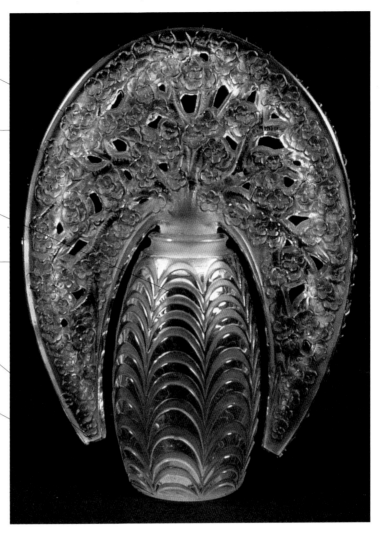

- *Collectors can compare potential buys with photos in the* Catalogue Raisonée *assembled by Felix Marcilhac to avoid manipulated or cut down pieces. One catch is worth the book.*
- *Medallions on the Forgeres Maison bottle illustrate the fine detail Lalique later designed on glass pendants. These can be found today for $500–1,500.*
- *A proposed tax on French family jewels in the late 1920s increased the popularity of Lalique's tax-free glass jewelry. This work shows up from time to time.*
- *The tiara bottle has been copied worldwide—Czech bottles with tiara stoppers were made in quantity and are less expensive as collectibles.*

A Glass Entrepreneur

Shortly after Lalique's enormous success at the 1900 Paris Universal Exhibition, he established a small glassworks on the outskirts of Paris. There he explored the "lost wax" method of glass sculpture called *cire perdue*, and delved into the mysteries of *pâte de verre*, neither of which required huge furnaces or extremely high temperatures.

In 1907, François Coty persuaded Lalique to design some labels for Coty's perfume bottles. Intrigued, Lalique designed the glass bottles as well. Lacking adequate facilities, Lalique contacted Auguste Legras, whose glass factories in Saint-Denis and Pantin employed more than 1,000 workers, to produce perfume bottles for him. By 1909, Lalique acquired better facilities for his own production, and his business expanded.

At the end of World War I, Lalique reopened his glass business. The addition of a large factory near the German border gave the company expansive facilities and new technology to develop glass production.

René Lalique—
1920s to the Present

René Lalique's transition from art jewelry to art glass occurred over time and with considerable overlap. But the opening of his factory in 1922 at Wingen-sur-Moder and his establishment of the "Verreries d'Alsace René Lalique & Cie" signaled a commitment to glass production, previously missing. Lalique had decided that his work should be available to the "common man."

The industrial development of post-war Europe in the 1920s encouraged mass production. While the artistic community mounted a decided resistance, Lalique believed that art could use industrial technology to produce decorative arts without artistic compromise, a belief in which he was not alone. For many, of course, this was as much a business decision as a philosophical statement.

Determined to retain quality, while both increasing the production and maintaining the cost of individual pieces, Lalique directed experiments with techniques and glass formulas. He emphasized the sculptural aspect of his designs without losing the precise detail of the patterns.

Today's interest in collectibles and the revival of art glass have coalesced to revive René Lalique's popularity. His designs allow for almost as many ways to collect as there are collectors: by form, color, pattern; by style, function, genre, or gender; or simply by availability.

Molded Art Glass "Serpent" Vase, *c.*1925

The raised, tapered top is polished at the rim and slightly faceted; the plain border balances the design.

The serpent's bulging eye, wide-open mouth, and naturalistic fangs add artistic impact.

Height and width of this vase contribute to the graphic force of the coiled, striking serpent, adding value for collectors.

A reddish-brown stain realistically fills the interstices of the minutely molded snakeskin.

The image of the snake required knowledge of the creature and its natural postures—a fact that increases the vase's value.

The base bears a molded mark, "R. Lalique," and the catalog number of the piece is 896, both of which assure authenticity.

Size: 9⅝ x 10in/
24.5 x 25.4cm
Value: $7,000–9,000

Opal "Deux Anneaux Lezards" Vase, c.1925

Note the raised rim on this elegant, understated vase. The addition of two shoulder rings to hold handles supports design.

Aside from form, all decoration occurs on the handles. Molded with grotesque lizards, this is a popular collectible motif.

Both handles are split in a unique geometric manner for removal from the vase.

Handles swing freely from their rings, making them potentially vulnerable ornaments—another reason for the rarity of this vase.

The frosted blue color applied as a patine in the recesses of the lizard designs provides a valuable accent for the creatures.

The molded glass is in a fiery, translucent opal color—not listed in the catalog and thus adding to rarity and value.

"Lalique France," inscribed on the base in a script signature, suggests a made-for-export piece that adds to its value.

Height: 13⅛in/33.3cm
Value: $25,000–30,000

• For the lizard-handled design shown above, Lalique created two other handles—scarabs and exotic pigeons.
• Treasure seekers might watch for any single handle that shows up. Advanced collectors happily pay for replacements.
• An unlisted color can indicate a rarity, or even a one-of-a-kind item. Check for other indicators of origin.
• Designs with birds, animals, mythical creatures, or people add substantially to value.
• Check catalog photos to be sure vases are of full height. If height is reduced, so is value.

In Pursuit of Excellence

With the 1922 opening of his new glass factory, René Lalique continued his pursuit of art glass excellence. Never a hands-on glass master, he created hundreds of designs, future collectibles all. His work included vases, bowls, boxes, ashtrays, bonbonnieres, dresser items, mirrors, trays, frames, card and menu holders, inkwells, bookends, paperweights, statuettes and sculptures, carafes, pitchers and tumblers, clocks, tableware, and lighting devices.

Lalique also received commissions for major architectural elements, interior decoration, commercial displays, and art glass design for several ocean liners. His displays for the 1925 Paris Exhibition included his own pavillion and a set of massive architectural art glass fountains. Lalique triumphed at the exhibition.

René Lalique died at 85, leaving the company to his son Marc, and later, his granddaughter Marie-Claude.

Auguste and Charles Legras

Legras & Cie (*cie* is the abbreviation in French for company) produced great quantities of art glass during the heyday of French production—roughly 1880 to 1930. Neither the best nor the least of the French makers, Legras remained in the mainstream, replicating popular styles and producing what was most in demand. The work was occasionally of highest caliber, and such pieces are sought after as avidly as Gallé or Daum items. Legras art glass has to be evaluated a piece at a time for design, workmanship, complexity, rarity, and condition.

Legras & Cie used a number of different marks and signatures to identify its products, causing some confusion. Pieces were sometimes marked with the product line name rather than "Legras." For example, "Indiana" referred to a line of art glass, but the additional identification "L & Cie" was often gilded, and it scrubbed off through the years. "Mont Joye" referred to more than one kind of

cameo glass produced by Legras, marked with a Mont Joye emblem that sometimes included the word "Pantin," the location of the Legras factory. This has led to incorrect attributions to one or other of many Pantin glass factories.

The Cornelian line, at right, has also caused confusion. Normally one would expect a script signature, "Legras SD," for example, designating the Saint-Denis factory. Occasionally the mark is reversed to "Sargel SD." A whimsy like this can be a collectible item in itself.

Yet another oddity in the Legras signature system is the mark "Leg" used in shallow etching or on a painted-and-fired vessel from the economy line of art glass. Again, these can be collected in their own right. They are identifiable as collectibles, made in all sizes, from miniature to monumental, and they turn up with some regularity. Happily, Legras items are usually reasonable—unlike more prestigious French art glass—in today's collectibles venues.

Mont Joye Cameo Etched and Enameled Vase, c. 1910

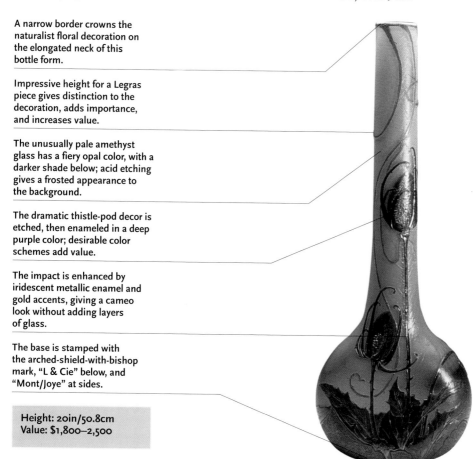

A narrow border crowns the naturalist floral decoration on the elongated neck of this bottle form.

Impressive height for a Legras piece gives distinction to the decoration, adds importance, and increases value.

The unusually pale amethyst glass has a fiery opal color, with a darker shade below; acid etching gives a frosted appearance to the background.

The dramatic thistle-pod decor is etched, then enameled in a deep purple color; desirable color schemes add value.

The impact is enhanced by iridescent metallic enamel and gold accents, giving a cameo look without adding layers of glass.

The base is stamped with the arched-shield-with-bishop mark, "L & Cie" below, and "Mont/Joye" at sides.

Height: 20in/50.8cm
Value: $1,800–2,500

Cornelian Cameo Glass Enameled Vase, *c.* 1907

This is a slender, curvaceous vase in the French Art Nouveau style with an inward turn at the top rim.

The height is monumental—always a value factor—and the decoration extends the full length and all around the vase.

The cornelian color of beige-pink simulates the gemstone, unusual in French glass and a Legras specialty; collectors seek rare colors.

The motif is acid etched, then colored in enamels and low-fired to preserve the decoration, a natural look that is much admired.

The signature "Legras SD," indicating it was made at the Saint-Denis factory, is at the back within the etched cameo design.

The curvilinear petticoat shape of the lower vase carries the Art Nouveau style and decoration to the edge, a nice completion.

Height: 25in/63.5cm
Value: $3,500–5,000

• Legras created art glass of such quantity and variety that no one "look" exists. Collectors need to do their homework.
• In the Legras "Indiana" line, a clear colorless glass body revealed a casing of red, aventurine green, or both, without acid etching the glass. Rare effects were achieved, making Indiana desirable.
• Legras used enamels on glass, with Art Deco or Secessionist motifs. Astute buyers collect these today for as little as $50–250. Most are signed "Legras" or "Leg."
• Prices for Legras art glass vary as much as the glass itself. Excellent pieces still bring top prices. Inferior work commands lesser prices.

The Legras Legacy

Auguste Jean-François Legras presided over the Legras company for 45 years, from 1864 until his retirement in 1909. The business employed over 1,000 workers, producing functional tableware and household goods, as well as significant art glass of the period.

Legras was consistently well received; the art glass won prestigious awards, including a Grand Prix in 1889 and 1900 at the Paris Exhibition.

The Legras company closed down during World War I. In 1919, Auguste's son Charles began anew as "Verreries et Cristallerie de St. Denis et de Pantin Reunis." The firm produced cameo glass, Art Deco vases and lighting devices, and crystal tableware.

Johann Loetz-Witwe

The primary means of promotion for art glass companies of the late 19th and early 20th centuries were the various international exhibitions and fairs held yearly throughout Europe and the Americas. As director of the Loetz glass factories after the retirement of his grandmother from the company in 1879, Max Ritter Von Spaun took advantage of these great meeting places to expose Loetz art glass broadly, winning awards and contracts for the Loetz product at every opportunity. He secured patents on many of his new processes before the major exhibition in Paris in 1889, attended by such notables as Louis Comfort Tiffany, Ludwig Lobmeyer, Émile Gallé, Thomas W. Webb, and others representing the major glass artists of the time. Von Spaun was awarded a Grand Prix for the Loetz exhibit that included the firm's hardstone replications and the unusual "Federzeichnung" art glass line. Better known as Octopus glass, the latter cleverly incorporated internal air channels in a technique

well ahead of its time. By the time of the U.S. exhibitions in Chicago in 1893, and Saint Louis in 1904, Loetz was exhibiting the iridescent art glass Spaun had patented previously. Loetz was awarded a Grand Prix at each of these World's Fairs, setting up important contacts and contracts in the American marketplace.

Thus it was that the Loetz glass factories produced extraordinary art glass that found distribution outlets throughout Europe and the Americas in the first years of the new century. What this means for serious art glass collectors is that this material is available in the current everyday marketplace. Certainly rarities occasionally show up in the antique auctions and upscale shows, but, for the novice and the conservative collector, many Loetz items with more reasonable price tags also exist. Loetz was a company of many product lines, not all of them terribly expensive. Even in the top-of-the-line patterns, some items can be found in the affordable price ranges.

Iridescent Tricolor Art Glass Vase, *c.*1900

A raised, wide rim shows the iridescent yellow interior, unusual for a Loetz product and an added-value factor.

The lemon-yellow glass has diagonally striped, honey-colored amber "fingers" above a dark purple border and foot; extra value for three colors.

Spiral striping around the vase adds drama, highlighted by horizontal waves within and a silver-gold lustrous surface.

The bowl-form vase is wider than tall, with a broad feminine shape tapering to a pedestal foot.

Note how the raised pedestal allows decoration in the lower quadrant to be seen at eye level, a good design element that increases collectibility and price.

The base is inscribed on polished pontil "Loetz Austria"; this does not change value significantly as it could be a late addition.

Size: 5 x 6in/12.7 x 15.2cm
Value: $8,000–10,000

Iridescent Phenomenon Vase, c. 1900

The skillfully crafted tricorn rim—a valued feature—was manipulated at the fire on the freeblown oval vessel.

The piece is tall and scarce in this form and line, more often found in diminutive items; collectors would consider this a treasure.

This extraordinary blend of shades of amber glass, internally decorated in horizontal blue bands, is a rare combination.

Six long-stemmed leaf forms of stylized water lilies decorate the vase at its widest point, providing graphic impact and increasing value.

There is artful subtlety in the water-lily forms above impressionistic blue waters with silvery, iridescent surface decoration.

No mark is seen or expected on the polished pontil at the base.

Height: 10in/25.4cm
Value: $15,000–18,000

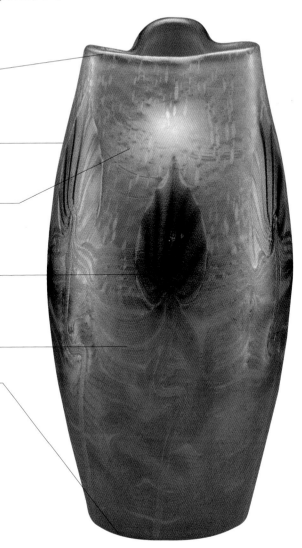

• Because so few early Loetz pieces are legitimately signed, an inscribed mark hardly changes value up or down.
• The rare double-arrow mark increases value on Loetz art glass, because it is difficult to fake accurately.
• Loetz pieces made before 1909 are generally most valuable because of better quality and variety. Designer pieces from after World War I are the exception.
• A patent or registry mark in English may be found on Loetz pieces, indicating U.S. or British patents. Such pieces are fine.
• Collectors wanting to score big-time with Loetz art glass should find reference books and study all the obscure product lines and ranges.

Max Ritter Von Spaun

Some 40 years after Johann Loetz purchased a glass factory complex in Klostermuhle, Austria, his widow (*witwe* in German) retired from the firm and left their grandson, Max Ritter Von Spaun, in charge. Von Spaun was an astute craftsman, designer, director, and promoter. He quickly focused on developing attention-grabbing lines of artistic glassware to display to commercial advantage in the various decorative and applied arts venues. Von Spaun concentrated on two techniques that broadly attracted private buyers and entrepreneurs alike. One was the replication of gemstones and natural rock formations in the glass lines known as onyx, jasper, and agate ware. The other technique involved using chemical chlorides or oxides to produce an iridescent lustre on an object's surface. These lines of art glass were, in large measure, the basis of the Loetz company's success from the 1880s until Max Ritter Von Spaun's death in 1909.

Johann Loetz-Witwe— 20th Century

The body of work created by the Loetz glassworks has attained a high reputation in the European art glass world. Its significance to European design was complicated, but indisputably important. Loetz innovated early with such techniques as iridescence. The company's craftsmen influenced the development and progression of the Secessionist movement by their skillful rendering of designs brought by artists and students without affiliation elsewhere. They similarly supported and contributed to the Wiener Werkstätte (Vienna Workshop). As early as 1904, Loetz introduced decorative art glass designs that were forerunners to Art Deco and Minimalist styles. The company's impact, craftsmanship, and foresight are sometimes overlooked or misunderstood. But art glass's current popularity may help correct oversights.

The collectibility of Loetz art glass took a small leap in the late 1960s with the publication of several reference books on art glass. Loetz became known, coveted, and collected, along with Tiffany, Steuben, Gallé, and Heisey. Loetz's collectibility took a huge leap in the late 1980s and again after the lull of the early 1990s. Major deep pockets existed in the international market at that time, and lesser items than the masterworks, like Loetz, benefited from a sort of ripple effect. Americans could find reasonably priced Loetz art glass, and the prices moved steadily upward, in keeping with the trends of inflation and the economy. In the economic downturn at the start of this century, prices took a dip; but, in general, Loetz has held its own in the collectibles marketplace. It may be a good time to buy, in anticipation of a decreasing supply.

Iridescent Blue Czechoslovakian Centerbowl, *c.*1920

The scalloped edge has 12 softly pointed curves around the broad rim, enhancing value.

This star-shape form is a popular choice among collectors.

The shallow bowl is designed for beauty, not functionality; it displays best upright as shown.

The bowl's width gives a broad expanse for the strong blue iridescence inside.

A lustrous silvery-blue "oil spot" motif on the exterior is typical Loetz coloration on the deep crimson-red base glass.

The base is stamped with the oval "Czecho/Slovakia" used after World War I, decreasing value for Loetz purists.

The strong brilliant-blue interior is mirror-bright and in perfect condition; bowls are hard to find without scratches and wear.

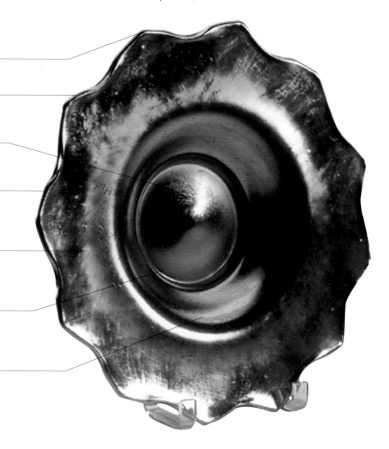

Size: 2 x 12in/5.1 x 30.5cm
Value: $700–900

Etched and Cut Czechoslovakian Vase, *c.*1920

The flared rim has symmetrically spaced, wheel-cut facets, as well as notches that create a scalloped border.

The floriform shape reflects the shape of the blossoms in the decor, a design element that increases value.

The colorless glass is cased with pastel yellow and layered in rose-pink on the exterior.

Collectors value the acid-etched texture that adds visual and tactile elements to the design.

The etched, stylized bellflowers and fanciful vertical stems are attributed to Josef Hoffmann, sending value high.

The "Loetz" signature, in etched script, appears at the lower edge, while the polished base is unmarked. Collectors have to do homework on this one.

Height: 6in/15.24
Value: $5,000–7,000

• *The Czechoslovakian designation on Loetz pieces can either increase or decrease value, as shown here. The 1920s design attributed to Josef Hoffmann increases value because of his stature.*
• *For Loetz collectors, early pieces gain value. For Czech glass buyers, early is less.*
• *The value of the etched vase above is enhanced because of a red example exhibited in Britain at Sunderland Museum and Art Gallery, and pictured in* The Art of Glass *(1996), by Victor Arwas.*
• *Loetz produced much cameo etched glass before and after World War I. Many are as collectible as industrial French cameo glass of the time.*
• *Czechoslovakian Loetz glass is especially valuable to collectors of Czech art glass.*

A Reinvented Glassworks

The Glasfabrik Johann Loetz-Witwe was directed by Max Ritter Von Spaun from 1879 until 1908, when Von Spaun turned over the operation to his son, Max. The company went bankrupt in 1911, but reorganized in 1913. With the breakup of the Austro-Hungarian empire at the end of World War I, the Loetz Glassworks, formerly Austrian, became Czechoslovak. Its hometown underwent a name change, from the German Klostermuhle to the Czech Klasterske. Nonetheless, the company reinvented itself, producing old successful designs, iridizing glass by old techniques, and introducing new designs by old friends and new artists.

Between 1919 and 1938, Loetz remained productive. The company reestablished ties with some of the Wiener Werkstätte designers, including Michael Powolny, Josef Hoffmann, and Otto Prutscher. Happily, some superb and wonderfully fresh new designs came out of these collaborations. The Loetz Glassworks exhibited in the International Exhibition in Paris, 1925, making contact again with European and U.S. galleries and export-import clients.

Ludwig Moser & Söhne

The Ludwig Moser and Sons Glassworks was well-established in Karlsbad, Austria, by the early 1900s, producing a wide range of decorative art. Their work graced royal palaces as well as local restaurants. The turn of the 20th century was a time of great artistic experimentation for Ludwig Moser. His mentoring relationship with designers and artists secured the company's leadership role in the art glass community at the beginning of the new century.

Moser art glass designs and subsequent product lines led to recognition in the international exhibitions of European decorative arts. The company exhibited in Paris, London, Belgium, Italy, and Vienna. Rather than give allegiance to a style or school of a given period, region, or aesthetic, Moser focused on quality and excellence.

Among Moser's most prolific and long-term designers was Josef Hoffmann, whose name sometimes accompanied the Moser signature on art glass pieces. Hoffmann created some of Moser's most popular lines, now highly collectible. His designs included the vertically faceted, jewel-toned vases, decorated with etched and gilt-enameled scenes of jungle animals and occasional nudes. The well-known "Amazon Warrior" is frequently attributed to Hoffmann, but was actually designed by Leo Moser in 1914. It, too, found immediate success and continued in the Moser production well into the 1970s.

Because such a wealth of Moser glass was imported into the United States, and respected, it is widely available today. Some is well-marked with the company name and/or product line designation. Many pieces can only be identified by knowledge of the form, shape, color, and quality. Moser glass has been much copied and replicated through the years by other glass enterprises. Collectors, as usual, have to work a little to distinguish the treasures.

Scenic Giraffe Vase, c.1920

A wide flare at the rim tops the trumpet form body.

A narrow strip of clear, polished glass sets off the acid-etched broadside area, which contrasts with the overall mural motif.

Choice of a tall, slender vessel for the tall, slender giraffe and trees adds to value.

The clear, thick-walled amber glass has flawless clarity.

Decoration has exotic animals for the 1920s, with two elephants at reverse and giraffe between coconut palm trees a plus.

Gold-enamel decoration on the raised scenic motif is further enhanced by red and green highlights; complexities add to the value of the piece.

The signature "LMK Moser Carlsbad" appears in the scene, and "Made in Czechoslovakia Moser Carlsbad [sic]" appears on the base.

Size: 14 x 8in/35.5 x 20.3cm
Value: $2,800–3,500

Scenic Jungle Vase, c.1920

The raised, flared rim balances the symmetry of the broad oval mold-blown vase.

The vase's size is impressive but not above average; note that the amber vase is taller but less valuable.

This brilliant dark-purple color provides a fine background for the decoration and is prized for vibrancy and clarity.

The artfully crafted and well-detailed band of etched and gilded jungle animals and tall palm trees adds value.

The naturalistic scene shows no stylized effort here; rather, this is a style of its own, with many collectors.

Molded ridges that are outlined in gold provide additional decoration around the lower vase.

The vase is signed twice: in the grasses with "LMK Moser Karlsbad RW," and on the base with "Moser Karlsbad made in Czechoslovakia."

Size: 11³/₈ x 7in/
28.9 x 17.7cm
Value: $3,500–4,500

• *Moser produced many lines of glass, most of them imported into the U.S. and available at a wide range of prices. Look for perfect pieces.*
• *Engraved intaglio floral designs on slender crystal vases proliferated from 1919–1939. Colored pieces with padded blossoms in contrasting color are more valuable than colorless frosted items.*
• *Moser's crystal stemware with cobalt, green, ruby, and amber overlaid bowls are especially fine. Look for these as collectibles.*
• *Moser perfume bottles, in patterns similar to the jungle line, are rare and valuable.*

Surviving Changing Times

During World War I, the Austrian glass factories were either closed or redirected into wartime production. Ludwig Moser, the patriarch of the Moser family, died at this time. At war's end, the Karlsbad area became part of the new nation of Czechoslovakia. The Moser firm reorganized under Moser's sons and grandsons and reinstated virtually all of its workers and most of its clients. Between the World Wars, the Moser firm prospered.

The Moser glassworks shut down again during World War II. After the war and the rise of Communism in Czechoslovakia, the government nationalized the glass industry. About 50 previously autonomous Czech glass companies were consolidated into 15 entities. The Moser firm maintained its autonomy, however. Today, in the now democratic Czech Republic, the Moser glassworks still produces high-quality glassware under family direction.

Muller Frères

The work of the Muller Frères (brothers) Glassworks of Lunéville and Croismire in France, is highly regarded by glass experts and advanced collectors. Muller art glass appears in major museums and scholarly publications throughout the world. Important pieces frequently come up in major auctions or appear in antique shows and upscale shops, selling for impressively high prices. They have not, however, acquired the distinction held by contemporaries Gallé or Daum. The work in the collectible marketplace today is rarely the "good stuff."

During Muller's most productive period, between 1895 and 1914, the company created extraordinary art glass. Talented artists to begin with, the brothers had been trained by masters. They introduced new techniques and embellished old methods, advancing the craft of glassmaking significantly. Among their most signature techniques was "fluogravure," a process in which colored enamels were overlayed on glass, heated to vitrification, and then acid etched, often more than once, to decorate the glass. This sophisticated process became Muller's tour de force, as illustrated in the vase at right.

Of course, in order to compete in a country with hundreds of other glassmakers, Muller Frères produced many lines of purely commercial art glass. The company made cased-glass items acid-etched with floral or scenic decorations for domestic and export trade. These are the pieces most often found today, and they suffer only by comparison to Muller masterworks. After purchasing the Hinzelin factory in Croismire in 1919, the company became well-known for lighting equipment. It produced molded light bowls for lamps and ceiling fixtures, using subtly colored mottled glass, molded in half-round design. These were usually signed with an acid mark, "Muller Frères Lunéville," or variations of that name. Muller's light fixtures work for interior decorating today, as they did during the Art Deco period when they were made.

Etched and Carved Poppies Vase, c.1905

The raised, tooled rim flares outward above an oval body, adding height and balance to the classic vasiform.

Average in height for Muller's production-line series, the broad oval form offers good area for the overall decoration.

This warm, fiery amber color was popular with French art glassmakers and buyers.

Poppies were among Muller's most popular lines for vases, lamps, and light bowls; they are still much in demand as collectibles.

Note the wheel cutting in addition to acid etching of orange and brown layers of glass; buyers pay more for these features.

The vase is prominently etched in cameo, "Muller Fres Lunéville," one of various signatures they used.

Height: 7³/₄in/19.6cm
Value: $1,500–2,000

Etched and Enameled Fluogravure Scenic Vase, c.1910

This flattened oval body has a raised rim with border band of finely detailed, etched bells and floral swags, an added value factor.

The piece is small for such a complicated art form, with its continuous scene in droll vignettes of heavenly life.

The colorless glass is overlaid in dark red and opaque white, with amber-brown enamels, vitrified and acid-etched.

The intriguing and unique scene of nude and robed angels increases value.

Serious collectors would be attracted to the child-like and humorous quality of the artwork.

The scene is marked in etched design, "Mvller," at the side edge, a valuable addition.

Size: 7¹/₈ x 7in/18.1 x 17.7cm
Value: $18,000–25,000

• *The prestigious Val St. Lambert Glassworks commissioned Henri and Désiré Muller to design for them. During 1906–1907, the brothers produced over 400 models marked "VSL." These are treasures today.*
• *Scenic designs, especially with people, are increasingly valuable.*
• *Muller's poppy line of cameo glass was a popular series. Collectors seek vivid colors that will increase in value.*
• *In the 1920s, Muller Frères made a limited quantity of etched, transparent glass in the Art Deco style with bright, stylized fish and animals— rare and valuable today.*
• *Another Muller line is decorated with specks of silver or gold foil sheets. These items are likely to increase in value.*

A Family of Glassmakers

One result of the German victory in the Franco-Prussian War of 1870 was that the border regions of Alsace-Lorraine passed from French to German control. To avoid German rule, many French families relocated west to France. Among these families were the glass-making Mullers, nine brothers and a sister, all of whom apprenticed with French glass masters during the 1890s. Five of the young brothers studied with Émile Gallé in Nancy. They were exposed to the techniques and aesthetics of the most competent glass masters and were taught in a period when Gallé was engaged in series production—creating quality art glass in great quantity. The Muller brothers were well on their way.

Henri Muller was first to establish his own workshop in Lunéville. The rest of the family joined him and began decorating art glass purchased from a company in Croismire that eventually became a part of their business. Until the outbreak of World War I, the Muller Frères Co. produced extremely popular cameo glass, acid-etched and wheel-carved. They produced pieces in the French Art Nouveau style, using the industrial-commercial methods being introduced throughout Europe.

Murano—Artisti Barovier

The glassworks that became "Artisti Barovier" began in 1896 on Murano—one of Venice's 118 islands and home to virtually all the city's glassworks. Ercole Barovier took over as director of his family business, "Artisti Barovier," after World War I. The well-traveled Barovier was familiar with French Art Deco. But his background in traditional Italian and Venetian decorative glass led him to opt for a sophisticated interpretation of the Viennese Secessionist aesthetic, which was more in tune with Italian Novecento style.

Barovier was especially intrigued by murrine—slices of glass that could be fused into shapes and forms to create a mosaic "painting." He had experimented with such decorations even before the war with glass master Vittorio Zecchin, who did such work before leaving Artisti Barovier for the newly established Venini glass house.

Surprisingly, today's enthusiasts of Murano art glass can occasionally find Artisti Barovier mosaic pieces in the collectibles marketplace, even though they were made in limited quantity and sold at elevated prices. Some of the best pieces of mosaic art glass landed in the United States. The two pieces illustrated here were found in the collectibles venue, and each is a great rarity in the scheme of Artisti Barovier historic and artistic development.

Some exceptional pieces of mosaic work are "signed" with an Artisti Barovier crown and "AB Murrine" embedded in the design. Otherwise, collectors find it hard to substantiate studios, designers, and dates of particular items. Comparisons with well-known identified pieces can aid in attribution. Photographs, exhibition records, and other legitimate documents are also helpful. Collectors should consult these whenever possible.

Mosaic Murrine Scenic Vase, c.1920

Three applied decorative handle ornaments, symmetrically spaced around the rim, add interesting sculptural detail.

The height of this piece gives an ample "canvas" for the whimsical, painterly design, which is attributed to Vittorio Zecchin.

The colorful design includes three white birds under green palms, and red flowers, all against tan, green, and yellow glass murrine; a great rarity.

The decoration is completely composed of colorful glass murrine fused together at the fire; complexity of technique and design increases worth.

The vase has a 4in/10.1cm annealing crack above the lower edge, which affects the price significantly, but not the historical value.

The vase is "signed" with the Artisti Barovier murrine mark included at lower edge: "AB" under a crown in a circle.

Height: 10in/25.4cm
Value: $7,000–9,000

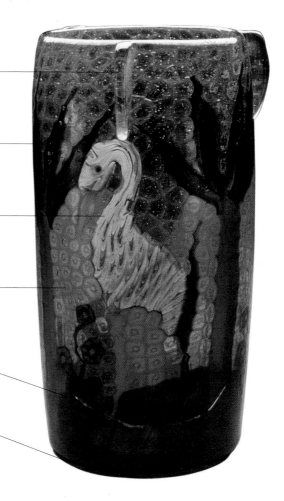

Murrine Goblet Vase, *c.*1920

An artfully applied band of blue glass rims the goblet-form vase with a slight flare at the top.

The Artisti Barovier design covers the entire bowl of the goblet-form; its impressive height increases value.

Colorful decoration presents an impressionistic, natural scene of yellow flowers on blue stems arising through blue-green waters.

Each murrine is smoothly fused into the integrated whole of the design, maintaining the artistic impact and increasing value.

Note that the knop and wafer attachments are pure Venetian-revival style elements in a modern surround.

The whole is raised on a classical inverted cup pedestal base, which is a traditional goblet form of value.

No identifying mark appears in the design or on the base.

Height: 18in/45.7cm
Value: $35,000–45,000

• *Mosaic murrine glass pieces required virtuoso glassblowers and skilled designers— look for the Artisti Barovier monogram on likely items.*
• *Many pieces that were exported to American retail outlets from 1919–1939 show up today, some marked or labeled, some not.*
• *Marina Barovier's book,* Art of the Barovier Glassmakers of Murano, *written in 1993, is an excellent reference book for collectors and historians.*
• *Remember that condition counts. A crack like the one in the bird vase, shown here, seriously affects the value. That vase, if perfect, could exceed the goblet vase in value.*

Ercole Barovier

The initial success of the Barovier family came from making the traditional Venetian glassware and crystal for which Murano was famous. Ercole Barovier rode the crest of art glass's popularity in the years between the World Wars. He concentrated on the export business in the 1920s, sending Artisti Barovier glassware to the United States and other countries. The firm also participated in European decorative arts exhibitions, including Italy's prestigious Biennales, gaining clients and taking its share of awards.

The worldwide economic decline affected Artisti Barovier as drastically as it did other Muranese companies. In 1936, Barovier entered into a merger with Ferro, Seguso, and Toso. The alliance lasted until 1939, when the company reorganized as Barovier & Toso, before closing down for the war.

After the war, Barovier & Toso experimented with modern techniques and designs. Ercole Barovier presented new designs that used bold colors and modern forms to attract customers at home and abroad. His efforts were rewarded. The company continued successfully into the 1960s. In 1972, son Angelo replaced Ercole and continues his involvement in the company today.

Murano—Vetri Soffiati Muranesi Venini

aolo Venini established his glassworks in the 1920s, when the decorative arts were attracting serious attention throughout Europe and the United States. In a strong economy, people were buying decorative items for their homes and collections, or for gifts. Travelers to Italy gravitated to Venice and the nearby island of Murano, where the great glassworks had been established in order to isolate Venice from the danger of fire. It was here that Venini started his business and launched a creative process that would be appreciated around the world.

Created in collaboration with designer and artist Vittorio Zecchin, Venini's early lines included delicate glass with traditional form and unexpected modern elements. Venini catered to conservative buyers while appealing at the same time to the more daring and progressive tourists. This duality served the company well.

Trade with the United States offered a particularly lucrative avenue for Venini. Venini's freeblown art glass was handcrafted to specific design guidelines. The glass was shaped primarily at the fire with a glass master directing the work of the *piazza*—the team who created the final product. For the duration of its production, Venini's art glass was popular, but it reached its height in the 1950s. That was when Fulvio Biaconi, Ricardo Licata, Massimo Vignelli, and others captured the spirit of the times in brightly colored free-forms and whimsical figurines. Paolo Venini added to the company catalog with his signature handkerchief vessels and mosaic and filigree designs.

Venini Incalmo Vase by Ricardo Licata, *c.*1955

This design with manipulated, oval rim above a round cylindrical body is Licata's signature tour de force and very collectible.

The clear green shows above a cobalt blue, with a medial band of black, white, and red glass squares—a winning combo of color, skill, and rarity.

The tripartite design is fused above and below a central row of fused murrines (*a doppio incalmo*), complex and valuable.

The center band has six rows of fused squares called murrine, each decorated in pseudo-Chinese characters.

The vase bears a label marked "Venini 3835"—very seldom found intact.

The acid-etched mark, stamped "Venini/Murano/Italia" in three rows on the base, can be elusive. Look for it.

Height: 9⁷/₈in/25.1cm
Value: $8,500–10,000

Venini Fasce Orizzontali Vase by Fulvio Biaconi, c.1953

The graceful rim on an elongated neck with bulbous bottle form is classic and masterfully blown.

This is a large piece to manipulate at the fire with such perfect symmetry. Advanced collectors value this.

The complex "orizzontali" design is integral to the vase, not applied or sandwiched within, and increases value.

The horizontal stripes of red, blue, green, and aubergine have maintained integrity and clarity, a technical coup.

The glass's transparency adds to the artistic impact, as the stripes are visible on both sides.

The base is stamped in three rows: "Venini/Murano/Italia"—this typical Venini mark aids identification and appraisal.

Height: 17in/43.1cm
Value: $15,000–20,000

• *Fulvio Biaconi became a major force in post-war Italian modern design. His colorful series of patchwork (pezzato) vases are collected worldwide.*

• *The Biaconi vase with horizontal stripes is a rare example of a design appreciated, but seldom executed, because of the skill required to complete it.*

• *Biaconi's costumed figures, designed from the "Commedia dell'Arte," were popular in the U.S. Originals are treasures, reproductions are not.*

• *Many Venini pieces have been reproduced and some are made under a conglomerate ownership. Collectors need knowledge and caution.*

• *The model of Licata's design at left is a rare form; most models are less valuable.*

Collecting Italian Art Glass

Collectors of Italian art glass in general, and particularly of pieces produced by the Venini glassworks, will find that it is available in some quantity in the collectibles marketplace. In addition to the real and virtual shops, shows and swaps, there are decorative arts venues that focus specifically on the extraordinary collectibles of the 1950s and onward. In such settings, Venini treasures can certainly be found. Interestingly, venues that concentrate on either Modernism or Art Deco also readily include Italian art glass, because it meets their criteria and artfully complements their styles. Collectors, too, find that this art glass makes a pleasing companion to other styles.

Murano—The Golden Years

The 1950s and '60s were the Golden Years of art glass production in the Murano studios. Post-war Italian glassmakers embraced a dynamic modernism that they expressed in their own very distinctive ways. It took the French time to adust to change. The Italians were off and running, and Venini led the way.

Vetri Soffiati Muranesi Venini had been led capably by owner-director Paolo Venini and a series of outstanding designers. Venini's art director, architect Carlo Scarpa, was arguably the most influential artist in the Venini stable, successfully executing lines never before attempted.

Barovier & Toso's production of the 1950s and '60s, especially its *pezzato* patchwork pieces, projected an exuberant modernism unexpected from Ercole Barovier's previous tradition-bound work. In Dino Martens, the firm of *Aureliano Toso* found a prescient artist to design their modern glass line. Martens's Oriente series was smashingly colorful, filled with pinwheels and aventurine powders. Its popularity continues in the collectibles market today.

Seguso Vetri d'Art exhibits the interfamily relationships inherent in the Murano glassworks. Archimede Seguso designed extraordinary filigree glass for his own company, and later for this 1950s Seguso family firm. *Gino Cenedese & C.* was established in 1946 with Alfredo Barbini as partner and artistic director. Barbini's sculptural designs became the company's tour de force. *Arte Vetreria Muranese*, better known as A.Ve.M., blossomed in the 1950s under Giorgio Ferro and the design genius of Anselo Fuga.

Also included among the Murano glass houses were *Vetreria Artistica Alfredo Barbini*, *Salviati & C.*, and *Vetreria Vistosi*. For collectors, identification is problematic, but they can avoid confusion by studying available materials.

A.Ve.M. Intarsio Vase, *c.*1960

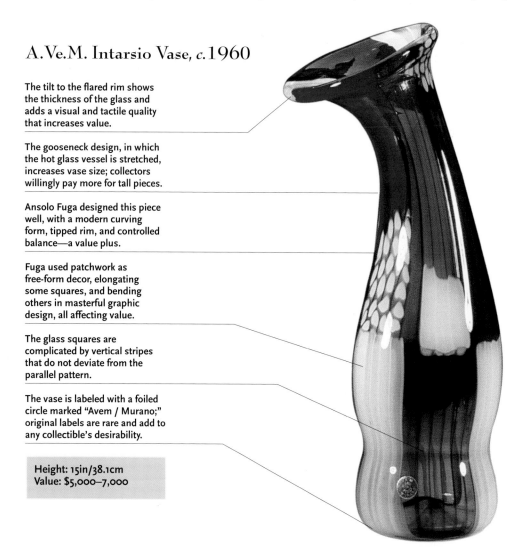

The tilt to the flared rim shows the thickness of the glass and adds a visual and tactile quality that increases value.

The gooseneck design, in which the hot glass vessel is stretched, increases vase size; collectors willingly pay more for tall pieces.

Ansolo Fuga designed this piece well, with a modern curving form, tipped rim, and controlled balance—a value plus.

Fuga used patchwork as free-form decor, elongating some squares, and bending others in masterful graphic design, all affecting value.

The glass squares are complicated by vertical stripes that do not deviate from the parallel pattern.

The vase is labeled with a foiled circle marked "Avem / Murano;" original labels are rare and add to any collectible's desirability.

Height: 15in/38.1cm
Value: $5,000–7,000

Barovier & Toso Intarsio Vase, c.1962

The top rim was smoothed at the fire and slightly turned inward, reflecting the curve at the lower edge.

The piece's height was determined by the four rows of fused squares on the regimented and symmetrical oval form.

Designer Ercole Barovier took a classical approach while using a modern aesthetic, a blend that can increase value.

Barovier used the Pezzato patchwork technique to best advantage here, alternating clear, colored glass with colorless bubbled glass.

Note that the bubbles form a rigid grid work—a skillful glass master was needed to complete this valuable decoration.

This unsigned vase is well-documented in catalogs, biennial records, and the Barovier reference book, all of which increases value.

Size: 8 x 5³/₄in/
20.3 x 14.6cm
Value: $6,000–8,000

• *A variety of artistic features contributed to Italian art glass in the 1950s and '60s, rather than one style or trend.*
• *Value features are constant, but the collectors are ever changing—personal choice and judgment affect price.*
• *For every masterwork created on Murano, thousands of ashtrays and bowls were made. Treasures await the patient collector.*
• *Some Murano glassworks were taken over in the late 20th century by conglomerates. Some produce art glass in the original styles and designs.*
• *Collectors need to be cautious about buying without clear provenance or history of the Murano piece in question.*

More About Murano Art Glass

In the 1990s, several books were published that had a significant impact on the market for Murano art glass. Intended to identify and promote the works of specific glassmakers, the books helped to stimulate an already interested audience.

Not surprisingly, prices for Italian art glass escalated. This was especially true for the masterworks and specialized pieces and product lines of the island's firms; but the increase in demand for Murano art glass trickled down to the more available middle lines and so-called lesser items.

Collector enthusiasm for Italian art glass remains high and is expected to continue on an upward trajectory.

For collectors interested in knowing more about this body of art glasswork and its history, any of the following would be valuable: Rosa Barovier Mentasti, *Venetian Glass 1890–1990*; Mark Heiremans, *Art Glass from Murano 1910–1970*, and *20th Century Murano Glass*; Franco Deboni, *Venini Glass*; Anna Venini deSantillana, *Gli Artisti Di Venini*; Helmut Ricke and Eva Schmitt, *Italian Glass Murano–Milan 1930–1970*.

Cristallerie de Pantin

The glassworks known as Pantin was producing an iridescent art glass long before many glass companies were aware of the technical possibility. Pantin's experimental work preceded much of that conducted by the Tiffany, Steuben, and Quezal companies in the United States. Pantin's process was patented in 1878 and involved the use of metallic oxides and particular heat reduction techniques resulting in a bronzed or golden sheen on the glass. At the same time, Pantin was issued another patent for inserting metallic foil sheets or powders between layers of glass to achieve a shimmering intercalary decoration the company called "Chine Métallique." Cristallerie de Pantin is seldom credited for its experiments in art glass decoration, yet Pantin's early work and technical breakthroughs had a major impact on later art glass production.

Under the directorship of Camille Tutre de Varreux, between 1909 and 1914, the factory at Pantin produced a great quantity of "De Vez" acid-etched cameo glass. Multiple layers of colored glass were acid-etched with natural decorations such as florals, landscapes, river views, animals and birds, and popular Art Nouveau designs of the period. These are sometimes found lightly wheel-etched to enhance the decoration. The "De Vez" signed pieces show up with some frequency in the collectibles marketplace today.

A Pantin product line frequently found and readily recognized is the iridized aquamarine art glass often decorated with subtle acid etching of the cased-glass surface. The example illustrated here is characteristic of Pantin's "Aigue Marine" product line and shows the delicacy of the crystal-clear glass coloration. These pieces are prized collectibles, much in demand, and not overly expensive—especially when compared to other well-known French art glass made by Gallé, Daum, Muller, Burgun, Schverer, and others. Through the years of art glass's resurgence, they have gained the respect and consideration of collectors worldwide. As authentic pre-World War I French art glass becomes scarcer, prices for the Pantin art glass lines are expected to escalate.

Aquamarine Etched Floral Cameo Glass Bowl, *c.*1910

The flared rim with an etched border band of irregular grass-like spikes accents the decoration below.

The bowl is wide and heavy enough to use as a flower vase, which adds value for some collectors.

The aqua-green transparent crystal bowl is cased in bright turquoise glass with a subtly iridescent surface.

The outer layer is acid-etched in stylized foliate decoration—skillful rendering adds value.

The background glass was frosted in an acid bath and compares nicely with the floral vase at right.

The base is marked "Cristallerie de Pantin" with "TSV & C." at center, which can add value.

Size: 3 x 6in/7.6 x 15.2cm
Value: $700–900

Acid-Etched Pond Lily Vase, c.1910

The unusual blob-top rim on this long-necked bottle vase helps make the form desirable.

The vase's opal color and distinct luminescent sheen were much admired originally, and are again in favor with collectors today.

Cased in pink-red and green layers of glass, the vase projects an aura of Art Nouveau style.

The vase is pleasantly diminutive but presents an effective decoration because of its "petticoat" flare—a popular but scarce form.

Three pond lilies perched on green pads in a watery surround are acid-etched and lightly wheel-cut, a valuable design.

The "De Vez" mark, etched prominently in the decoration, gives subtle credibility to the maker and value to the piece.

Note that the vase is raised on an integral pedestal base; this feature increases value.

Height: 6in/15.2cm
Value: $900–1,200

- *De Vez art glass was marked on the body of the work, etched or intaglio.*
- *Cameo-etched scenic decorations were specialties of Pantin's De Vez glass house. In great demand by collectors, these bring strong prices.*
- *Pantin marks usually involve the TSV&C monogram, and "Cristallerie de Pantin." "Pantin" alone does not indicate the company. Collectors need to research and identify the true maker.*
- *Pantin produced a coiled figural snake of iridescent amber art glass in 1880—a treasure for any collector.*
- *Pantin art glass is not known to be forged, thanks to the prevalence of marks.*

An Art Glass Pioneer

The Cristallerie de Pantin was established by E.S. Monot in 1851 at La Villette, then relocated in the town of Pantin near Paris in 1855. Monot's son and entrepreneur M. Stumpf joined the company in the next decade, which led to experiments in new lines of art glass and patents for new processes.

After the elder Monot's retirement, the company added new partners to become Stumpf, Touvier, Viollet & Cie. Until 1900, Touvier served as designer and artistic director, and Stumpf as managing director. Camille Tutre de Varreux succeeded Stumpf, and the company became Cristallerie de Pantin, but still used the initials TSV&C in the company emblem.

The tenure of de Varreux at Pantin revitalized an already progressive and successful commercial enterprise. Pantin's acid-etched cameo glass achieved popularity and commercial success. After World War I, the company redirected its focus toward crystal and colorless glassware, and was headed in a conservative direction by the Depression years of the 1930s.

Marius Ernest Sabino

The success of a genius like René Lalique motivated hundreds of art glass entrepreneurs to reproduce the success first of his jewelry, then of his perfume bottles, and finally of his art glass. One of those dubbed an "imitator" is Marius Ernest Sabino. It is a bum rap.

Italian by birth, Sabino established his glass company in Paris in 1919, where he produced metal-mounted lamps and architectural accessories. He arrived on the scene just in time to participate in one of the most creative periods in European decorative arts—the interwar years between 1920 and 1939.

Building on his metalworking business, Sabino began to produce large objects—chandeliers, doors and window framing devices, columns and building accessories, even furniture and wall partitions. During the post-World War I reconstruction boom, in which the Art Deco style flourished, Sabino designed and produced decorative objects in the popular styles of the day. At the same time, he became intrigued by art glass and its sculptural

potential, and acquired the furnaces needed to produce art glass. Golden opal glass—his legacy in the collectible marketplace today—was born during this period.

Today's collectors were led to Sabino art glass of the interwar period through the figurines produced by the family business in and after the 1960s. These glass animals, birds, fish, and the occasional nudes were produced primarily in opal glass that is decidedly different from the opalescent color of the earlier production. Many were sold in the United States, accounting for the large numbers found in the American collectible markets today. From these later figurines, collectors made the leap to the earlier art glass pieces. Sabino can now be found in antique shops and auctions, swap meets and flea markets, estate sales and consignment shops, as well as Internet sites. The pieces are virtually always signed and are therefore identified readily. Collectors should watch for the early work, because it is often undervalued in the American collectibles marketplace. Prices will escalate as supply dwindles.

Molded and Applied Art Glass Vase, c. 1925

This form, with a top mold ridge and raised band, allows a press-molding technique for more detailed results.

This popular vase is elliptical in form, wider than tall, with heavy glass that carries a romanticized scene in transitional style.

The low-lead glass is colorless with a frosted garden area; applied nudes are selectively polished and frosted in typical Sabino fashion.

The full-bodied women cling to each side in unusually fine, sculptural detail.

The mold design suggests a classical genre rather than an Art Deco scene, which could decrease value.

"Sabino Paris" appears in script in the mold on the base; collectors like molded marks for authenticity.

Size: 7 x 9in/17.7 x 22.8cm
Value: $1,800–2,500

"Gaiete" Opalescent Vase, *c.*1925

The deeply curving top flares above a sensuous oval vase in the French Art Nouveau style.

The heavy-walled vase has great visual impact, allowing dramatic presentation in a value-plus size.

This translucent golden opal glass is Sabino's signatory color—quintessential Art Deco style and highly desirable.

Collectors especially seek this popular design titled "Gaiete," with its eight dancing women.

The extra detail in the mold design—especially at the lower border and in the draped women—shows craftsmanship.

An inscribed signature, "Sabino Paris," appears at the center of the bottom and increases value.

Height: 14⅛in/35.8m
Value: $2,500–4,000

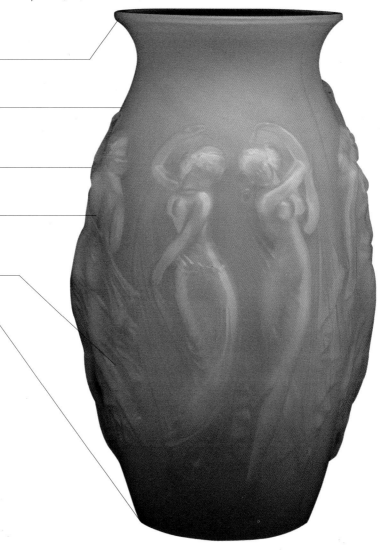

• *The elegance of a design, such as the nudes on "Gaiete" (above), increases the relative value of the work.*

• *Larger scale that allows the decoration on a work of art glass to extend to the full length of the piece will add both interest and value.*

• *Sabino's opalescent glass is a major value factor in appraising his work. The handled vase's value would increase were it opal.*

• *Sabino's colored art glass (red, amber, green, blue) is often priced reasonably in the marketplace but is poised to increase in value.*

• *Collectors looking for an investment that will appreciate might consider early Sabino a good buy. It's the right price on the market today.*

• *Collectors expecting their 1960s Sabino figures to skyrocket in value would do well to be patient.*

Sculptural Art Glass

Marius Sabino adapted the techniques he used in the production of lamps and lighting devices to decorative art glass of all kinds. His work was freeblown and molded, using primarily low-lead glass for its sculptural qualities rather than lead crystal. While his art glass included a range of colors, styles, and forms, it was the unique opal-colored glass that became Sabino's signature, shown and recognized worldwide.

Sabino was one of the few art glass producers to emerge unscathed by the Great Depression. Through the 1920s and '30s, he continued to display in international exhibitions, winning prestigious awards and medals everywhere he went. The Sabino factories finally closed down at the start of World War II, precipitating Marius's retirement. Shortly after his death in 1961 at the age of 83, the Sabinos reopened the glassworks, attempting to resurrect the opal-colored glassware for which the company had become famous.

Scandinavian Glass—Early

The artistic impact of Scandinavian art glass production in the interwar years was based on timing and quality. Sweden remained neutral in World War I, so the country did not suffer the economic hardships endured elsewhere. Swedish glass output dipped, but the factories remained open, and experimentation and production continued. The key players at the Orrefors Glassworks—Knut Bergqvist, the master glass craftsman, designer Simon Gate, and artist Edward Hald—all joined the Orrefors team during the worst war years. Technology that was put on hold in France, Britain, and Holland advanced at Orrefors during that period. By the time of the armistice, Scandinavian art glass was off and running.

Scandinavia's impact on the global art glass trade was also due to the quality of its crystal. Scandinavian glass formulas resulted in a product of great purity and clarity, with innate responsiveness and malleability that endured the stress of the engraver's wheels and new mass-production methods. This glass did not chip at a touch, could be deeply cut or sandblasted without shattering, and exhibited a clarity and brilliance that carried 20th-century art glass significantly forward. It was an artistic success that continues to be a collector's favorite today.

Over time, the workmanship of Orrefors designers, glassblowers, cutters, and engravers produced glass objects admired at home and abroad. Simon Gate's nudes were presented in many styles and settings. Vicke Lindstrand's originals, including the Shark Killer and the Pearl Diver, sell in the thousands. Edward Hald's paperweight fish vases in the Graal technique have become popular collectibles. Edvin Ohrstrom's extraordinary designs in the Ariel technique have sold for impressive prices at auction. Current prices for Scandinavian art glass will increase as the older designs become more difficult to find.

Orrefors Engraved Vase, *c.*1933

Note the folded rim on this flared freeblown vase of pristine colorless crystal, a perfect foil for the decoration.

The piece is large by Orrefors standards, and allows a fine area for artistic placement of the motif.

Selective and aesthetic use of frosted and polished areas increase visual impact and value.

Simon Gate's design, "The Javanese Dancer," is one of a series of exotic semi-nude women in ethnic headdress and diaphanous gowns.

Gate's design employs engraving to create an impression of movement in the flowing garment, hair, and arms.

The base is inscribed "Orrefors/ S. Gate/1387 C2 ea," all important appraisal information. Good marks increase price and appreciation.

Size: 10 x 11in/25.4 x 27.9cm
Value: $2,500–4,000

Orrefors Ariel Vase, *c.*1945

The top rim of this heavy oval vessel has been tooled into square form; added artistic factors increase price.

The height is average for Ariel, but allows fine presentation of the painterly decoration within. Many collectors seek this rare line.

Clear, colorless glass with an aqua-blue layer provides a "seawater" background for the underwater scene.

Both the scene and colors are desirable here—a purple-aubergine air-trap design of two mermaids swimming among aquatic plants.

The reverse decoration portrays King Neptune, a rare design that will continue to increase in value.

The base is fully signed, "Orrefors/Edvin Ohrstrom/ Ariel No. 491 F," which gives a collector all the needed information and adds value.

Height: 8in/20.3cm
Value: $10,000–12,000

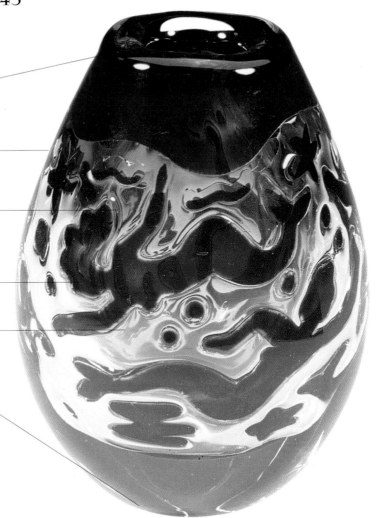

• *Orrefors Ariel art glass resembles "paintings in glass" that charm collectors.*

• *Scenic or portrait Ariel pieces as intricate as the one above are rare, potential treasures.*

• *Orrefors copper-wheel engraved glass was made in great quantity. Prices depend largely on complexity.*

• *The Indonesian nude dancers designed by Simon Gate do not have great current value, but would seem to be a good investment.*

• *Collectors need to buy the best engraved art glass if they expect increases in value.*

• *Serious collectors should invest in books explaining the marking system of Orrefors glass if they hope to find treasures.*

Orrefors Glassworks

The Orrefors engraving shop included the most updated equipment and methods available and employed notably competent workmen. Soon Orrefors was exhibiting brilliant crystal glass, copper-wheel cut in a range of decorations, featuring natural scenes and nude maidens. The Swedish public loved it, and word spread to the Continent and abroad.

In 1916, Simon Gate invented the "Graal" technique. This involved acid etching a design, then reheating and casing clear glass over the design. The resulting "internal" decoration could be filled with slip color, bubbles, geometric elements, and more. At the 1925 Paris Exhibition, Orrefors artists won the Grand Prix and Gold Medals.

In the 1930s, after Edvin Ohrstrom joined the company, he directed the development of the "Ariel" process. This involved sandblasting design pathways on glass vessels to form air pockets of decoration to be colored or left clear. Sven Palmqvist was largely responsible for developing the Kraka and Ravenna lines. Nils Landberg pursued an approach that would create links with European studio artists.

Scandinavian Glass—Late

Orrefors production of all art glass lines increased in the 1930s and beyond, in spite of economic reverses and the interruption of World War II *(see pages 138-139)*. Advances in technique, innovative new lines, international exhibitions, and well-placed public relations promotions increased export of the Orrefors art glass throughout the world. The eventual consolidation of Sweden's glass factories late in the 20th century created a new entity called Orrefors AB and led Scandinavian glassware in a new creative direction.

Collectors have responded favorably to Scandinavian art glass as it has gotten increasing attention in the antiques media, especially during the period of art glass revival and discovery in the late 1980s and 1990s. Books and articles informed the public of the aesthetic concepts being expressed in art glass designs from Scandinavian factories, even as the products were being exported and sold worldwide in department stores, gift shops, and galleries. Visitors to Scandinavia purchased the exciting glassware and carried it home, where it quickly won new admirers. Incipient collectors spread the word.

For today's collectors, nothing makes the hunt more pleasurable or profitable than information about the objects that form the focus of their collections. Fortunately for them, much of the Scandinavian glass was signed, dated, and numbered according to strictly followed systems that are well-recorded in their respective company publications and reference books. The interested collector can gain access to these identifying markings by visiting a local library or bookstore, or by going online for an appropriate website. With a little more effort, relevant out-of-print books can also be located.

Kosta Trad I Dimma Autumn Scenic Vase, *c.* 1955

A small opening is employed at the top of this heavy-walled oval vessel of brilliantly clear glass.

The height of this piece is slightly below average for this design, but not so as to decrease its value.

The internal decoration of tall, slender trees is the hallmark of this design; treatment of the leaves is its variation.

The darkest purple-black trees are nearly bare, while colorful leaves appear to be falling and piling up on the ground.

Note how the leaves on the ground maintain their integrity, a tricky use of color.

The vase is inscribed on its base, "Kosta Lu 2011." It is unusual that the Lindstrand name is not included, and this detracts from value slightly.

Height: 7in/17.7cm
Value: $3,000–4,000

Kosta Trad I Dimma Vase, *c.*1955

An asymmetrical ovoid opening at the top rim of this freeblown vessel shows an ethereal quality that appeals to many.

Taller than average, this model emphasizes a slender and shadowy design that increases its artistic merit and value.

The colorless glass is manipulated within by addition of opal-white coloration, achieving a ghostly appearance and a feeling of motion.

Aubergine-black trees with elongated leafless branches decorate the vase, creating a valuable graphic impact.

The white foggy background extends nearly to ground level in the forest setting in an effective, artful design.

The base is acid-marked, "Lind/Strand/Kosta," and is inscribed, "Lu 2005"; collectors expect this information on Swedish glass.

Height: 13in/33cm
Value: $3,500–4,500

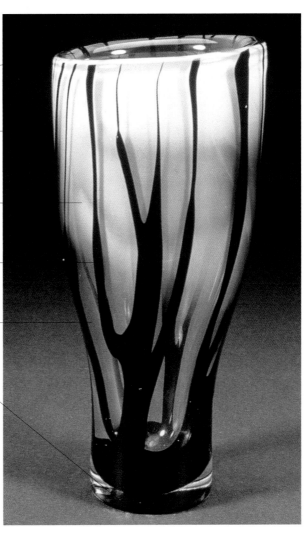

• *Lindstrand pieces are now considered rare and have increased in value greatly in the last 50 years.*
• *Scandinavian glass is famous worldwide for its very high quality and deft artistic touches. Both assets are clearly illustrated by the examples shown on these pages.*
• *The work of Italian artists in the 1950s is compatible with Scandinavian design, a result of the international decorative arts exhibitions of the post-war years.*
• *The quality of Scandinavian glass was based on secret formulas that moved from factory to factory with the workers. Clarity and brilliance became shared characteristics of Scandinavian art glass.*

Kosta Glasbruk

Kosta Glasbruk (glassworks) evolved from a prestigious Swedish company founded in 1742. It began producing art glass after 1897, and its etched cameo glass in the Art Nouveau style earned international awards at the "Celebration of Electricity" in Paris in 1900. Kosta designers played a critical role in the Swedish Arts and Crafts movement of the time, helping to create a style that revealed the superb quality of Scandinavian glass and designs. Edward Stromberg became Kosta's most significant designer.

In the Art Deco mid 1920s, when Sweden achieved notable success at the Paris Exhibition of Modern Decorative and Industrial Arts, Vicke Lindstrand, then 24 years old, became one of Orrefors's new designers. He stayed for over a decade, before leaving to try his hand at ceramic design. In 1950, Kosta hired him as its senior designer. Among his most notable contributions were the sleek "Trad I Dimma" and "Trad I Autumn" designs. Lindstrand effectively directed Kosta to the forefront of Scandinavian glass design.

Verrerie Schneider

The Verrerie Schneider, founded by Charles Schneider and his brother Ernest, thrived during the 1920s, when Art Deco designs were most popular in Europe. The brothers were well-trained for success in glass-making, having worked for both Gallé and Daum. In the interwar years, Ernest managed accounting and promotion, while Charles was art director and technician—an ideal division of labor.

Acid-etched cameo glass decoration had been a favorite of French glass houses since its introduction in the late 1800s. Charles Schneider made it look like a new technique when he etched brilliantly colored layers of glass cased to thick mottled glass vessels. His stylized designs in Art Deco colors were popular, and they were copied.

The Le Verre Français line of Schneider's glass is considered a distinct collectible area. Virtually always inscribed on the lower edge of the item, the mark is a script signature, "Le Verre Français." An elite selection of this line is additionally signed "Charder," a contraction of CHARles SchneiDER, and presumably indicates a piece designed by Charles himself.

The "Schneider" signature is reserved for the line of art glass without acid etching, usually internally decorated or bearing applications. Such work attracts collectors who favor simplicity and elegance. Some of it is mounted with metal fittings, adding both interest and artistic impact. The art glass of the Verrerie Schneider is highly respected and valued. This is likely to continue as supply dwindles.

Two Contrasting Charder Etched Vases, c.1925

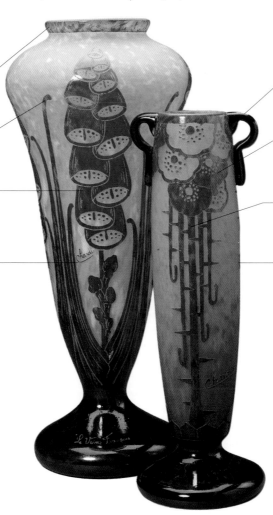

The larger vase has a raised rim above a broad oval body of mottled white, a size that helps compensate for the lack of handles.

The bright orange shading to aubergine/purple of the larger piece is a value enhancer.

The stylized foxglove decoration in three repeats on the larger piece uses the tall form effectively.

Each vase has an etched "Charder" at the side and is inscribed, "Le Verre Français," in script on the foot—value factors for each.

Height: 19in/48.2cm
Value: $2,800–3,500

The smaller vessel has applied glass handles in dark purple that match the base. Handles usually increase value.

Stylistic blossoms above thorned stems on the smaller piece display a contrasting design of equal value to the larger.

The pink cased with lavender shading to dark purple of the smaller compares favorably to that of the larger vessel as a valuable color treatment.

Each vase is listed in the Bertrand reference book; inclusion in collector's guides increases appraisal value.

Height: 15in/38.1cm
Value $2,000–2,500

Etched and Enameled Vase, c.1928

The rim is pulled at the fire in three symmetrical points around the oval body, a rare design that increases the value

The diminutive size can be an added-value factor—not all collectors prefer larger pieces.

The oval body of creamy yellow glass shading into a mottled orange and brown displays Schneider's expertise at blending opaque colors.

The unusual decoration of aubergine-black olives clustered with green leaves in a medial band increases the vase's desirability.

The decoration is lightly etched, enameled, and fired, a technical rarity especially valued in the marketplace.

The disk foot of aubergine color is signed "Schneider France," probably made for export and desired by advanced collectors.

Height: 5³/8in/13.6cm
Value: $4,000–5,000

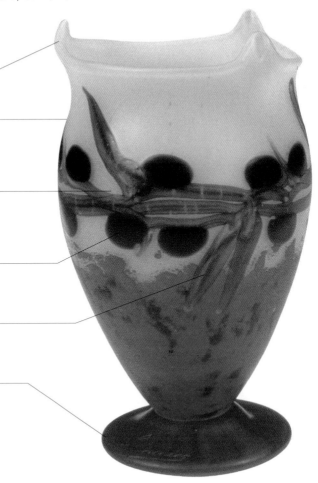

• *The Schneider signature in script or block letters is usually present on all lines, thus aiding treasure hunters.*
• *A "Candycane" mark was used for certain anonymous shops; other marks were used for upscale stores in New York, London, and Brussels.*
• *Schneider fitted metal mounts on lamps, light shades, vases, compotes, and centerbowls. These are increasing in value.*
• *The "Le Verre Français" line was made throughout the 1920s when Schneider was especially prolific, which helps explain current availability.*
• *The compatibility of the "Charder" Art Deco designs with modernist and contemporary art contributes to the popularity of the line.*

After World War I

In the 1920s, the Verrerie Schneider quickly gained a reputation for well-designed art glass, popular with the buying public and design critics alike. The company found ways to market its art glass to best advantage, stocking local shops and galleries and creating major clients abroad. As the Art Deco style became ever more fashionable, Schneider designs followed suit. The company's profitability exceeded all expectations, as did the number of awards and accolades it earned.

After the 1925 Paris Exhibition, rival glass companies began to imitate Verrerie Schneider's art glass. Most blatant was David Gueron, who not only "borrowed" designs for his Degue art glass, but also recruited Schneider workers. The Schneiders sued, but the legal action moved slowly, nearly destroying both companies.

Times and tastes were changing by the 1930s. After Ernest Schneider died in 1936, the Verrerie Schneider switched to producing the colorless glass made popular by the Scandinavian producers. During World War II, France was invaded, and the German occupiers nearly demolished the company. After the war, family members reestablished a glassworks that continued through the 1970s, albeit in diversified glass production.

Almeric Walter

Almeric Walter had a great advantage over the major glass masters, credited with the rediscovery of the *pâte de verre* technique in the late 19th century. At the time that Walter was involved in experimentation at Daum, much of the *pâte de verre* work of others was available for study and interpretive investigation. Walter was subsidized at Daum, where he was encouraged to make use of industrial advances and mechanization. Unlike some artists, Walter was not troubled as a *pâte de verre* master by the seeming conflict between art and industry.

The *pâte de verre* ("paste of glass") art glass made by Walter, both for Daum, and later for his own company, was highly successful for a number of reasons. The work—created from glass that had been ground and reheated into a moldable paste—became available during a period of relative prosperity. Its design appealed to the general public. The colorful, natural designs of creatures,

vegetation, and occasional figures, were all popular, affordable collectibles that could be easily acquired and displayed. They received excellent promotion, first by the Daum businesses, and later by Walter's outlets.

The reasons for Almeric Walter's popularity in the 21st century are basically the same as in the 20th. The figural pieces appeal as much today as when they were made, with their fresh naturalistic designs and timeless style. Walter's proficiency with the *pâte de verre* method is as easily appreciated by the neophyte collector as by the connoisseur. Except for the rare plaques and tiles of his earliest work, Walter's pieces can be found in the marketplace at auctions, antique shops, shows, and websites. Prices have consistently increased since the collecting surges of the 1960s and 1990s. Walter's work is popular internationally, a significant factor in driving prices upward in the collectibles market.

Pâte de Verre Lizard Decorated Vase, *c.*1925

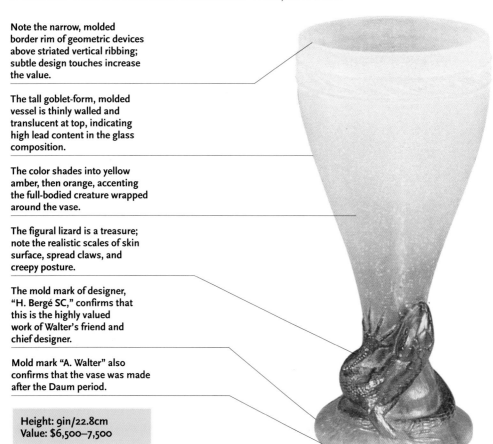

Note the narrow, molded border rim of geometric devices above striated vertical ribbing; subtle design touches increase the value.

The tall goblet-form, molded vessel is thinly walled and translucent at top, indicating high lead content in the glass composition.

The color shades into yellow amber, then orange, accenting the full-bodied creature wrapped around the vase.

The figural lizard is a treasure; note the realistic scales of skin surface, spread claws, and creepy posture.

The mold mark of designer, "H. Bergé SC," confirms that this is the highly valued work of Walter's friend and chief designer.

Mold mark "A. Walter" also confirms that the vase was made after the Daum period.

Height: 9in/22.8cm
Value: $6,500–7,500

Pâte de Verre Figural Mouse Sculpture, *c.*1928

Collectors value the fine craftsmanship of this full-bodied gray mouse, molded with crisp detail and anatomical precision.

The signature mark appears in the mold—"A. Walter Nancy"—adding to value; this is surely a Henri Bergé design.

The realistic, appealing portrayal of the mouse, nibbling from a walnut shell, raises appraisal value.

Colors are strong and enhance the naturalistic style: gray mouse, brown nutshell, green grass, all with realistic shading.

The designer perched the mouse on a grassy green knoll, raised for impact and presentation.

The figural item appeals to a wide range of collectors, not only *pâte de verre* enthusiasts.

Height: 3in/7.6cm
Value: $7,500–9,000

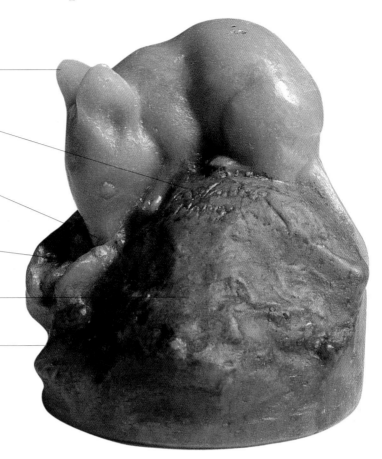

• **Pâte de verre** *is not in great supply; few glass houses mastered the technique to produce enough quality pieces to make it profitable.*
• *Few pieces from Walter's Daum period—marked with a molded or incised "Daum"—exist. These are especially valuable on today's market.*
• *Walter's figural pieces appeal to a variety of collectors: the mouse would be collectible as an animal, paperweight, Bergé design, or French whimsy.*
• **Pâte de verre** *is susceptible to occasional bubbles and blemishes, especially in the early work. Collectors are tolerant of minor flaws.*
• *Walter made* **pâte de verre** *pendants to be worn as jewelry, decorated with natural motifs, and mold-marked "AW." Quite collectible, they bring $300–$1,000 or more.*

Walter and *Pâte de Verre*

Almeric Walter was trained early. He studied under artist Gabriel Lévy, then later joined with Lévy to experiment with the glass paste technique. The Walter and Lévy work was exhibited in 1903 and caught the attention of the Daum brothers. Walter and Lévy went to work for Daum but maintained a degree of control over their work.

Even after Lévy went his own way, Walter stayed with Daum. Walter's work became far more sophisticated and technically proficient as he worked with Daum designers and learned from Daum's modern equipment and production advances. By 1914, when the company closed for the duration of the war, Walter was well-established.

After World War I, Almeric Walter set up his own *pâte de verre* workshop with Daum's consent and assistance, acquiring the molds he had previously used and continuing his relationship with several Daum designers, most importantly Henri Bergé. By 1920, Walter was producing *pâte de verre* commercially and winning awards at exhibitions. During this time, he produced small decorative works of art glass, often sculptural depictions of animals, birds, reptiles, insects, and flowers, all in great quantity that sold well. Walter's business thrived until the Depression. The death of Henri Bergé, and his own failing health caused him to curtail and then end his glass work.

Thomas Webb & Sons

The glassworks of Thomas Webb & Sons was at the forefront of British production of "fancy" glass during the late 19th century. Britain had its own version of the Art Nouveau movement, and Thomas Webb & Sons meant to supply the demand. Along with their closest competitor, the Stevens & Williams Co., Webb produced an enormous quantity of art glass from 1880 through 1910. Their Victorian art glass included: cased, satin, opalescent, threaded, applied, agate, mother-of-pearl, zipper, nailsea, crackle, coralene, rainbow, spangle, spatter, and marble. They also patented glassware by color or technique. Then cameo glass swept the British Isles from Stourbridge to Sandringham, and the glass companies found new product lines that would sell wonderfully.

While Thomas Webb & Sons's Woodall teams, headed by George and Thomas Woodall, focused on the creation of masterworks, the company also produced popular cameo glass in quantity. Its output included acid-etched vases, bowls, lamps, and lighting devices, perfume bottles and dresser items, and other decorative items for the home. Decorations ranged from floral designs to neo-classical scenes, portraits and nautical images, Islamic, Persian, Egyptian, and Oriental motifs, and many naturalistic animal and aviary tableaux.

After exhibiting at the Chicago World's Fair in 1893, Webb became very popular the United States. His cameo glass and other lines were much in demand. Among Webb's innovations were an "Ivory" line of vases, treated to simulate aged ivory ware, and a line of colorless crystal glass forms "padded" with areas of colored glass, wheel-carved in intricate designs, and polished to resemble rock crystal. Collectors avidly seek this fanciful, elegant work.

Carved Cameo Glass Exhibition Vase, c.1889

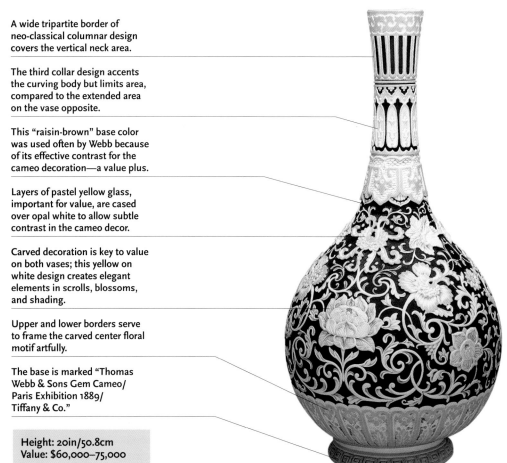

A wide tripartite border of neo-classical columnar design covers the vertical neck area.

The third collar design accents the curving body but limits area, compared to the extended area on the vase opposite.

This "raisin-brown" base color was used often by Webb because of its effective contrast for the cameo decoration—a value plus.

Layers of pastel yellow glass, important for value, are cased over opal white to allow subtle contrast in the cameo decor.

Carved decoration is key to value on both vases; this yellow on white design creates elegant elements in scrolls, blossoms, and shading.

Upper and lower borders serve to frame the carved center floral motif artfully.

The base is marked "Thomas Webb & Sons Gem Cameo/ Paris Exhibition 1889/ Tiffany & Co."

Height: 20in/50.8cm
Value: $60,000–75,000

Carved Cameo Glass Exhibition Vase, c.1889

The border design's geometric and fretwork motif accents the carved decoration below.

The classic forms of this and the vase opposite suggest that they were planned for display in the Paris Exhibition.

The unusual sapphire-blue base color provides a strong contrast for the carved decoration—compare this with the brown combination opposite.

Layers of pleasing rose-red upon opal white glass offer strong contrast for the cameo design and heighten visual impact.

The dramatic carved decoration in red on white is a key value factor.

The lower border design emphasizes the red, while maintaining the restrained style of the smaller collar at the vase's top.

The base is marked "Thomas Webb & Sons Gem Cameo/ Paris Exhibition 1889/Tiffany & Co."

Height: 19in/48.2cm
Value: $70,000–85,000

• *Collectors can find treasures like these two vases; many such items are still tucked away in attics and vaults.*
• *It took the Woodall team a reported three years to produce these vases—this explains why such vases are no longer produced and cost so much.*
• *Marks on these vases were probably added after the Paris exhibition, when they were sent to Tiffany & Co. The marks increase value.*
• *These vases were included in John Loring's book,* Tiffany's 150 Years, *Sir Geoffrey Beard's* Nineteenth Century Cameo Glass, *and the Grover's* English Cameo Glass. *This adds value.*

British Art Glass

The town of Stourbridge in England was the center of British glass-making in the late 19th century. Three men played pivotal roles in the development of that industry: John Wilkes Webb (Thomas's father), John Northwood, and Joseph Silvers Williams-Thomas *(see page 149)*. Northwood had established his glassworks by 1860 and became famous for his virtuosity in the ancient art of cameo glass decoration.

After inheriting his father's glassworks, Thomas Webb commissioned Northwood to create a cameo glass masterwork for Thomas Webb & Sons. The resulting Pegasus vase took Northwood six years to carve and was exhibited incomplete in Paris in 1878, where it won a Grand Prix and the French Legion of Honor for Thomas Webb.

The Webb company has maintained its reputation throughout the years and continues to produce fine glassware today, now operated under the name of Webb and Corbett.

Thomas Webb—Cameo Glass

In England, the Golden Years of cameo glass started in the late 1870s and lasted until about 1914, when World War I began in Europe. Cameo technique changed dramatically during that period, a reflection of changes taking place in both technology and attitudes. Artist-craftsmen often grudgingly adapted new techniques as a necessary economic evil. New equipment made possible the repetitive etching of designs on glass, saving time without necessarily sacrificing quality. Profits increased as production time decreased.

But after the end of World War I, the collecting public let it be known that what they had wanted before the war was not what they wanted after. In the United States, cut glass was out. In England, cameo glass was passé. The glass factories had to move on to new styles for emerging collectors. The British resisted the Art Deco styles sweeping the continent. They preferred the Arts and Crafts style of the Glasgow "Mac's." The glass houses at Stourbridge shifted to more crystal decorations, pressed-glass materials, and the "modern" department store goods suitable for domestic and international markets.

The export of English cameo glass to the Americas has given this art glass a significant presence in the American antiques market. Given the quality, beauty, and relative affordability of the pieces, cameo glass has become a popular collectible. In addition, publication of such books as *Art Glass Nouveau*, followed by *English Cameo Glass*, by Lee and Ray Grover, and Victor Arwas's *Glass: Art Nouveau to Art Deco*, published in 1977 and updated in 1987, have stimulated interest in British art glass. Exhibitions and major sales of collections have furthered the trend. Prices are expected to continue appreciating in the future.

Unique Gem Cameo Glass Giraffe Vase, *c.*1898

A raised, cuffed rim is carved with linear bands above and below the acanthus leaf border, accentuating the scene below.

The pedestaled ovoid body offers a broad "canvas" for the painterly natural scene, which Woodall uses to great effect.

This typical "raisin brown" color is a perfect foil for the opal white scene.

The desert palms and giraffes—one eating from a tree—is unique to Webb / Woodall and adds to its value.

The "G. Woodall" signature appears in the scene at lower right; the base is also marked with "Thomas Webb & Sons—Gem Cameo" in a circle; both increase value.

A repeating foliate design decorates the rim of the pedestal foot, symmetrically balancing the top rim.

Height: 7in/17.7cm
Value: $45,000–55,000

Cameo Glass "Serpentina" Portrait Vase, *c.*1895

The deeply flared rim, decorated with repeating scrolling devices, balances the flared base below.

Woodall artfully created this design to conform to classic oval form.

Webb's signature deep-purple color enhances the expressive motif.

The ethereal scene of a nude woman dancing with sheer veils swirling around her body in exquisite detail is masterfully executed.

Opal white glass layer is hand carved in precise minutiae.

Note the shaded crescent cloud on which the woman dances, adding subtle nuance.

The signature, "Geo. Woodall," at lower right increases value greatly. The base is also signed with the name, "Serpentina," a dramatic touch adding to the Woodall mystique.

Height: 7in/17.7cm
Value: $50,000–60,000

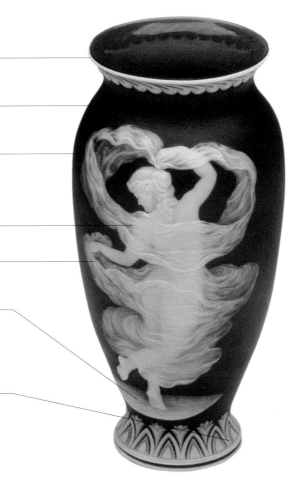

• *Thomas Webb masterworks seldom come to market but have consistently increased in value whenever they appear.*
• *Woodall's giraffe vase has a companion piece with deer decoration; both are pictured in Sir Geoffrey Beard's* Nineteenth Century Cameo Glass, *long out of print. Collectors might watch for that pricey volume, a collector's item itself.*
• *These vases, of similar size, quality, rarity, condition, and provenance are also similarly appraised. All these attributes count for a potential purchase.*
• *If the Woodall decoration were replaced with a simple floral design, the value of each vase would drop to about $1,500–2,000.*

Stevens & Williams Company

Headed by Joseph Silvers Williams-Thomas, Stevens & Williams was located in the Stourbridge district, home to the most prestigious English glassworks. S&W's output, like Webb's, was vast and excellent. Research suggests that from about 1860 to 1880, the company introduced some 4,800 designs in cut glass, engraved glass, and acid-etched glass. In the following two decades, it introduced approximately 1,000 designs a year, for a total by 1903 of 23,500 designs. Through these years, from 1880 and as late as 1910, Thomas Webb & Sons and Stevens & Williams ran neck-and-neck in terms of innovation and productivity.

Meanwhile, in 1878, decorative artist John Northwood was represented at the Paris Exhibition with three extraordinary carved cameo glass masterworks: the Portland Vase, the Milton Vase, and the Pegasus Vase, the last a commission for Thomas Webb & Sons. In 1881, Joseph Williams-Thomas astutely offered Northwood the position of art director and production manager for S&W. Northwood's 20-year tenure at S&W had a great deal to do with the quality and size of the company's creative output. Hiring Northwood virtually assured Stevens & Williams a formidable niche in the English glassmaking competition.

Württemberg
Metal Goods Factory

The Württemberg Metal Goods Factory (WMF) introduced its art glass department at exactly the best time for success—the interwar period, between 1918 and 1938. Economic factors and artistic developments came together to create a climate especially friendly to creativity. The Art Deco style was attracting much attention in the wake of the 1925 Paris Exhibition, and the Arts and Crafts style continued to gain popularity.

While the decorative arts in Austria were moving in new directions, in Germany, the trend was conservative. Myra-Kristall, for example, WMF's iridescent glass, was far from revolutionary in form or design. It was the Ikora line that caught the public's eye. The company increased production and began to export to the American market. That step led to the line's remarkable collectibility in the U.S. market today.

The artistic significance of Württemberg art glass was its eclectic appeal. Ikora, and later the Lavaluna line of the 1930s, were compatible with many of the styles of the period. This may also explain the current popularity of the WMF art glass as an interior decorating ornament. Collectors find that the clean lines and crisp internal decoration of Ikora fit comfortably in modern or contemporary homes, and a heavy-walled glass bowl, with artfully crafted decoration, is a beautiful addition to an Arts and Crafts environment.

Collectors seeking Württemberg glassware today need to know what they are looking for. Generally, the glass is not signed, marked, or labeled. Ikora, however, has an identifiable look, as shown on these pages. Because of the Württemberg export business of the 1930s, WMF treasures continue to be available in the 21st century.

Ikora Vase, c. 1927

The skill needed to make the smooth rim and broad opening above a symmetrical oval body adds value to Ikora.

The top border band contains a valuable balanced blending of maroon powders enclosed in colorless glass.

The white powders in the medial band flow into the colors above and below, adding visual impact.

The moss green, mottled and striated, appears to blend upward into the white row in a shadowy progressive mix.

The vase is raised on a round disk foot of integrated color and balanced form that was applied at the kiln, a value factor.

No label, mark, or signature appears here; an original label is rare and would add value and historical interest.

Height: 8in/20.3cm
Value: $450–600

Ikora Centerbowl, *c.*1927

From above, this bowl presents the entire design, color, and decoration configuration, an Ikora characteristic.

The edge of the freeblown bowl is folded under, adding a pleasing tactile quality and protection to the rim.

Maroon powders were trapped and melded into the glass body at the outer border.

The internal crackled appearance is idiosyncratic.

An appealing secondary band of white powders is also captured within the colorless glass surround.

The central area has six segmented white panels in a pinwheel pattern on a moss-green background— a value factor.

The base (not seen here) has a colorless glass, disk-form pedestal foot applied at the fire over the pontil; fine craftsmanship increases value.

Size: 4 x 13in/10.1 x 33cm
Value: $700–900

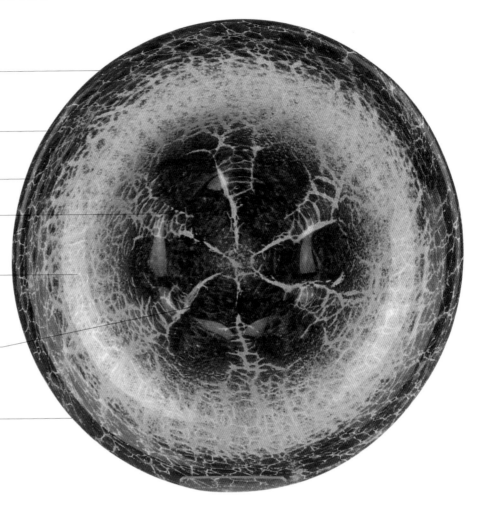

- *The WMF art glass may be mistaken for Austrian or Czech items. Ongoing research on WMF patents should help in the future.*
- *The iridescent Myra-Kristall WMF line of amber glass with gold luster and purple-blue highlights is difficult to locate unless well-attributed.*
- *Ikora pieces are relatively inexpensive as collectibles, but their value is expected to increase.*
- *Ikora is usually free from integral flaws or condition problems. Any chips or cracks decrease value significantly.*
- *WMF pieces with metal mounts from their foundry are potential treasures in the U.S. marketplace.*

Ikora Art Glass

Founded in 1853, WMF began making glass in Goppingen, Germany, in 1883. At first, the company focused on utilitarian glass and decorative items with metal mounts and accessories. In the interwar period, WMF produced such successful art glass lines as the iridescent Myra-Kristal and a mother-of-pearl lustered glass, Perlmutter.

In 1926, Württemberg introduced its tour de force line, Ikora art glass. Ikora was a freeblown, heavy-walled glass, internally decorated with a unique configuration of bubbles, swirls, and colored powders. Ikora came in a limited range of colors and included

vases, bowls, lampshades and bases, plates, pitchers and tumblers, and some tableware pieces. WMF also added a popular group of souvenir miniatures to the product line, along with small jewelry items and whimsies.

Largely as a result of Ikora's success, Karl Wiedmann became the Württemberg Glass Works manager in 1927. Innovative by nature, Wiedmann recruited well-respected designers, architects, and artists for technical research and artistic development purposes. It was a dynamic move and one that translated quickly into positive growth for the company.

▶ *Dale Chihuly Art Glass Basket, 1983. This piece is from Chihuly's Macchia Series, and is spotted, horizontally ribbed, and integrally wrapped in yellow with blue interior. $9,000–12,000. 17 × 19in/43.1 × 48.2cm.*

Contemporary
International Studio Artists

Dale Chihuly

The extraordinary art glass of Dale Chihuly seems at first blush to be a confusion of beautiful objects. But there was a progression to what he created. His first vessels were his Navajo Blanket Cylinders, inspired by Northwest Coast Indian objects. Horses were an unusual inclusion, as were actual woven strips of glass, as seen at right. The Pilchuck Basket series, similarly inspired, was known as the Soft Cylinders. These pieces are less representational and more colorful than the earlier series.

By 1981, the Cylinders had evolved into the Sea Form series, presented in unified color groups, each piece representing a different sea creature or shell. Later Sea Forms were ribbed designs. Chihuly's style was abstract and modernistic, but with naturalistic themes. The ribbed Sea Forms led to the Macchia, or spotted, series. Loosely unified by a basket-like form with undulating rim, these were usually wrapped in a brilliantly colored cord of glass. A short step led to the Persian series, with spreading rims and freely "slumping" vessels. These were subtly Venetian-revival in style and led to the superb Venetian series.

The Venetians were vases in retro shapes, but bigger than life, and often filled with oversized exotic glass flowers or flower-forms. Empty vases were "filled" with surface decorations, applied randomly or in symmetrical swirls, leafy arrangements or abstractions. Chihuly then added putti to the Venetian series, as below.

A statement for the new millennium, Chihuly's angular, monumental Jerusalem cylinders featured applied chunks of shard-rocks. In 1992, he joined ten other artists in creating room-size sculptures for the Corning company. As his work finds homes in prestigious museums around the world, Chihuly's creativity continues to flow unabated.

Venetian Vase with Putti, *c.* 1989

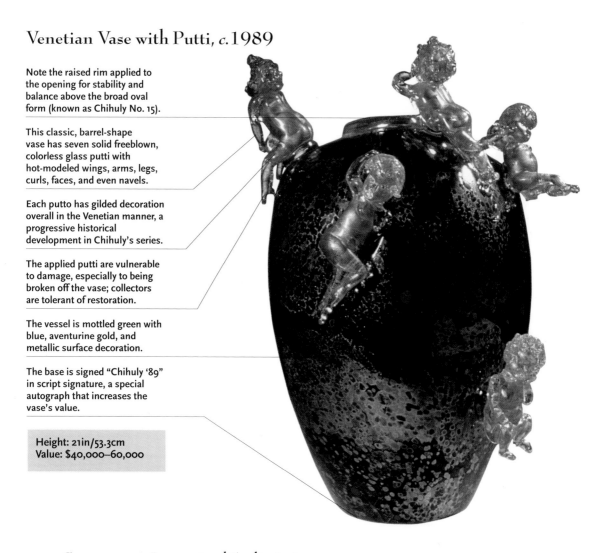

Note the raised rim applied to the opening for stability and balance above the broad oval form (known as Chihuly No. 15).

This classic, barrel-shape vase has seven solid freeblown, colorless glass putti with hot-modeled wings, arms, legs, curls, faces, and even navels.

Each putto has gilded decoration overall in the Venetian manner, a progressive historical development in Chihuly's series.

The applied putti are vulnerable to damage, especially to being broken off the vase; collectors are tolerant of restoration.

The vessel is mottled green with blue, aventurine gold, and metallic surface decoration.

The base is signed "Chihuly '89" in script signature, a special autograph that increases the vase's value.

Height: 21in/53.3cm
Value: $40,000–60,000

Navajo Horse Blanket Glass Cylinder, *c.*1976

Green translucent glass at the rim shows the opal core below that accents the decoration.

The cylinder is a generous size for Chihuly's first series, with classic form, primitive decor, and simplistic graphics.

Dramatic use of the Western brands above the horses conveys the "cowboy" theme.

Color is a valuable decoration factor here: note the blue sky and the two-tone pintos typically ridden by the Navajo people.

Ten speckled-yellow glass triangles are meaningful Native American symbols frequently used on rugs, pottery, and baskets.

Yellow-brown-blue glass threads woven together effectively use the glass as an art medium.

The base is inscribed "Chihuly 1976" in script; this piece of his earliest series is especially coveted by collectors, museums, and even the artist.

Size: 10 x 8in/25.4 x 20.3cm
Value: $60,000–75,000

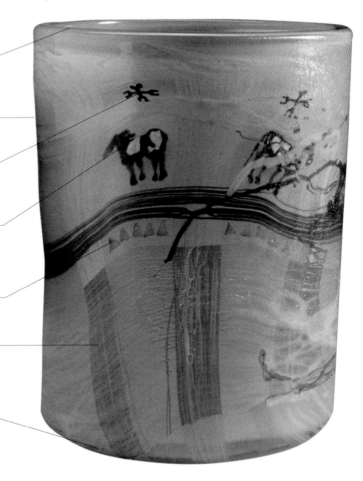

• *Chihuly was known to barter glass and to give it away, so astute collectors near RISD in Rhode Island and probably in Seattle can find early examples of Chihuly's work near where he made it.*
• *Some Venetian vases were made at Pilchuck with Lino Tagliapietra. Many pieces were damaged, making the survivors even more valuable.*
• *Some Chihuly sea forms and Persian series are intended as groups. Collectors should beware buying a partial set at a complete-set price.*
• *Chihuly's "paintings" are hot collectibles. His works on paper sell for about $3,000. On the secondary market, they are a bargain at $900–1,200.*

Artist and Teacher

Dale Chihuly, born in Tacoma, WA, in 1941, earned his MFA in 1968 at the renowned Rhode Island School of Design. A Fulbright Fellowship took him next to Murano, Italy, where he interacted with glass masters of the Venini company under the direction of Ludovico Diaz de Santillana.

Returning to RISD the following year, Chihuly worked closely with Jamie Carpenter, a brilliant student, architect, and glass aficionado. That summer, Chihuly headed the glass program at Haystack Mountain School in Maine, an interdisciplinary art community. There Chihuly conceived the idea of a similar retreat/school specifically for art glass. In 1971, he returned to Washington, where John and Anne Hauberg donated land and co-founded with Chihuly the Pilchuck Glass Center.

Chihuly remained head of the glass department at RISD until 1982. Finally, in 1987, he established his first hot shop in Seattle. This evolved into The Boathouse by the Lake Union ship canal, which houses his business, his glass furnaces, and his private residence. Here his various art glass series are developed, completed, and eventually sent around the world.

Dan Dailey

an Dailey's work is among the most aesthetically challenging for collectors of American Contemporary Studio Glass Art. His work does not repeat the "same old stuff." In 1979, he produced a whimsical wall relief titled "Cafe." It is composed of Vitrolite and plate glass, cut, polished, sandblasted, and assembled with stainless steel accoutrements. It portrays a cartoon character in shades and harlequin costume. In 1987, the Corning Museum of Glass and the Toledo Museum of Art presented an exhibition entitled "Thirty Years of New Glass 1957-1987," and included Dailey's "Cafe" on the cover of the catalog. Two years later, Dailey completed another wall relief called "Study."

In 1989, a banner year for Dailey masterworks, he introduced a series that would add up to at least 22 Mythology Head vases freeblown and applied. These led in 1990 to the Abstract Head series. Meanwhile, also in 1989, Dailey and Lino Tagliapietra collaborated on wonderful scenic vases decorated with enameled cityscapes and hot-applied devices. In this series, both artists are restrained and symmetrically oriented. The work is European in style and locale, as seen in the two examples presented here.

Dailey's recent work has incorporated metals and mounted glass ornamentation. Like other contemporary studio glass, Dailey's work appears rarely in the collectibles market. Such pieces, after all, are available in galleries and directly from the artists. They occasionally appear on the secondary market: auctions, estate sales, websites, and modern art venues. Collectors should study studio artists' work so they'll be able to recognize future treasures.

"Vista Di Sopra" Enameled Blown Glass Vase, c.1989

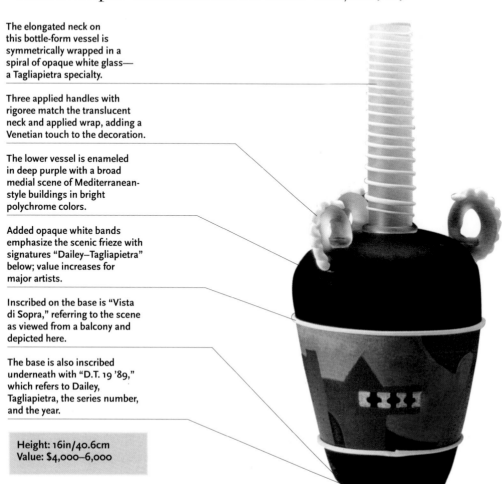

The elongated neck on this bottle-form vessel is symmetrically wrapped in a spiral of opaque white glass—a Tagliapietra specialty.

Three applied handles with rigoree match the translucent neck and applied wrap, adding a Venetian touch to the decoration.

The lower vessel is enameled in deep purple with a broad medial scene of Mediterranean-style buildings in bright polychrome colors.

Added opaque white bands emphasize the scenic frieze with signatures "Dailey–Tagliapietra" below; value increases for major artists.

Inscribed on the base is "Vista di Sopra," referring to the scene as viewed from a balcony and depicted here.

The base is also inscribed underneath with "D.T. 19 '89," which refers to Dailey, Tagliapietra, the series number, and the year.

Height: 16in/40.6cm
Value: $4,000–6,000

"Vedetta" Enameled Blown Glass Vase, c.1989

The flared rim with purple lip wrap is tooled to an elliptical shape to conform with the design of the vessel.

Height adds to the stature of this vessel, shaped as a lighthouse to accent the depicted scene.

The scene refers to *Vedetta*— Italian "sentinel," or outpost. Applied glass balls suggest lights at the scene.

The medial scenic view of buildings and architectural elements is enamel hand-painted in strong primary colors.

Applied purple glass borders frame the scene and match the wraps above, as well as the cased purple headlight balls.

Engraved at the lower edge is "Dailey–Tagliapietra," and inscribed on the base is "D.T. 20–'89 / Vedetta." The piece identifies artists, series number, date, and scene—a value plus.

Height: 19in/48.2cm
Value: $6,000–8,000

- *Collaborations between major artists are rare. Only 20 pieces appear to have been made by Dailey with Tagliapietra, including the pieces seen here, so any collector would treasure one.*
- *Dan Dailey's known use of vitrified enamels in his work is a rarity. Like condition, rarity always influences value.*
- *Dailey's work emphasizes form above all, with color and reflected light in supporting roles. His art speaks of humor and pleasure, a step many artists never reach, or care to.*
- *Collectors can find Dailey's work in modern art galleries and shops catering to contemporary decorative arts. Remember the Internet— online searches can help locate virtually anything.*

The Path of a Master

The son of an industrial designer, Dailey was born in Philadelphia in 1947. In 1967, he enrolled at the Philadelphia College of Art. By this time, the Studio Glass Movement was well underway. While a student, Dailey received a grant to set up a glass studio. He subsequently went in full pursuit of glass-making excellence, earning an MFA from the Rhode Island School of Design, then traveling to Murano to study with masters.

After Murano and two trips to France, Dailey took a job with the Daum glassworks. He returned to the United States in 1973 and accepted a position in Boston at the Massachusetts College of Art. He founded their advanced glass art program and served as director and master teacher, a position he held for the next 10 years. During his tenure, Dailey designed and executed progressively more complex art forms—work that continues today.

Dominick Labino

In scientific circles, Dominick Labino is best known for his work with tiles for the Apollo Space program. His artistic legacy, however, lies in the development, with Harvey Littleton, of the small furnace for handblowing glass. This crucial advance allowed artists to produce glass art outside of the industrial complex. It also launched the Studio Glass Movement of the late 1960s that sped across the United States and through Europe with the speed of light, reflected.

Once started, Labino became a prolific studio craftsman. His best-known work is probably the glass mural he assembled for the Gallery of Glass at the Toledo Museum of Art. Created in 1970, the mural was an architectural installation before its time, one of the first such works to emanate from the Studio Glass Movement.

Labino's "Emergence" series of glass sculptures includes his most recognizable pieces and the ones most frequently found in today's collectibles marketplace. They arose from Labino's artistic vision of colored levels contained within a single blow of glass, emerging from the central core in a series of veils of color. These multicolored sculptures were created throughout the 1970s and illustrate the progression of Labino's proficiency, and sense of order and symmetry. In early vessels, the veils recalled the Sommerso vases of Flavio Poli for Seguso, while the form suggested Tapio Wirkkala's work for Iittala. Once Labino changed the form from vessel to solid sculpture, his work became truly unique and free of precedent. The example illustrated at right shows the subtlety of the design and coloration.

Collectors can find Labino's work in the usual venues, especially where modern decorations and art forms are presented. Glass enthusiasts are anxious to have even a single piece of Labino glass as an historical memento. Most of the work is reasonably priced, especially pieces like the mold-blown animal series he made in his later years. Most of his pieces are inscribed with his name and the date.

Freeblown Green Studio Glass Vase, c.1965

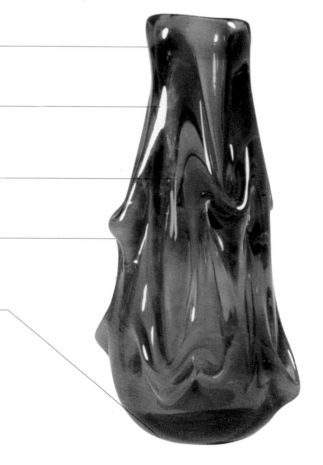

This is a good size for a freeblown vessel.

This green is strong and clear, with occasional opal inclusions that add visual impact. Collectors want this.

The surface is pulled and tooled into decorative protrusions and swirling ridges, softened at the furnace; such hot decor adds value.

This is a unique but not rare example of Labino's work; he made many pieces, but few masterworks. Value reflects this.

The base is inscribed "Labino 5-1083," reflecting the model and color number systems used to record results of experimentation.

Height: 7in/17.7cm
Value: $500–700

Emergence Series Sculpture, c.1976

The flattened oval shape comes to a symmetrical apex not often found in Labino's sculptural pieces.

Height is average for this series and works well for completion of the design motif.

The central teardrop bubble is perfectly positioned, evoking a flame image; the unusual offset bubble above left adds interest and value.

Pink shades predominate, with the tallest veil in the palest color, and contrast with the clear glass, to increase impact and value.

The sculpture is smooth and weighty—both desirable tactile features that increase value.

The polished base is inscribed "Labino 4-76," dating the piece within the Emergence series, a collector's plus.

Height: 7in/17.7cm
Value: $4,500–5,500

• *Labino's significance to the Contemporary Studio Glass Movement derived mostly from his research and development, which heightened the collectibility of his glass.*

• *Labino's Emergence pieces have been highly collectible since they appeared in the 1970s. As works-in-progress, the sculptures appealed to knowledgeable collectors and fellow artists. Look for variations on the theme.*

• *A cover story on Labino's work in the* National Geographic Magazine *(Vol. 184, #6) created an instant collectible of the Emergence sculpture on the magazine's cover.*

• *Contemporary Glass, by Ray and Lee Grover, lavished attention on Labino that gave further impetus to the collectibility of his work.*

The Studio Glass Movement

Two men are generally credited with the development of what we know as the Contemporary American Studio Glass Movement. Harvey Littleton, a ceramics teacher at the University of Wisconsin, saw an analogous relationship between the sculpting of clay and the manipulation of hot molten glass. In 1962, Littleton arranged a series of glass workshops at the Toledo Museum of Art. He called on Dominick Labino, then a vice president and research director at the the Johns-Manville Fiber Glass Corp., to act as a technical consultant.

Labino provided the workshop with samples of shard-marbles used in the production of fiberglass and advised on adjustments needed to blow glass with the small furnace facilities at hand. Thus was born the technique that allowed artists to create their glassware in small studios without huge furnaces and industrial apparatus.

Dominick Labino started blowing glass in his personal laboratory in 1963. To create a viable studio, he designed a small furnace, blowpipes, tooling devices, and annealing equipment that he made available to other studios as well. He provided workshops for the Toledo Museum of Art and their School of Design. After his retirement from Johns-Manville in 1965, Labino promoted the Studio Glass Movement at every opportunity.

Paul J. Stankard

In the last quarter of the 20th century, collectors discovered a new kind of paperweight, made by Paul J. Stankard. Not always small, not always round, it employed an artistic vocabulary that celebrates the poetic nature of the environment. To achieve this, Stankard researched and experimented for years, seeking out the flameworking secrets of the paperweight masters of old. Once found, he updated and perfected those secrets with modern equipment and capabilities. Then, Stankard shared.

In 1981, a London gallery, Spink & Son Ltd., presented a retrospective exhibition of Stankard paperweights dating to 1974. Their small hardcover catalog included photographs in exquisite color and detail of some 70 different paperweights, the earliest dating from 1971 to 1973. The exhibition and its catalog brought advanced collectors to Stankard's work, many for the first time, and gave significant impetus to its collectibility.

In 1986, Stankard led a workshop at the Wheaton Village complex in Millville, NJ, where he demonstrated the secrets of paperweight production. He frequently offers programs and demonstrations of flameworking there, as well as at the well-known Penland School of Handicrafts in Asheville, NC. He is a participating faculty member at the Pilchuck School of Glass outside Seattle, WA, and a Fellow of the Corning Museum of Glass in Corning, NY. His paperweights are exhibited in museums globally.

Beginning in the 1980s, Stankard introduced two innovations to his paperweights that have significantly increased the popularity and value of his work. First, he introduced bees in his weights—naturalistic, full-bodied glass insects, with the floral inclusions. In the same period, Stankard expanded his botanicals, including full-root systems with his flora. To this realistic representation, Stankard added "root people," poetic creatures that suit the spirit of nature, if not its laws. Paperweights with root people sell for increasingly high prices and seem to be headed for greater heights, in value and appeal, in the collectibles marketplace.

Stankard Botanical Paperweight, *c.*1983

The squared top has polished beveled edges and side corners; such detail increases value.

This is smaller than later examples of this form, a product of Stankard's experiments.

Flameworked glass depiction shows prickly pear cactus in botanically perfect design.

The colors in the blossoms are accurate representations; each petal, filament, and anther is correctly placed.

The glass "sand" layer and two levels of this compound paperweight increase its value.

The lower section shows a botanically correct, detailed root system—a value plus.

The early mark inscribed at the lower edge, "Stankard 58 1983," precedes copyright-marked pieces and numbering systems.

Height: 3⁷/₈in/9.8cm
Value: $3,000–5,000

Morning Glory Paperweight with Root People, *c.* 1986

This two-part paperweight uses sandy glass "soil" as a natural separation between levels, a rare piece in Stankard's production.

These flamework glass morning glories with three flowers in separate stages of development are a Stankard specialty.

Colors of pale lavender stripe on white are botanically accurate and artistically exceptional, and the subtle green shading true to nature.

Extremely fine details created in flamework by the artist and undamaged in the process of casing with clear glass add considerable value.

The underside of this early weight depicts a botanical garden with four dancing root people (not seen)—very collectible.

The inscription at the lower edge, "Paul J. Stankard Y335 1986," is an early mark for root people and possibly unique.

Size: 3in/7.6cm dia.
Value: $4,000–6,000

• *Both of the pieces shown here, with "root people" and botanicals, have become popular collectibles at increasingly high prices.*
• *Limited edition collectibles are tolerated by collectors if the series includes relatively few pieces—the lower the number, the higher the price.*
• *Collectors, always after unique pieces, pay higher prices for "early" examples and experimental work.*
• *The more categories a collectible piece fits, the stronger the price. Stankard's work sells to collectors of paperweights, studio glass art, botanists, and enthusiasts.*
• *Paperweights with chips or scratches lose value proportionate to the damage.*

Flamework

By 1964, Stankard was working in Vineland, NJ, a town with a long history of glass-making. Among the locals were the T.C. Wheaton Glass Factory in neighboring Millville, the Vineland Glass Works of Durand Art Glass fame, and Wheaton Village, eventual home of the Creative Glass Center of America. Glass-making had supported the area since the 1800s.

As Stankard worked at the Andrews Scientific Glass Company, his interest in the technique of flameworking grew. He learned to manipulate glass in the flame of a lamp-like device similar to a Bunsen burner. The so-called "lamp-working" had been used for years, but was underemployed by artists and guarded by artisans who created paperweights, marbles, buttons, and similar ornamentals, usually cased in clear glass. Stankard spent some five years perfecting original techniques. At age 28, he made financial arrangements that enabled him to work full time on his paperweights. By 1976, he had his own studio in the countryside of Mantua, NJ.

The success of Paul J. Stankard paperweights is due to three primary factors: his mastery of glass flameworking, his intimate knowledge of local flora, and his ability to express nature's beauty poetically in his glass.

Lino Tagliapietra

For collectors, Lino Tagliapietra's work is difficult to pin down. He was something of a rolling stone, studying here, teaching there, and collaborating with various artists in Italy, the United States, Scandinavia, and elsewhere. He gave freely of his knowledge, gaining the respect of studio glass workers all over the world. He taught at the Pilchuck School of Glass beginning in the 1970s and worked with Dale Chihuly at the Rhode Island School of Design.

During the 1970s, while Tagliapietra was artistic director and glass master at Effetre International, he designed and produced a number of limited edition lines. His "Saturno" designs were among the most popular— large platter-like planet-vessels in numerous colors surrounded by broad, flat rings. Also produced in large numbers were his parallelepiped, squared vessels with horizontal banding, and the "Stone of Venice" group created with Marina Angelin. Into the 1980s, Tagliapietra collaborated with a number of glass artists in "series"

productions. The turquoise vase illustrated here is an example of this kind of work. These studio "repeats" often show up on the secondary market. Most can be readily identified by the inscription on the base that names the artist, collaborating artist if any, studio, date, number of pieces in the series, and the sequential number of the particular piece. This is valuable information. Tagliapietra also produced collaborative glass in multiples of similar design that represent variations on a theme. These items come on today's market from time to time and are usually more valuable than limited edition series.

In 1998, Peter Aldridge, Steuben's Vice President and Creative Director, invited Tagliapietra to create a group of Steuben crystal designs at the Corning glassworks. The resulting masterworks are brilliant examples of dexterity and virtuosity, and of the purity and clarity, of perhaps the finest crystal in the world. Today, 50 years after he began, Tagliapietra has begun to produce his own masterworks in his own studio on Murano.

Vaso a Incalmo Limited Edition Vase, c.1984

The folded rim at the top repeats the squat form of the vessel.

The bowl-form vase has a good heft and a polished surface that appeals to collectors.

The turquoise color evokes the Native American gemstone, derived from Tagliapietra's visit to the Southwest, perhaps.

The squat form conforms to that of a variety of baskets and pottery, adding value.

The black stripes in the central incalmo band are aligned symmetrically and add value.

This vase is number 10 in a limited series of 100 pieces; low numbers offer most value.

Marina Angelin's joint involvement is indicated on the base with the mark, "Tagliapietra / Angelin Murano 10 / 100 1984 Effetre International."

Size: 9 x 13in/22.8 x 33cm
Value: $2,000–2,500

Collaborative "Venetian" Vase with Dale Chihuly, *c.*1989

The applied twisted-rope rim at top is repeated on the base edge, both of solid blue that match internal splotches.

The cylindrical form appeals to collectors as a typically assertive Chihuly design.

The base glass is transparent with splotches of brilliant red, blue turquoise, and with gold-foil squares interspersed.

Tagliapietra has applied the ribbon swirls in an apparently haphazard way but maintains a balanced symmetrical alignment.

Five spiral-twirled glass ribbons both match and complement the cylinder; this artful design increases value.

The base is inscribed "Chihuly '89;" Tagliapietra made the vase at RISD under Chihuly's direction.

Height: 19in/48.2cm
Value: $18,000–25,000

• *Tagliapietra's limited edition items will continue to increase in value, largely because so few exist.*
• *Tagliapietra's multiples are one-of-a-kind pieces with variations in each specimen of a design. This makes them more valuable as collectibles.*
• *Recently, Tagliapietra has been manipulating the work after it cools, as with his 1998 Steuben masterworks. These are partially engraved, a desirable addition.*
• *Tagliapietra's use of new treatments is reflected in recent work. Andries Copier and Venetian revival influences appear in some pieces.*
• *Collectors should be aware that new studio work is difficult to find and expensive to acquire. A secondary market has not yet been established for the Tagliapietra masterworks.*

Master Glass Blower

After Paolo Venini died in 1959, his successor opened the Venini glass house to artists, visitors, and students as never before. Meanwhile, the American Studio Glass Movement was under way, with glass artists looking toward Murano. For Tagliapietra, this was a two-way street. After achieving master status, Tagliapietra worked with Venini, Galliano Ferro (A.Ve.M.), La Murrina Moretti, and especially Effetre Internazionale, where he served as chief artistic designer and master glass blower throughout the 1970s. In the late 1970s, he was invited to teach at the Pilchuck Glass School, co-founded by Dale Chihuly and the Hauberg family near Seattle. Thus began a series of demonstrations and tours to studios around the globe, as well as chances to collaborate with studio glass artists.

In 1996, Tagliapietra built his own studio on Murano, where he continues to create unique forms in studio glass.

▶ *Steuben* **Cire Perdue**
Translucent Glass
Sculpture of Three Dolphins,
signed "F. Carder 1947."
$25,000–28,000.
5¼ × 7¼ in / 13.3 × 18.4cm

Sources & References

Where to See and Buy Art Glass

Where to See

It was my good fortune to travel to 27 U.S. cities with Antiques Roadshow™ as an appraiser of art glass. While appraisers do not have much time for sightseeing, the first thing our group always did after we checked in was to go directly to the art museum recommended by the locals. This is exactly what I recommend to you as potential art glass collectors whenever you travel to a city or town. Find the locally respected museums, historical societies, and galleries associated with your area of special interest. You will be glad you took the time to visit.

Before you travel, check websites for local chambers of commerce, or call the 800 numbers for them (call 800-555-1212). If you have a contact in the town where your favorite glass was made, great! If not, find one. Check the local public library or chamber of commerce, or look in the local Sunday paper.

So many museums and galleries display art glass, it is impossible to mention any without slighting many more. Following are just a few I have visited with some frequency and, therefore, can confidently recommend:

The Art Institute of Chicago
Chicago, IL
This museum could be the focus of an entire vacation. The triptych window of Frank Lloyd Wright, commissioned for the Coonley children's playhouse, by itself is worth the visit. The entire art glass collection at the Institute is outstanding.

The Chrysler Museum of Art
Norfolk, VA
A museum complex made up of 55 galleries and several historic homes. To an art glass aficionado, this museum offers rare and unusual pieces gathered throughout the years from outstanding collections. Once located in New England, the museum has a fine base of late 19th-century American art glass.

The Corning Museum of Glass
Corning, NY
A great museum for all ages. The museum has recently undergone an extensive renovation and expansion program in honor of its 50th anniversary, so if you visited in the past, you are in for some surprises. The Rockwell collection of Frederick Carder's Steuben art glass has moved into the new quarters. Next door, The Studio is a working glassblowing facility where you can observe the making of art glass from start to finish.

The Currier Gallery of Art
Manchester, NH
A gallery that lays claim to one of the choice collections of American art glass, with Amberina, Burmese, Peachblow, and Crown Milano in pristine condition. Call ahead to make sure the collection is on the scene, as it seems to travel a bit. Contemporary Studio art glass is part of the mix.

The High Museum of Art
Atlanta, GA
A permanent collection of art glass full of outstanding examples and many of them. The architecture is wonderful as well.

The Jones Museum of Glass and Ceramics
Douglas Hill, ME
A charming museum with a wonderfully laid out arrangement of art glass that gives historical perspective to the collections. A special exhibit of fakes and reproductions arranged in careful juxtaposition with the originals is especially effective and informative. Dorothy-Lee Jones has arranged symposiums, study groups, and various activities for collectors; you might want to make contact before your trip.

The Lightner Museum
St. Augustine, FL
An eclectic museum, housed in one of the Flagler resort hotels built in 1888. This venue has a little of everything and an especially superb collection of American Brilliant Period cut glass.

The Metropolitan Museum of Art
New York, NY
An amazing museum that presents, among many other treasures, a collection of spectacular art glass.

The Charles Hosmer Morse Museum of American Art
Winter Park, FL
Commonly called the Tiffany Museum, this museum houses the most extraordinary collection of the work of Louis Comfort Tiffany to be found. Assembled by Jeanette Genius McKean and her husband, Hugh McKean, the museum installed the entire Tiffany room exhibited at the 1893 Columbian Exposition.

The Portland Museum of Art
Portland, ME

A small but choice collection of art glass. Not far from the waterfront, up the street from the Old Port, and next door to the Children's Museum, the PMA's selection will surprise you.

Wheaton Village
Millville, NJ

A museum complex that includes the Museum of American Glass, with more than 6,500 items on display at any given time, including an extensive collection of Durand art glass. The Creative Glass Center of America is located in the village, and the T.C. Wheaton Glass Factory operates all day, every day.

The Wolfsonian
South Miami Beach, FL

A small but dynamic museum that draws from some 70,000 objects in an ever-changing display, presented in the heart of the Art Deco/SoBe area of Miami. Don't think if you go once, you've seen it all. It warrants checking out as often as you have opportunity.

Where to Buy

For the potential collector of art glass, there are a great many venues and opportunities for acquiring new pieces. You probably already know about most of them, but a few tips might be helpful:

First, do your homework. Knowing what you are looking for will assuredly help you find it. Making use of bibliographies *(see pages 170–171)* and museums can give you a good start. Or obtain more specific materials from your local bookstore and library; aside from printed resources, you can use their Internet connections. Do not hesitate to ask for help.

If you know what you want but just can't find it, *check out the antique shows and shops, the galleries, studios, and consignment shops,* and talk to professionals who are reliable dealers in your sought-after collectibles. Allow them to add you to their list if you like. The same applies to the auction galleries. Professional auction houses provide a great service for their customers, gathering in one place the materials the collectors and buyers are actively seeking. Request their brochures so you will know what they have coming up, and when.

Subscribe to the appropriate journals, magazines, and collectors' guides. One way to find these materials is to check out the entrance tables at shows, shops, and auction galleries. Publishers of specialty journals always leave "freebies" in the locations frequented by buyers and collectors. Check them all out, find the ones that interest you, and make your choices.

Join a club. The National American Glass Club provides an "Organization Director,"—compiled by *Glass Collector's Digest*—of collector's clubs and associations. These groups are always looking for members to add to their rosters. They offer a link to like-minded people with whom to share your specialty enthusiasm. They organize meetings, symposia, study groups, conventions, and swap meets; they also take tours, publish newsletters, and establish websites. You can participate as much or as little as you wish.

Contact the National American Glass Club directly at: Box 8489, Silver Spring, MD 20907.

Akro Agate Collectors Club
10 Bailey Street
Clarksburg, WV 26301

Aladdin Knights
3935 Kelley Road
Kevil, KY 42053

American Carnival Glass Association
P.O. Box 235
Littlestown, PA 17340

American Cut Glass Association
P.O. Box 482
Ramona, CA 92065-0482

Antique/Art Glass Salt Shaker Collectors Society
2832 Rapidan Trail
Maitland, FL 32751

Cambridge Collectors, Inc.
P.O. Box 416
Cambridge, OH 43725

Candlewick Club
275 Milledge Terrace
Athens, GA 30606

Collectible Carnival Glass Association
2360 North Old S.R. 9
Columbus, IN 47203

Collectors of Findlay Glass
P.O. Box 256
Findlay, OH 45939-0256

The Corning Museum of Glass
One Museum Way
Corning, NY 14830-2253

Czechoslovakian Collectors Guild International
P.O. Box 901395
Kansas City, MO 64190

Early American Pattern Glass Society
P.O. Box 340023
Columbus, OH 43234-0023

Fenton Art Glass Collectors
P.O. Box 384
Williamstown, WV 26187

Fostoria Glass Collectors, Inc.
P.O. Box 1625
Orange, CA 92668

The Fostoria Glass Society
P.O. Box 826
Moundsville, WV 26041

Fostoria (OH) Glass Association
109 Main Street
Fostoria, OH 44830

H.C. Fry Glass Society
P.O. Box 41
Beaver, PA 15009

Glass Collectors Club of Toledo
6122 Cross Trails Road
Sylvania, OH 43560-1714

Glass Museum Foundation
1157 N. Orange, Box 921
Redlands, CA 92373

Glass Research Society of New Jersey
Wheaton Village
Millville, NJ 08332

Heart of America Carnival Glass Association
3048 Tamarak Drive
Manhattan, KS 66502

Heisey Collectors of America, Inc.
169 West Church Street
Newark, OH 43055

International Carnival Glass Association
Box 306
Mentone, IN 46539

International Perfume Bottle Association
Box 529
Vienna, VA 22183

The Jones Museum of Glass and Ceramics
35 Douglas Mountain Road
Sebago, ME 04029

Lightener Museum
P.O. Box 334
St Augustine, FL 32084

Marble Collector's Society
P.O. Box 222
Trumbull, CT 06611

Mt. Washington Art Glass Society
P.O. Box 24094
Fort Worth, TX 76124

National American Glass Club
P.O. Box 8489
Silver Spring, MD 20907

National Depression Glass Association
P.O. Box 8264
Wichita, KS 67208

National Duncan Glass Society
P.O. Box 965
Washington, PA 15301

National Fenton Glass Society
P.O. Box 4008
Marietta, OH 45750

National Greentown Glass
1807 West Madison Street
Kokomo, IN 46901

National Imperial Glass Collectors Society
P.O. Box 534
Bellaire, OH 43906

National Milk Glass Collectors
1113 Birchwood Drive
Garland, TX 75043

National Westmoreland Glass Collectors Club
P.O. Box 100
Grapeville, PA 15634

New England Carnival Glass Club
10 Seminole Road
Canton, MA 02021

Old Morgantown Glass Collectors Guild
P.O. Box 894
Morgantown, WV 26507

Paden City Glass Collectors Society
P.O. Box 139
Paden City, WV 26159

Paperweight Collector's Association
P.O. Box 1263
Beltsville, MD 20704-1263

Phoenix and Consolidated Collectors
P.O. Box 182082
Arlington, TX 76096-2083

Rose Bowl Collectors
1111 Delps Road
Danielsville, PA 18038

Stretch Glass Society
P.O. Box 573
Hampshire, IL 60140

Tiffin Glass Collectors Club
P.O. Box 554
Tiffin, OH 4883

Toothpick Holder Collectors
Red Arrow Highway, Box 246
Sawyer, MI 49125

The Toy Dish Collectors
P.O. Box 159
Bethlehem, CT 06751

Vaseline Glass Collectors, Inc.
P.O. Box 125
Russellville, MO 65074

Westmoreland Glass Society
513 Fifth Avenue
Coralville, IA 51141

Whimsey Glass Club
20 William Street
Danville, NY 14437

You can also buy art glass for your collection at auction galleries, large and small, local and international, throughout the United States and, indeed, throughout the world. Auction houses provide not only the opportunity to purchase collectible items, but also a most important learning experience. Before the auction begins, you will be able to see the art glass on public exhibition and, within certain guidelines, actually handle the pieces. The "hands-on" approach is absolutely the best way to learn about your chosen field of collecting. You may also, of course, ask questions, check out the catalog descriptions, and learn from the knowledgeable gallery experts.

The following auction galleries are among the best in the United States, and several also present their specialty auctions abroad:

Bonhams & Brooks
Montpelier Street
London SW7 1HH
www.bonhams.com

Frank Boos Gallery
420 Enterprise Court
Bloomfield Hills, MI 48302
www.boos.com

Butterfields
7601 Sunset Boulevard
Los Angeles, CA 90046
www.butterfields.com

Christie's
20 Rockefeller Plaza
New York, NY 10020
www.christies.com

William Doyle Galleries
175 East 87 Street
New York, NY 10021
www.doyles.com

Ken Farmer Auction Gallery
105A Harrison Street
Radford, VA 24141

Northeast Auctions
93 Pleasant Street
Portsmouth, NH 03801

Phillips Auction Galleries
406 East 79 Street
New York, NY 10021
www.phillips-auctions.com

Skinner, Inc.
63 Park Plaza
Boston, MA 02116
www.skinnerinc.com

Sotheby's
1334 York Avenue
New York, NY 10021
www.sothebys.com

Weschler's
909 E Street NW
Washington, DC 20004
www.weschlers.com

Other Sources of Information

Arwas, Victor. *Art Deco.* New York, NY: Harry N. Abrams, Inc., 1992.

Arwas, Victor. *Glass: Art Nouveau to Art Deco.* New York, NY: Harry N. Abrams, Inc., 1987.

Arwas, Victor. *The Art of Glass.* Berks, England: Andreas Papadakis, 1996.

Avila, George C. *The Pairpoint Glass Story.* New Bedford, MA: Reynolds-DeWalt Printing, Inc., 1968.

Baldwin, Gary, and Carno, Lee. *Moser: Artistry in Glass.* Marietta, OH: Antique Publications, 1988, revised 1997.

Barlow, Raymond E., and Kaiser, Joan E. *The Glass Industry in Sandwich, Vol. 1–4.* Windham, NH: Barlow-Kaiser Publishing Co., 1983.

Barovier, Marina. *Art of the Barovier.* Venice, Italy: Arsenale Editrice, 1993.

Beard, Sir Geoffrey W. *Nineteenth Century Cameo Glass.* London, 1977.

Blount, Berniece (sic) and Henry. *French Cameo Glass.* Des Moines, IA: Wallace-Homestead Co., 1968.

Brunhammer, Yvonne, et al. *Art Nouveau Belgium France.* Houston, TX: Rice University, 1976.

Cudd, Viola N. *Heisey Glassware.* Brenham, TX: Herrmann Print Shop, 1969.

Daum, Noel. *Daum: Mastery of Glass.* Edita, Switzerland, 1980.

Dawes, Nicholas M. *Lalique Glass.* New York, NY: Crown Publishers, 1986.

Deboni, Franco. *I Vetri Venini.* Torino, Italy: Umberto Allemandi, 1987.

Deboni, Franco. *Venini Glass.* Torino, Italy: Umberto Allemandi, 1996.

Diaz de Santillana, Anna Venini. *Venini: Art and Design in Glass from Venice.* Tacoma Art Museum, 2000.

Dimitroff, Thomas P. *Frederick Carder and Steuben Glass.* Atglen, PA: Schiffer Publishing Ltd., 1998.

Duncan, Alastair, and de Bartha, Georges. *Glass by Galle.* New York, NY: Harry N. Abrams, Inc., 1984.

Eidelberg, Martin, et al. *1935–1965: What Modern Was.* New York, NY: Harry N. Abrams, Inc., 1991.

Fauster, Carl U. *Libbey Glass Since 1818.* Toledo, OH: Len Beach Press, 1979.

Frantz, Susanne K. *Contemporary Glass.* New York, NY: Harry N. Abrams, Inc., 1989.

Fusco, Tony. *Art Deco.* New York, NY: Avon Books, 1993.

Forsythe, Ruth A. *Made in Czechoslovakia.* Galena, OH: Ruth A. Forsythe, 1982.

Gardner, Paul V. *The Glass of Frederick Carder.* New York, NY: Crown Publishers, 1971; reissued 2002.

Grover, Lee and Ray. *Art Glass Nouveau.* Rutland, VT: Charles Tuttle Co., 1967.

Grover, Lee and Ray. *Contemporary Art Glass.* New York, NY: Crown Publishers, 1975.

Grover, Lee and Ray. *English Cameo Glass.* New York, NY: Crown Publishers, 1980.

Hajdamach, Charles R. *British Glass 1800–1914.* Antique Collectors Club, 1991.

Heiremans, Marc. *20th Century Murano Glass.* Stuttgart, Germany: Arnoldsche, 1996.

Herlitz-Gezelius, Ann Marie. *Orrefors: A Swedish Glassplant.* Stockholm, Sweden: Atlantis, 1984.

Hillier, Bevis. *Art Deco.* London, England: Studio Vista Ltd., 1968.

Koch, Robert. *Louis C. Tiffany: Rebel in Glass.* New York, NY: Crown Publishers, 1964.

Koch, Robert. *Louis C. Tiffany's Art Glass.* New York, NY: Crown Publishers, 1977.

Koch, Robert. *Louis Comfort Tiffany's Glass—Bronzes—Lamps.* New York, NY: Crown Publishers, 1971.

Lalique, Marc and Marie-Claude. *Lalique Par Lalique.* Paris, France: Societé Lalique, 1977.

Leier, Ray, Peters, Jan, and Wallace, Kevin. *Contemporary Glass.* Madison, WI: Guild Publishing, 2001.

Mac Neil, Malcolm Neil. "Quezal Art Glass: Part 1," *Antiques.* January 1998.

Madigan, Mary Jean. *Steuben Glass: An American Tradition in Crystal.* New York, NY: Harry N. Abrams, Inc., 1982.

Marcilhac, Felix. R. *Lalique 1860–1945.* Paris, France: Les Editions de Lameteur, 1989, 1994.

McClinton, Catherine Morrison. *Lalique For Collectors.* New York, NY: Charles Scribners, 1975.

McKearin, George S. and Helen. *American Glass.* New York, NY: Crown Publishers, 1941, 1948.

Mentasti, Rosa Barovier. *Venetian Glass: 1890–1990.* Venice, Italy: Assenale Editrice, 1992.

Meschi, Edward J. *Durand: The Man and His Glass.* Marietta, OH: Antique Publications, 1998.

Neuwirth, Waltraud. *Loetz Austria 1900.* Wein, Austria: 1986.

Neuwirth, Waltraud. *Loetz Austria 1905–1918.* Wein, Austria: 1986.

Opie, Jennifer Hawkins. *Scandinavia: Ceramics and Glass in the Twentieth Century.* New York, NY: Rizzoli, 1990.

Padgett, Leonard. *Pairpoint Glass.* Des Moines, IA: Wallace-Holmstead Co., 1979.

Pepper, Adelaide. *The Glass Gaffers of New Jersey.* New York, NY: Charles Scribner, 1971.

Revi, Albert Christian. *American Art Nouveau Glass.* New York, NY: Thomas Nelson, 1968.

Revi, Albert Christian. *Nineteenth Century Glass.* New York, NY: Thomas Nelson, 1959.

Rheims, Maurice. *The Flowering of Art Nouveau.* New York, NY: Harry N. Abrams, Inc., 1965.

Riche, Helmut, and Schmidt, Eva. *Italian Glass: Murano-Milan.* Munich, Germany: Prestal, 1997.

Spillman, Jane Shadel. *The American Cut Glass Industry and T.G. Hawkes.* Corning, NY: Corning Museum of Glass, 1996.

Spillman, Jane Shadel, and Farrar, Estelle Sinclaire. *The Cut and Engraved Glass of Corning, 1858–1977.* Corning, NY: Corning Museum of Glass, 1977.

Stankard, Paul J. "Flora in Glass: Paperweights by Paul J. Stankard," Spink & Son Ltd. Exhibition, London, England, 1981.

Taylor, Gay LeCleire. "Distinctively Durand: The Art Glass of Vineland, New Jersey," Museum of American Glass Exhibition, 1988.

Truitt, Robert and Deborah. *Collectible Bohemian Glass 1880–1940.* Kensington, MD: B&D Glass, 1995.

Warmus, William. *The Venetians: Modern Glass 1919–1990.* New York, NY: Muriel Karasik Gallery, 1989.

Wilson, Jack D. *Phoenix and Consolidated Art Glass, 1926–1980.* Marietta, OH: Antique Publications, 1989.

Wilson, Kenneth. *American Glass 1760–1930.* New York, NY: Crown Publishers, 1994.

A Glossary of Terms

The terms included in this glossary focus primarily on decorations, both integral and added on, that are most often associated with art glass produced between 1880 and the present. For the most part, these are words you will encounter in the collectibles marketplace, rather than highly technical or scientific terminology. Only a few names of particular lines or series of art glass have been included, and only because they are specific to a glassworks and can be easily identified as you seek them out. It might also be helpful to obtain a pocket dictionary for translating from Italian, French, or another language to English. Using such a resource often allows you to better understand the language of glassmaking.

Annealing: the tempering process required for glass to cool down and adjust to the heat and stresses of glassblowing. Cooling-off takes place in a special oven called a *lehr.* An annealing crack that occurs during the annealing process is considered damage.

Aventurine: glass containing tiny particles of shiny metallic dust, sometimes inserted between layers of glass as decoration, appearing golden or silvery and sometimes adding color.

Cameo carved: descriptive term for glass decoration achieved by carving or acid etching through one or more layers of colored glass.

Canes: rods of glass with internal decorations that can be sliced off and inserted into or between layers of glass at the fire. The rods fuse with the surround as decoration. Used in paperweights, Millefiori decorations, and signature murrines.

Cased glass: layers of glass fused at the fire inside or upon the core body of glass. Cameo glass may be cased with several layers, which are then carved or etched.

Cire perdue: literally, "lost wax;" a technique of warm work in which melted glass is poured into a mold created from a wax sculpture. A sculpture of glass replaces the wax figure.

Cluthra: glass with bubbles—large or small, uniform or at random—added to the mix at the fire. Often used in Scottish glass, called *clutha,* it was also made by Steuben and many European glassworks.

Crackled: term for glass purposely decorated with fine cracks overall, achieved by abruptly lowering the temperature during processing. Durand's crackle ware is a collectible example. *Craquelle* was made by many European glass factories, not the least of which were Gallé, Leveille, and Rousseau.

Cold decoration: refers to work with glass that occurs after the annealing process; includes acid or machine etching, carving, sandblasting, handpainting, and various applications.

Corroso: rough textured surface on art glass created by the application of acid or abrasive materials; used often by Murano artists. Tiffany's Cypriote and Lava glass are examples.

Crizzled: term for glass with a network of tiny lines caused by a faulty batch or stress in the blowing process. These cannot be seen except in strong light, cannot be felt, and are found only occasionally in colorless crystal, Intarsia, and similar ware.

Diatreta: Roman technique of cold-glass under-carving of a layered vessel by removing all but structural struts for support. Frederick Carder at Steuben achieved this; Barry Sautner has perfected the methods with pinpoint sandblasting and minute in-sculpting.

Enameling: a mixture of powdered colored glass, wetting agents, and vitrifying material used to color and "paint" decoration on art glass, then heated to fuse decoration to the object.

Favrile: trade name Louis Comfort Tiffany chose for his art glass, bronze and enamel work, pottery, and jewelry. It is a variation of the German word *fabrile,* meaning handmade. It often appears as part of the signature mark inscribed on Tiffany glass.

Flamework: also called *lampwork,* a warm-work technique whereby glass rods are manipulated and shaped in the heat of a burner. Extremely fine detail-work can be achieved by this method and is often used by studio glass artists.

Flashing: application to a vessel of a thin layer of glass or paint, which can then be etched or decorated by simple techniques; often found on Bohemian glassware using dark red or amber on colorless glass.

Fluogravure: technique of acid-etching enamel-painted glass objects with decorative designs or scenes; used most effectively by the Muller Glassworks.

Frosted glass: glass with a clouded surface achieved by application of hydrofluoric acid and ammonia (do not try this at home!); used frequently to highlight and contrast design features. René Lalique was master of this technique, copied by many, surpassed by none.

Fusing: the bonding of two or more sections of glass. Murano Glassworks fused glass in *mosaica, incalmo, pezzato,* and *zanfirico* techniques; contemporary kiln work uses warm fusing with extraordinary results.

Iridescence: the lustrous metallic surface decoration on glass achieved by the judicious use of metallic oxides and employed to simulate ancient glasses; used extensively by Lobmeyr, Tiffany, Loetz, Webb, Quezal, Steuben, Kew

Blas, Trevaise, Durand, Imperial, and numerous Bohemian companies.

Martele: the French decorative method of carving a "hammered" texture into glass. Gallé used the technique to perfection. On the island of Murano, the cut design was named *battuto*.

Marquetry: the technique of implanting colored glass into a vessel at the fire so that it may later be carved during the decoration of the surface.

Millefiori: canes, or rods, of glass, usually depicting flowers, that are made to be sliced and inserted into vessels at the surface or between layers of glass. Tiffany and Steuben pieces are especially collectible.

Mold-blown glass: glass made by blowing hot molten glass into a mold to create uniformity of form, pattern, size, or shape; also called blow-molded glass.

Overlay: a layer of glass applied over the main core-glass. The overlay can be decorated at the fire or after the annealing (cooling) process, by wheel cutting, acid etching, hand-carving, engraving, and/or painting, sandblasting, or applying surface designs.

Overshot: decorative technique in which small granules of glass are picked up on the hot glass surface at completion of the glassblowing. If reheating takes place, the overshot becomes smooth; if not, the surface is rough textured. Sandwich, Wheeling, Portland, and other American glassworks used the technique, as did British, Bohemian, and later, Czechoslovakian glassmakers.

Pâte de verre: literally "paste of glass," an ancient technique of molding glass. Ground glasses are mixed with adhesives and additives, then poured or pressed into a mold and slow-heated to vitrification. This can be achieved without the extremely high temperature required for blowing glass; the technique is used in studios around the world.

Prunt: a piece of glass applied during the blowing process to decorate or to strengthen a vessel, sometimes in the form of a berry, lion head, wafer, or teardrop.

Punty rod: metal rod used for fashioning hot glass.

Reactive glass: glass that changes color as it is heated because of chemical reaction. Burmese and amberina are examples of heat reactive glass; Tiffany glassblowers used heat reactive glass in paperweight vessels to achieve internal color in fish, morning glories, or other decorations.

Sick glass: term for glass vessels, such as decanters, bottles, cruets, pitchers, or vases, whose interior becomes clouded with a white stain after exposure to liquid; caused when wine, vinegar, cider, lemonade, or even water left too long with flower stems produces acid strong enough to etch the glass. This is especially noticeable in colorless crystal or cut glass; removal is virtually impossible.

Slumping: a warm-work technique of slow-heating studio flat glass over a mold to create a conforming shape. Harvey Littleton's 1974 sculpture, "Upward Undulation," inspired many studio glass artists to master the technique.

Sommerso: a line of art glass characterized by a layer of colored glass cased to the interior of a heavy, colorless or transparent vessel; made popular by Seguso Glassworks on Murano in the 1950s and by the Scandinavian factories in the same period.

Spangling and spattering: techniques in which decorative material is enclosed within two layers of glass: *spangling* includes pieces of mica, silver or gold foils, or other metallic bits and pieces; *spattering* includes bits of colored glass that melt into splotches of color. Victorian glass used these techniques often; Murano studios revived the techniques.

Stone glass: glass made to simulate natural gemstones or mineral formations, such as green malachite, blue lapis, opal, multicolored agate, or striated granites; produced by many European glassworks, often in Bohemia.

Tessera: pieces of glass used in mosaic decoration, applied to an object at the fire, picked up on the hot glass, or fused together as surface decoration. Artisti Barovier made superb examples of the work, as did other Muranese glassworks.

Textured glass: glass whose surface is textured by the use of acid finish, metallic oxides, applied materials, or cold decoration, including sandblasting, engraving, and wheel cutting. The textural complexity of the glass becomes the decoration.

Threading: method of decorating exterior surface of glass with threads of the same or contrasting color glass, in either random or structured design. Steuben, Fry, Durand, and others used threading often, especially on art glass lamp shades.

Tooling: manipulation during the glassblowing and shaping process. The gaffer, or glassblower, forms the item, using special tools for specific purposes to create a flared rim, footed base, pinched neck, pouring spout, or other design.

Warm work: any glass-making technique that does not require the extreme heat necessary for glassblowing. Examples include: flameworking (lampwork), *pâte de verre, de cristal* and *d'email,* enameling, slumping, and *cire perdue* sculpting. Many contemporary glass artists use hot, warm, and cold techniques to create a single design.

Wafer pontil: the round blob of glass added to an art glass piece to strengthen the base where the punty rod is attached after the blowing process; the wafer is usually polished smooth. Often referred to as a Tiffany characteristic, this is virtually always used on Trevaise art glass, as well as on art glass by other companies.

Index

Acknowledgments

My sincere thanks to:
My friend and hero, Nancy Skinner, and the late Robert W. Skinner, Jr.;
Karen Keane, Skinner CEO, for permission to use the Skinner photo archive;
Neil Grossman, who took at least 99% of the photographs;
Anne Trodella for finding 100% of them and arranging to duplicate every one;
and especially to my husband, Robert L. Luther, who kept me focused, on time, and smiling.